Dialogues in the Philosophy of Religion

16 JUN 2022

WITHDRAWN

*Also by John Hick*

AN INTERPRETATION OF RELIGION

ARGUMENTS FOR THE EXISTENCE OF GOD

CHRISTIANITY AND OTHER RELIGIONS (*co-editor with Brian Hebblethwaite*)

CLASSICAL AND CONTEMPORARY READINGS IN THE PHILOSOPHY OF RELIGION (*editor*)

CHRISTIANITY AT THE CENTRE

DEATH AND ETERNAL LIFE

DISPUTED QUESTIONS IN THEOLOGY AND PHILOSOPHY OF RELIGION

EVIL AND THE GOD OF LOVE

FAITH AND KNOWLEDGE

FAITH AND THE PHILOSOPHERS (*editor*)

GANDHI'S SIGNIFICANCE FOR TODAY (*co-editor with Lamont C. Hempel*)

GOD AND THE UNIVERSE OF FAITHS

GOD HAS MANY NAMES

PHILOSOPHY OF RELIGION

PROBLEMS OF RELIGIOUS PLURALISM

THE EXISTENCE OF GOD (*editor*)

THE EXPERIENCE OF RELIGIOUS DIVERSITY (*co-editor with Hasan Askari*)

THE FIFTH DIMENSION: An Exploration of the Spiritual Realm

THE MANY-FACED ARGUMENT (*co-editor with Arthur C. McGill*)

THE METAPHOR OF GOD INCARNATE

THE MYTH OF CHRISTIAN UNIQUENESS (*co-editor with Paul F. Knitter*)

THE MYTH OF GOD INCARNATE (*editor*)

THE RAINBOW OF FAITHS (= A CHRISTIAN THEOLOGY OF RELIGIONS)

THE SECOND CHRISTIANITY

THREE FAITHS – ONE GOD (*co-editor with Edmund S. Meltzer*)

TRUTH AND DIALOGUE IN WORLD RELIGIONS (*editor*)

# Dialogues in the Philosophy of Religion

John Hick

palgrave

First published 2001 by
PALGRAVE
Houndmills, Basingstoke, Hampshire RG21 6XS and
175 Fifth Avenue, New York, N.Y. 10010
Companies and representatives throughout the world

PALGRAVE is the new global academic imprint of
St. Martin's Press LLC Scholarly and Reference Division and
Palgrave Publishers Ltd (formerly Macmillan Press Ltd).

ISBN 0–333–76103–0 hardback
ISBN 0–333–76105–7 paperback

This book is printed on paper suitable for recycling and
made from fully managed and sustained forest sources.

A catalogue record for this book is available
from the British Library.

Library of Congress Cataloging-in-Publication Data
Hick, John.
    Dialogues in the philosophy of religion / John Hick.
        p. cm.
    Includes bibliographical references and index.
    ISBN 0–333–76103–0 (cloth)
    1. Religious pluralism—Christianity. 2. Christianity and
other religions. 3. Religion—Philosophy. I. Hick, John.
    BR127 .D544 2001
    210—dc21
                                                    00–054521

10    9    8    7    6    5    4    3    2    1
10    09    08    07    06    05    04    03    02    01

Printed in Great Britain by Antony Rowe Ltd, Chippenham, Wiltshire

# Contents

# Preface

In recent years I have been engaged in dialogue, discussion, debate, argument with others on the question, 'How can we best understand the fact that there is not just one but a plurality of great world religions?' All world religions claim to be paths to a supremely good fulfilment in relation to the ultimate transcendent reality. Are none of the religions such paths because there is no such reality and no such fulfilment; or only one's own; or several of them to some extent but not so fully as one's own; or are they all, so far as we can tell, equally such paths? This last is the pluralist view. But what can it mean and, in view of the obvious great differences between the religions, how can it possibly be the case? My project has been to investigate and advocate the pluralist position. And so this book collects journal articles and contributions to composite books, together with new material, in which I try to present it coherently, to persuade others of it and to meet counter-arguments.

Because there are such different points of view and such intense debates between them, the book is argumentative. But it is worth adding that most of those with whom I have been arguing are also friends. For over the years, within the international philosophy of religion and theological communities, one comes to know and interact freely with the main contributors to the ongoing debate. This happens at conferences, in lengthy one-to-one discussions, in relaxed conversations over meals, in public debates, in e-mail and snail-mail exchanges; and out of all this we have usually come to respect one another and often to become friends. And this despite the fact that we still disagree philosophically or theologically as much as it is possible to disagree.

So the book is dedicated to all those friends who are also foes – many more than feature in this book – some being of my own generation, others younger, including a number of my former students. For as a result of discussions with them I have considerably developed some of my positions, and some of them have likewise developed their positions in response to my own arguments. So let the dialogue continue!

JOHN HICK

# Acknowledgements

I am grateful to the following publishers and authors for permission to reprint, or to publish for the first time, the material in this book:

To the Macmillan Press Ltd of London and St. Martin's Press, Inc. of New York for 'Transcendence and Truth', which first appeared in D.Z. Phillips and Timothy Tessin (eds.), *Religion without Transcendence?* (1997), and 'Climbing the Foothills of Understanding', which first appeared in Jon R. Stone (ed.), *The Craft of Religious Studies* (1998).

'Religious Pluralism for Evangelicals' first appeared as 'A Pluralist View', taken together with Clark Pinnock's Response, from *Four Views on Salvation in a Pluralistic World*, edited by Dennis Ockholm and Timothy R. Phillips. © 1995, 1996 by Dennis L. Ockholm, Timothy R. Phillips, John Hick, Clark H. Pinnock, Alister E. McGrath, R. Douglas Geivett and W. Gary Phillips. Used by permission of Zondervan Publishing House.

To *Faith and Philosophy* (Journal of the Society of Christian Philosophers, USA) (July 1997) for 'The Epistemological Challenge of Religious Pluralism' and the Responses by William Alston, Alvin Plantinga, Peter van Inwagen and George Mavrodes, and to William Alston and George Mavrodes for their further Responses, now published for the first time.

To *New Blackfriars* (November 1997 and December 1998) for 'Response to Cardinal Ratzinger on Religious Pluralism' and 'The Latest Vatican Statement on Religious Pluralism'.

To Westminster John Knox Press, Louisville, Kentucky, for 'The Theological Challenge of Religious Pluralism' by John. H. Hick. Reproduced from *An Introduction to Christian Theology*, edited by Roger Badham. © 1997 Roger Badham. Used by permission of Westminster John Knox Press.

To *Religious Studies*, published by the Cambridge University Press, for 'Religious Pluralism and the Divine: a Response to Paul Eddy' (December 1995), 'The Possibility of Religious Pluralism: a Reply to Gavin D'Costa' (June 1997) and 'Ineffability' (March 2000).

To *Theology* (September/October 1998) for 'Is Christianity the Only True Religion?'.

To Orbis Books, Maryknoll, New York, for 'Paul Knitter on the Person of Christ', which first appeared as 'Five Misgivings', in *The Uniqueness of Jesus – A Dialogue with Paul F. Knitter*, edited by Leonard Swidler and Paul Mojzes (1997), and for part of Paul Knitter's Response to his critics.

# Introduction: Climbing the Foothills of Understanding – An Intellectual Autobiography

The particular subdivision of the wide field of religious studies in which I have worked is the philosophy of religion. During the past 40 years the subject has changed considerably in both scope and internal variety. I have been conscious of this particularly in producing revised editions of my small students' text on the philosophy of religion in Prentice-Hall's Foundations of Philosophy series, the first edition appearing in 1963 and the fourth in 1990.

My own books, reflecting these same developments, are of three kinds. First, there are those, coming at roughly ten-year intervals, in which I have made my own contribution, such as it is, to religious thought: *Faith and Knowledge* (1957, 1966), *Evil and the God of Love* (1966, 1977), *Death and Eternal Life* (1976) and *An Interpretation of Religion* (1989), together with smaller books applying some of these themes to Christian theology. Second, there are collections of mostly previously published articles in which I have repeated, anticipated, elaborated or defended aspects of that contribution, and also some edited and co-edited works dealing with the same issues. And third, there are students' texts and books of readings.

I shall refer here only to the first group. These have all been problem-driven, in the sense of being attempts to contribute to the solution of acutely felt problems facing religious persons. The facing of each has led on to the next, like climbing a mountain range and finding that as soon as you reach a summit another higher mountain comes into view – but with the compensation that each stage of the climb opens up a wider view of the territory, and yet also with the awareness that only the foot-hills of truth have been reached.

## The mediated character of our awareness of reality

The climb began at Edinburgh University, where as part of preparation for the Presbyterian ministry I took the four-year honours course in philosophy. This was under the guidance of Norman Kemp Smith and then, after a wartime gap in the Friends' Ambulance Unit from 1942 to 1945, under his successor A.D. Ritchie, and John Macmurray in ethics. (Macmurray's writings are now being read and appreciated again after a period of relative neglect. In addition to philosophers, his social thought has influenced Prime Minister Tony Blair. My impression, attending his lectures and seminars as an undergraduate, was that he had some very important insights, which we, his students, gladly absorbed, but that there were also considerable vaguenesses and lacunae in his larger metaphysical system.) Of these three teachers, the most influential, so far as I was concerned, was Kemp Smith. He was not primarily an original thinker, but he was a major historian of philosophy and had a massive, coherent mind formed at the end of the idealist period in British philosophy. Kemp Smith was an important interpreter of Kant (his translation of the *Critique of Pure Reason* is still widely used), his book on Hume revolutionized Humean studies and his work on Descartes was also significant. However, what I chiefly received from Kemp Smith was the basic Kantian insight that the mind is not passive in perception but continuously active so that the world as we are aware of it is partly a human construction. The diverse impacts upon us of our environment come to consciousness in terms of the system of concepts that are necessary for those impacts to be unified within a finite consciousness. The central point that took hold in me is that all awareness of our environment is an interpreted awareness. Already at Edinburgh it occurred to me that this could have an application to the epistemology of religion; and in a notebook filled during a slack period in Italy in 1944, I sketched out the basic idea of what was later to be my doctoral dissertation at Oxford.

That there was such a dissertation was due to one of those unpredictable accidents which account for so much of the shape of our lives. During my final year at Edinburgh someone died, triggering the endowment of the Campbell-Fraser scholarship to enable an Edinburgh graduate in philosophy or classics to go to Oriel College, Oxford for two years of research, and I had the good fortune to be the first recipient. My Oxford supervisor was H.H. Price, the author of major books on epistemology.

Price was independent of the Oxford school of linguistic philosophy, then headed by Gilbert Ryle, although of course fully *au fait* with it.

His independence from that movement suited me very well, for the kind of linguistic analysis then dominant in Oxford would have had no place for my own project. Though Price had a much broader outlook than the dominant school, in his own work he set the highest standard of conceptual clarity and verbal precision. Then after three years of theological study I turned my dissertation, on 'The relation between faith and belief', into a book while serving as a Presbyterian minister with a rural congregation at Belford in Northumberland, and took it with me to my first teaching post, in the philosophy department at Cornell University, where it was published by the Cornell University Press, and has been in print ever since, currently in a second edition from Macmillan in London. (It may be encouraging to some graduate students to know that before being accepted by the Cornell University Press the book was rejected by several British publishers, and that there were seven years between the completion of the Oxford dissertation and its eventual appearance as *Faith and Knowledge*.)

The Kantian distinction between the noumenal thing in itself, and its phenomenal appearance(s) to consciousness, the latter depending upon the cognitive equipment and conceptual resources of the observer, later connected in my mind with Wittgenstein's concept of 'seeing-as', which Wittgenstein illustrated with Jastrow's duck/rabbit picture, which we can see *as* the picture of a rabbit's head facing right or *as* the picture of a duck's head facing left; and, as he said, 'we see it as we interpret it' (1953: 198).

I expanded the notion of seeing-as into that of experiencing-as, involving several or all of our senses together. In experiencing an object as having a certain character (for example, being a knife) we are identifying it as having a specific meaning or significance. This is not semantic meaning, the meaning of words and sentences, but the practical meaning in terms of which we live all the time. For to see what is there as a knife and fork includes being in a dispositional state to behave in relation to them in ways appropriate to their being a knife and fork, namely by using them as implements with which to eat. However, the world of meaning within which we live most of the time is composed of *situations*, which are more complex than individual objects and which have a practical meaning over and above that of their constituent objects. The multilayered sphere of overlapping meanings within which we live is jointly created by the impacts of our environment upon us and by the conceptual system formed within us by our own cognitive choices, most of which however are made for us by our cultural and linguistic world.

## Religious faith as 'experiencing-as'

The correlative notions of experiencing-as, and of the forms of meaning which it half-discovers and half-creates, can I believe be applied to the analysis of religious experience. The religious mind experiences both objects (the bread and wine in the eucharist, statues of saints, of the Virgin Mary, of Hindu gods, the sacred icons in an Orthodox church, Buddhist *stupas*, the tombs of Sufi saints, and so on) and situations (from life as a whole to particular occasions – the birth of a new life, the closure of a life in death, the experience of worship, of human goodness, 'miraculous' recoveries and escapes from injury, viewing the starry heavens above and being conscious of the moral law within, being struck by the beauty of nature – as mediating the presence of God or the enlightenment of the dharma or the requirements of heaven or aware-ness of the Tao . . .). In experiencing in this way, the religious person is making a (usually unconscious) cognitive choice. For the situation itself is always objectively ambiguous, capable of being experienced either in purely naturalistic or in religious terms, presupposing but going beyond its purely natural character. To take an ancient biblical example, the prophet Jeremiah's experience of the Chaldean army's attack on Jerusalem as Jahweh's punishment of faithless Israel did not cancel, but added a further dimension to, his awareness of the political and economic significance of the event. And at the other end of the religious spectrum, when an 'awakened' person within the Mahayana Buddhist tradition comes to experience *samsara* (the process of ordinary life, with all its anxieties and suffering) selflessly, as *nirvana* (the blessed state of joyful serenity), the ordinary world is not obliterated but, on the contrary, is more intensely experienced, but in a completely new light.

In such cases the religious and non-religious minds are experien-cing the same situation, but experiencing it differently because at a pre-conscious level they are interpreting in fundamentally different ways. And I identify this voluntary interpretive element within our conscious experience as faith. It follows that the purely naturalistic experience of the world is as much a matter of faith as the religious; for *all* our con-scious experience is experiencing-as. This conception of faith does not replace but should be added to the traditional ideas of faith (*fides*) as believing propositions with a strength that exceeds that of the evidence for them, and also of faith (*fiducia*) as trust in someone or something.

In *Faith and Knowledge* this understanding of religious faith as an uncompelled interpretative choice led to the notion of 'epistemic distance', the idea that in order to preserve our human cognitive freedom in relation to the divine we exist at a distance from God – not however a spatial distance, but a distance in the dimension of knowledge. And that in turn is related to the idea that the universe is, from our present point of view within it, religiously ambiguous – that is, capable of being comprehensively understood both religiously and naturalistically – so that both options are objectively possible and both alike incur the risk of being profoundly mistaken.

## Eschatological verification

This conception of faith has to face the dilemma of verifiability versus factual meaninglessness which was being so powerfully posed by Logical Positivism. This movement, launched into the English-speaking world by A.J. Ayer in the 1930s and 1940s, was rapidly fading in Britain in the 1950s. But whereas many philosophers of religion thought that it could now simply be forgotten, it seemed to me that the fundamental positivist insight, that to exist is to make an in principle experienceable difference, posed a challenge to religious belief that had never been satisfactorily answered. This challenge was renewed in 1955 by, for example, Antony Flew in *New Essays in Philosophical Theology*. Flew and others said in effect: 'You believe that God exists; but how would the world be different if God did not exist?' If there is no observable difference, then the statement that God exists is empty or, as the Positivists had put it, meaningless. It was not good enough to say that the *belief* that God exists makes a difference to us, for that difference could be made even if the belief is false. The correct religious response to the challenge seemed to me to lie in what I called eschatological verification. The basic idea is that although the human situation is religiously ambiguous from our present standpoint within it, the religions teach that its total structure is such that there will be continued human experience beyond this life and that this will be either instantly or, more likely, progressively incompatible with a naturalistic understanding of the universe. Thus the basic religious claim is, if true, experientially confirmable to the point of excluding rational doubt – although not of course falsifiable if false, since if it is false no one will ever be in a position to note this fact. In illustration I offered the parable of two travellers on the same road, one believing that it leads in the end to the Celestial City the other believing that it leads to a precipice and then nothingness. Neither can predict what will happen round each next corner except the last; but in the end it will be evident that one of the two travellers has been right and the other mistaken throughout. It follows that the difference between their beliefs was all the time a genuine and not a merely empty or meaningless difference.

## Religious experience as the basis for religious belief

Given the religious ambiguity of the universe from our present position within it, and the ultimate *post-mortem* resolution of this ambiguity, together with the fact that many people now experience life, or some elements or moments within it, religiously, the next question is whether they are rationally justified in living on the basis of an understanding of it prompted by their religious experience. I have argued that the basic principle that it is rational to base beliefs on our experience, except when we have positive reasons not to,[1] applies impartially to all forms of putatively cognitive experience, including religious experience. The debate about the rationality or otherwise of religious belief thus hinges upon possible reasons to distrust religious experience. There are a number of possible reasons – particularly the obvious differences between sense experience and religious experience – but these can, I believe, be dissolved. I developed this argument within the context of Christian belief, and was thus working on parallel lines to William Alston in his many articles over the years leading up to his definitive statement in *Perceiving God* (1991).[2] I particularly value being in the same camp as Alston, so far as the epistemology of religion is concerned, because I regard him as the most important and successful contemporary thinker in this area. He has worked out the argument for the possibility of veridical experience of God much more fully and rigorously than I have; though I also think that he has faced less fully the further implications of this position arising from the fact that the people of other religions are equally justified in basing beliefs on their own religious experience, and that many of the beliefs thus justified are mutually incompatible. This is the epistemological problem of religious plurality to which I shall come presently.

There are two other main recent developments in the epistemology of religion which all of us working in the field have had to take note of. One is the 'Reformed epistemology' of Alvin Plantinga (see his essay in Plantinga and Wolterstorff, *Faith and Rationality*, 1983 and many later writings) and a number of others. This holds that there are 'properly basic beliefs', which are foundational and thus not in need of external justification, and that belief in God is of this kind. This is open to two interpretations. On one interpretation properly basic religious beliefs are 'free-standing', not grounded in anything else and therefore not in religious experience; and this position does not seem to me to be defensible. But on the other interpretation – which is, I feel sure, the intended one – what makes a belief *properly* basic is its occurrence in appropriate circumstances. Thus 'I see a tree before me' is properly basic if I am having the experience of seeing what appears to me to be a tree before me. And 'I am in God's presence' is properly basic if I am experiencing what seems to me to be God's presence. This is very close to Alston's position, and is in my opinion basically sound when taken with the various qualifications that Alston spells out.

The other recent development has been Richard Swinburne's attempt to show by means of Bayes' theorem that the probability of divine existence is more than half; and more broadly that the entire scheme of basic Christian theology constitutes the most probable picture of reality. This programme seems to me not only to be anachronistic, a throwback to medieval Scholasticism and unrelated to the needs of the modern mind, but also not to succeed even in its own terms, as I have argued elsewhere (in *Interpretation of Religion*, 1989, and my essay in Padgett, *Reason and the Christian Religion*, 1994).

Both these developments, which are technically superb and constitute impressive philosophical exercises, are however seriously limited, in my opinion, by very conservative theological presuppositions. They belong to philosophy of religion in the now old-fashioned sense in which this is understood to be the philosophy of the Christian (or at most the Judaeo-Christian) tradition, and they do not face the problems created by the fact that Christianity is one major world religion among others. Indeed Alston, Plantinga, Swinburne and the many others who are working solely within the confines of their own tradition are for the most part really doing philosophical theology rather than philosophy of religion. But if one claims to have established the epistemic propriety of believing, on the basis of religious experience, in the reality of the Christian deity, one should face the fact that there are others who believe, likewise on the basis of their own religious experience and with equal epistemic justification, in the reality of what are phenomenologically different deities, and also of even more different non-personal religious ultimates.

## The Irenaean theodicy

But before coming to that, the next problem to hit me – not through any one particular event, but just by being part of the human race – was the ancient and unavoidable problem of evil. This surely constitutes the biggest obstacle that there is to religious belief. I had begun to address it in my lectures at Cornell University, and then at the Princeton Theological Seminary, and seized the opportunity of a year's sabbatical leave (helped out by a Guggenheim fellowship) to confront it more fully. With the two summers before and after the academic year I had almost 18 months available, which were spent with the family in Cambridge, where I was made a Bye-Fellow at Caius College. The result was *Evil and the God of Love*, in which I contrast the traditional Augustinian type of theodicy with what I call the Irenaean type. The Augustinian scheme hinges upon a catastrophic rebellion against God, first by Satan and his angels, and then by humanity. This has resulted both in the fallen and sinful state of human life and also in a disordering of the entire physical world, producing 'natural' evil – life preying upon life, diseases, earthquakes, droughts, famines, and so on. (There are, of course, other important themes in Augustine, particularly his privative conception of evil as a lack of good, which I also discussed at some length.) This traditional Augustinian and Calvinist picture, which is still held by many conservative Christians, is open to obvious serious criticisms. There is no evidence for, and much against, the claim that there was once an 'unfallen' human race living in a right relationship with God and with one another. And the notion that natural evils are a result of the Fall is ruled out by the fact that they existed long before there was any human life. But more basically, the idea that God initially created a perfect universe – in the sense of a dependent universe that was as God wanted it to be – which then went radically wrong through the choice of free beings within it, is self-contradictory. Finitely perfect beings in a finitely perfect environment, although free to sin, will not do so. If they do, they were not perfect after all. And so if God is the creator *ex nihilo* of everything other than God, then God cannot escape the ultimate responsibility for the entire history of the universe, including the 'fall' of the free creatures who are part of it. We remain, of course, individually and corporately responsible, in varying degrees, for what we freely do. But on a different level, which does not clash with our own human responsibility, God must have the final responsibility for having created such beings as us: this is where the buck stops!

In the writings of some of the early Greek-speaking Church fathers, particularly Irenaeus and Clement of Alexandria, but others as well, writing long before Augustine, there is the beginning of a different Christian theodicy. Instead of presenting Adam's fall as a crime of cosmic proportions which has ruined human life and its environment, Irenaeus saw it as more like an understandable slip.[3] Adam and Eve were immature creatures (pictured at one point as children), created only at the beginning of a long process of growth and development. And human history is a phase of this second stage of creation in which beings made in the 'image' of God, as rational, ethical and religious animals, move freely towards the finite 'likeness' of God. Humanity was created, through the evolutionary process, as a 'fallen' creature, programmed for survival, and thus with the basic self-centredness from which what we call sin ultimately derives.

If, then, the purpose of human life is that we may grow through our own free choices towards our perfection, what kind of world would provide a suitable environment for this? Not an earthly paradise devoid of any pain or suffering, without problems, difficulties, uncertainties, setbacks, disasters of any kind. For moral and spiritual growth always comes through challenge and response; and our world is a challenging environment. This does not, of course, mean that God has planned the particular challenges and hardships that we each face. It means that God has created a world-process that is, from our present point of view, very imperfect in that it is not designed for our comfort but includes unpredictable elements both of natural contingency and of the inputs of human free will.

But the final responsibility for both our human sinfulness and for the harsh and challenging world in which we live, has to be God's. The 'free will defence' is valid on the human level, but does not extend to God's *ultimate* responsibility. We have to accept that the divine love is a 'tough love' whose goodness, from our human point of view, lies in its eventual success in bringing us through what Keats called this 'vale of soul-making' to the infinite, because eternal, good of perfected existence.

Clearly, this type of theodicy has an inescapable eschatological dimension. For it is evident that the person-making process is not completed in this life, so that if it is ever to be completed there must be a continuation of human existence beyond bodily death. I do not think that any religious response to the problem of evil can avoid this conclusion: 'No Theodicy without Eschatology'.

## Death and eternal life

The whole subject of death and the idea of life after death was neglected by most twentieth-century theologians, though not by the philosophers of religion. This is perhaps because the latter can discuss it as a purely intellectual issue whereas theologians must treat it with existential seriousness if they treat it at all – and so many prefer not to treat it. But Ludwig Feuerbach (1957) was right in noting that the idea of immortality is essentially involved in the idea of a loving God (see pp. 174–5). For human nature includes immense potentialities, which we see realized in varying degrees in remarkable men and women whom we regard, in our customary western term, as saints, or in eastern terms as *mahatmas*, or *bodhisattvas*. It follows that if our existence ceases at death, the full human potential is only realized by those few who are able to do so in this present life, so that in the great majority of men and women the higher potentialities must remain forever unfulfilled. Such a situation is clearly incompatible, not only with a Christian belief in the limitless love of God, but equally with Jewish or Muslim belief in the divine love and mercy, and with an advaitic Hindu or a Buddhist belief in a universal destiny in union with Brahman or in the attainment of Buddhahood. There can be no loving God, and more generally no ultimate reality that is benign from our human point of view, if there is no continuation of human spiritual growth beyond the point reached at the time of bodily death.

But what kind of eschatology? This large, even though unanswerable, question was the subject of my next book, *Death and Eternal Life* (1976). Here for the first time, benefiting from extended study visits to India and Sri Lanka, I tried to take account of eastern as well as western thought. I distinguished between eschatologies (conceptions of an ultimate state) and pareschatologies (conceptions of that which occurs between bodily death and that final state). The world religions differ greatly in their pareschatologies – purgatory or some kind of intermediate state, reincarnation of the personality, rebirth of a karmic structure, or a nil pareschatology through an immediate translation to heaven or hell. Concerning the final eschatological state there is the major divide between the broadly western religious belief (in Judaism, Christianity and Islam) that individual personality, having attained or received its perfecting, continues eternally, and the broadly Eastern belief (in advaitic Hinduism and in Buddhism) that individual personality is ultimately transcended in the eternal consciousness of Brahman or in the presently inconceivable *parinirvana*.

These different conceptions are, however, only 'broadly' eastern and western, because 'Hinduism' includes the large stream of thought classically expressed by Ramanuja (eleventh to twelfth centuries CE), according to which individual *jivas* continue eternally within the life of Brahman, who is conceived of as personal. And western mysticism, Jewish, Christian and Muslim, includes the thought that personal individuality is ultimately transcended as the soul, empty of self, is filled with the divine presence.

In this book I made more extended and sympathetic use of the Hindu conceptions of reincarnation and the Buddhist conceptions of rebirth than most other western philosophers so far. The speculation – and it can, of course, only be speculation – offered in the last part of the book is based upon the thought that our human moral and spiritual growth can take place only under the pressure of the ever-approaching boundary of death and that therefore, if it continues beyond our present earthly existence, it is likely to do so in a series of such bounded lives. These might occur by reincarnation in this world. But there are difficulties in that idea, and another and perhaps preferable speculation involves further lives in other worlds or indeed (as some contemporary scientific cosmologies permit) in other sub-universes. However I am now inclined, more than 20 years later, to stress more strongly the distinction between, on the one hand, the ego (that is, the now consciously thinking and acting personality) and, on the other hand, an underlying dispositional (or karmic) structure, which both affects and is affected by the former. One can then speculate that it is the latter that continues through a number of lives, being expressed in a new conscious personality each time – as much Hindu and Buddhist thought suggests. The connection between the members of this particular series of lives consists in their being fully recorded within the continuing psychic structure and able to be remembered at an advanced stage of the process – as is said of the Buddha's enlightenment at Bodhgaya. (I am not, however, impressed by most of the present life claims of ordinary people to remember a previous life.) It could also be, as is suggested by some of the parapsychological research, as well as by such religious sources as the Tibetan *Bardo Thödol*, that consciousness persists for a limited time between the embodiments of the continuing dispositional, or karmic, structure. According to this picture, I have to learn to accept that my present conscious self, or ego, will not live forever (even if it survives bodily death for a while), but that the deeper self of which I am a temporary expression is being modified all the time by the ways in which I am responding to my present options. I am thus continuously affecting my own future selves, whose nature will benefit from or be harmed by my present thoughts, emotions and actions. And all this within the continuum of mutual influences, mental and emotional, within which we are continuously (unconsciously) affecting one another for good and ill.

If we now ask to what end, if any, the whole process is moving, we do well, I think, to heed the agnosticism recommended long ago by the Buddha. Buddhism speaks of many rebirths of the karmic structure, leading towards an eventual universal nirvanic liberation or awakening. But when the Buddha, Gotama, was asked by a monk, Vaccha, in what kind of world or state the Tathagata (a fully enlightened being) arises after death, he rejected the question as having no answer because it was formed in terms of categories which do not apply (Horner 1957: 162–3):

> 'Arise', Vaccha, does not apply.
> Well then, good Gotama, does he not arise?
> 'Does not arise', Vaccha, does not apply.
> Well then, good Gotama, does he both arise and not arise?
> 'Both arises and does not arise', Vaccha, does not apply.
> Well then, good Gotama, does he neither arise nor not arise?
> 'Neither arises nor does not arise', Vaccha, does not apply.
>                                           (*Majjhima Nikaya*, II, 484–5)

In other words, *parinirvana*, or *nirvana* beyond the round of rebirths, cannot be encompassed by our present set of concepts, which involves entities of some kind being in various states, or substances having various attributes. Rather, *'Freed from denotation by consciousness* is the Tathagata, Vaccha, he is deep, immeasurable, unfathomable as is the great ocean' (Horner 1957: 166; emphasis added). Such talk of realities that lie beyond our present conceptual systems and powers of imagination seems to me to be realistic. We must free ourselves from the assumption that our human capacities are adequate to the nature of reality beyond its present impingements upon us (for a fuller discussion, see Hick 1993).

As this reference to the Pali scriptures of Buddhism may suggest, I had become intensely interested in the great world religions in addition to Christianity. Apart from a good deal of reading, I encountered Islam in Birmingham, where about 10 per cent of the population are Muslim, and also in Los Angeles; and Judaism in Britain and in the Los Angeles area, which has the third largest Jewish population in the world, and also briefly in Israel; and Hinduism and Sikhism in India, as also in Birmingham and in California; and Theravada Buddhism in Sri Lanka, and the Mahayana (mainly Zen and Tibetan) in the United States and in Japan. It seems clear to me that the philosophy of religion is not properly just the philosophy of the Christian (or Judaeo-Christian) tradition, but in principle of religion throughout history and throughout the world. For the philosophy of religion, on analogy with the philosophy of science, philosophy of law, philosophy of art, philosophy of education, philosophy of mind, and so on, is properly the philosophy of *religion*, and not just of one particular form of it. Of course, the philosopher of religion cannot hope to have a detailed, first-hand knowledge of all the major, let alone minor, religious traditions, any more than the philosopher of science can hope to have a detailed first-hand knowledge of all the natural sciences. But he or she should have a general knowledge of the major religious traditions and should know how to acquire more detailed knowledge of particular aspects of any of them when necessary. This need is met to a reasonable extent today by most US graduate programmes in religion, though not by many of their European equivalents, which are still often confined to (Christian) theology, still treated in religious, even if no longer in sociological, isolation.

## Religious pluralism

As I indicated earlier, the fact of religious plurality creates a fundamental problem for any religious apologetic hinging upon the rationality of basing beliefs on religious experience. A Christian philosopher can respond to this situation positively or negatively. The negative response is to feel threatened by the existence of other streams of religious experience, producing as they do belief-systems which are at many points incompatible with the Christian belief-system. This has been Alston's (1991) reaction. He accepts that the other world religions are as experientially well based as his own; and he sees this as 'the most difficult problem for my position' (p. 255), which is conceived as a defence of specifically Christian theism. His response to the problem of religious diversity is determined by the assumption that there can be at most one 'true religion', in the sense of a religion teaching the truth. Given this assumption, he has to justify privileging the Christian stream of religious experience, in which he participates, over all others. And his justification is that, in the absence of any way of establishing objectively that one stream is epistemically more reliable than another, it is rational to stay with the one in which one already participates. This seems to me to make good pastoral sense, but to be at the same time a counsel of philosophical despair in face of the challenge of religious plurality. It seeks to justify one's belief that doctrines based on Christian religious experience are true, whilst those based on non-Christian religious experience, at least in so far as they are incompatible with

Christian beliefs, are false. But this makes one's own belief-system the sole exception to a general rule that beliefs based on religious experience are false! Thus the carefully defended principle that religious experience generally produces true beliefs is converted into the arbitrary principle that religious experience generally produces false beliefs – except in the case of Christianity! This does not seem to me to be a position in which a rational person can comfortably rest. (However, see chapter 2 for Alston's response to this criticism.)

Already in my inaugural lecture as H.G. Wood Professor at Birmingham in 1967 (see Hick 1973) I had identified the relation between the world religions as one of the four main problems facing Christian thought today. It was also the one that I had not yet then begun to address. Hence the period, mentioned above, of learning about the world religions – in particular, Judaism, Islam, Hinduism, Sikhism and Buddhism – and of reflecting on what can be called the philosophy of religions and the theology of religions.

This gave rise to successive publications, culminating in my Gifford Lectures, *An Interpretation of Religion* (1989). I was seeking a *religious* (as distinguished from a naturalistic) interpretation of religion in its various forms. By this I mean one based on the faith that human religious experience is not purely an imaginative projection (though this is certainly an element within it) but is also a response to a transcendent reality. The generic term that I have preferred for the ultimate religious referent is the Real – rather than such equally suitable alternatives as Ultimate Reality, the Transcendent, the Divine – mainly because the English term 'the Real' is not only acceptable within Christianity but also corresponds sufficiently to both the Sanskrit *sat* and the Arabic *al Haqq*.

Each of the great post-axial religions exhibits a soteriological structure, being concerned with the radical transformation of human existence from its state of 'fallenness', or of the spiritual blindness of *avidya*, or of subjection to *dukkha*, to a limitlessly better state in right relationship to, or identity with, or consciousness of, the ultimately real. And each seems, so far as we can tell from their spiritual and moral fruits in human life, to be more or less equally successful (and also equally unsuccessful) as contexts of this salvific transformation of individuals and through them to a lesser extent of societies. Again, each has its own unique belief-system, arising from the immensely powerful religious experience of its founder(s) and their successors in the developing tradition.

In order to do justice to these data, it seems to me necessary to appeal to a distinction, found in some form within each of the great traditions, between the Real as it is in itself and the Real as humanly thought and experienced. This is supported by Aquinas's epistemological principle that 'Things known are in the knower according to the mode of the knower' (*Summa Theologica*, II/II, Q.1, art. 2), which implies a distinction between God *a se* and God as conceived and experienced in accordance with the mode of the human knowers. It is also supported by the Kantian distinction between a thing *an sich*, the noumenal reality as it is in itself, and that reality as a phenomenon of human experience. It therefore seems to me that we should distinguish between the Real in itself, beyond the scope of our human conceptual systems, and the Real as variously humanly thought and experienced. For in religion the 'mode of the knower' is differently formed within the different traditions, producing a corresponding range of ways in which the Real is humanly thought, and therefore experienced, and therefore responded to in life.

## The humanly experienced *personae* and *impersonae* of the Real

The two main concepts in terms of which religious experience is structured are the concept of deity, or of the Real as personal, and the concept of the absolute, or of the Real as non-personal. But we are never conscious of deity or of the absolute in general. Each becomes concretely experienceable or in Kantian language schematized in terms, not (as in Kant's system) of abstract time, but of the filled time of history and culture. Thus in one stream of thought and experience deity has become the figure of Jahweh who, developing through history, chose the Jewish people, entered into a covenant with them, rescued them from slavery in Egypt, led them into a new land, and who has through the centuries punished them when they strayed from his allegiance and blessed them when they have been faithful to him. The Jahweh phenomenon exists in relation to the Jewish people and cannot be extracted from that relationship; he is part of their history, and they are part of his; and in the biblical accounts he shows no awareness of, for example, the peoples of China or India or the Americas. In quite a different strand of history deity became concretized as the Vishnu of India, God of a thousand names who has become incarnate on earth in times of human crisis (but always in India), for example as Rama and as Krishna. Vishnu, as pictured in the Hindu scriptures, shows no awareness of the Jews, or of the peoples of China or of Europe or the Americas. Again, the Holy Trinity of Christian faith, and the strictly unitary Allah of Islamic faith, are yet other phenomenologically different historical concretizations of deity. In each case, awareness of the Real as personal has taken a specific form provided by the human imagination as formed within a particular religious culture. Other religious cultures again have experienced the Real in non-personal terms, which have become specific as the Tao, or as the Brahman of advaitic Hinduism, or as the *dharmakaya*, or *sunyata*, or *nirvana* of Buddhism. All these various *personae* and *impersonae* of the Real have formed at the interface between the Real and different realms of human consciousness. Each is the joint product of the universal presence of the Real and of a particular religious tradition with its own specific conceptuality together with its associated spiritual practices, exemplars, scriptures, history, culture and form of life.

On this hypothesis the Real in itself is, in western terms, ineffable, or in eastern terms, formless in that it is outside the scope of our human conceptual systems. We cannot apply to it any of the attributes of its manifestations as the God-figures and the non-personal absolutes. It cannot be said to be personal or impersonal, good or evil, purposive or non-purposive, substance or process, even one or many – though it can of course be said to have such purely formal, linguistically generated, attributes as 'being able to be referred to' and 'being ineffable'. The main argument for the ineffability of the Real is that it would be impossible to attribute to it the qualities of its *personae* and *impersonae*, because, taken together, these are at many points mutually incompatible. There is however a sense in which the Real can be said, from our human point of view, to be good or gracious, namely as the necessary condition of our highest good, which the great religious traditions variously speak of as eternal life, *moksha*, *nirvana*, union with the divine. And there is a sense, pointed out by Maimonides, in which the Real can be said to be one rather than many: 'In our endeavour to show that God does not include a plurality, we can only say "He is one", although "one" and "many" are both terms which serve to distinguish quantity' (1904: 81). The Upanishads meet the same problem by speaking paradoxically of 'The One without a second' (*Chandogya Upanishad*, VI, 2. 4). And if we ask why, from a religious point of view, we should suppose there to be a transcendent reality about which we can say so little, the answer is that the Real is the necessary postulate of the religious life. The difference between affirming and denying the Real is the difference between a religious and a naturalistic interpretation of religion.

On this view, the function of religion is to be an enabling context of salvation/liberation, which consists in the transformation of human existence from self-centredness to a new orientation centred in the Real as variously manifested through the different religious traditions. And because the great world faiths seem to have proved over the centuries to be more or less equally salvific (and also more or less equally infected by human greed, cruelty, pride and selfishness), it seems to me proper to hold that they constitute, so far as we humans can tell, equally valid even though very different responses to the Real.

## Implications for Christian theology

If so, the pluralistic hypothesis inevitably reflects back into the religious traditions, and those who accept a view of this kind will want to de-emphasize and eventually filter out that aspect of their own trad-ition which implies its unique superiority over all others. In the case of Christianity, this is the idea that Jesus of Nazareth was God (that is, the second person of a divine Trinity) incarnate. For it follows from this that Christianity alone, among the religions of the world, was founded by God in person and is thus God's own religion in a way in which no other can be. I have accordingly tried, in my capacity as a theologian, to contribute to the new self-understanding of Christianity as one 'true' religion among others.

This has involved a critique of the three basic interrelated doctrines of Incarnation, Trinity and atonement. The traditional doctrine of the Incarnation holds that Jesus of Nazareth was the second Person of a divine Trinity living a human life. The Council of Chalcedon, which definitively formulated the official doctrine, supported it by affirming that this is 'as the Lord Jesus Christ taught us'. And until within the past 150 years or so virtually all instructed (as well as uninstructed) Christians believed that Jesus himself had taught his own deity in such statements as 'I and the Father are one' (John 10: 30), 'He who has seen me has seen the Father' (John 13: 9). However, today almost all New Testament scholars are agreed that these are not words of the historical Jesus, but words put into his mouth some 60 or 70 years after his death by a Christian writer expressing the theology that had by then developed in much of the Church. Jesus probably thought of himself as the final prophet, proclaiming the imminent coming of God's kingdom on earth, and would have regarded as blasphemous the idea that he was himself God in either a unitarian or a trinitarian sense. He is reported to have said at one point, 'Why do you call me good? No one is good but God alone' (Mark 10: 18). And long before the Gospels were written, in the period between about AD 70 and 100, the early church thought of

Jesus as, in the words attributed to St Peter in the Acts of the Apostles, 'a man attested to you by God with mighty works and wonders and signs which God did through him in your midst' (Acts 2: 22).

Jesus himself spoke of God as his *abba*, father, and taught his followers to pray to God as their heavenly father. But it has only been widely known in modern times that it was common in the ancient world to speak of outstanding individuals as sons of God. In the wider Mediterranean world great rulers – Egyptian pharaohs and, in Jesus's time, Roman emperors – and great philosophers (for example, Pythagoras and Plato), and great holy men were spoken of as divine or as a son of God; and within Judaism Adam, and Israel as a whole, and angels, and the ancient Hebrew kings, and indeed any outstandingly pious Jew, was often called a son of God. Within Judaism the phrase was clearly intended metaphorically: 'son of' meant 'in the spirit of' or 'true servant of'. But when the gospel went out beyond Israel into the Gentile world, where the term was often used much less clearly metaphorically, and when the gospel had to be expressed in philosophical terms to appeal to the sophisticated classes of the Empire, Jesus the metaphorical son of God was transformed into the metaphysical God the Son, second Person of a divine Trinity, having two complete natures, one human and the other divine. However, the relationship between these two natures has never been satisfactorily explained. Did Jesus have two consciousnesses? Did he have two wills? Was he, as genuinely human, able to sin? Was he, as genuinely divine, unable to sin? If so, does not the latter annul the former? If he was divinely omnipotent and omniscient, how was he also humanly weak and limited in knowledge? Such questions have never been given agreed answers, and for most Christians the doctrine is accepted as a sacred mystery which we must believe, but must not expect to understand.

The traditional doctrine takes the idea of divine incarnation literally. It holds that Jesus was literally (not metaphorically) human and literally (not metaphorically) divine. But this literally understood idea has not only proved to be inexplicable, but has also proved to be readily exploited to validate great human evils. The ancient charge of deicide presupposes a literal doctrine of Jesus's deity, and was used throughout medieval Christendom to justify the persecution and slaughter of Jews, thereby forming the continuing mind-set in which the secular anti-Semitism of the nineteenth and twentieth centuries could flourish and in which the Nazi holocaust of the 1930s and 1940s could take place. The doctrine of the deity of Christ was also used to inspire the European colonists who conquered and then exploited so much of what today we call the Third World. And the idea that God became a man (not a woman) has been used to justify the ecclesiastical suppression of women down to our own day. None of this shows that the doctrine, thus literally understood, is false, but it does induce a certain 'hermeneutic of suspicion', and prompts us to ask whether this is the only way to understand the idea of divine incarnation.

It is evident that it is not the only way. Incarnation, or embodiment, is a familiar metaphor. Great men, it has been said, 'incarnate' the spirit of their age. George Washington 'incarnated' the spirit of American independence. Hitler was evil 'incarnate'. Winston Churchill, in 1940, 'incarnated' the British will to resist Hitler. And so on. And in this metaphorical sense God was incarnate in the life of Jesus in several interrelated respects. In so far as Jesus was doing God's will, God was acting through him and was thus 'incarnate' in Jesus's life. Again, in so far as Jesus was doing God's will he 'incarnated' the ideal of human life lived in openness and response to God. And again, in so far as Jesus lived a life of self-giving love, or *agape*, he 'incarnated' a love that is a finite reflection of the infinite divine love. Indeed, in this metaphorical sense, whenever a man or a woman freely does the divine will, God becomes incarnate on earth in that action; and among these Jesus is the one who has captured the imagination of the millions who call themselves Christians.

Given a metaphorical understanding of divine incarnation, the traditional doctrine of the Trinity ceases to have any point. For its purpose was to safeguard a literal doctrine of Jesus's deity. And again, the various transactional understandings of atonement – as a ransom to the devil, or a satisfaction to God for the sins of the world, or a substitute bearing on our behalf the just punishment for human sin – likewise lose their point, for they all presuppose the literal deity of Jesus. One can then return to the teachings of Jesus himself, who taught (for example in the Parable of the Prodigal Son and in the words of the Lord's Prayer) that whenever there is genuine penitence for sin there is genuine and free divine forgiveness, without any need for an atoning death.

And so as well as working as a philosopher of religion I have also functioned as a theologian, taking part along with many others in the modern re-understanding of Christianity as one valid context of human salvation among others. A parallel task exists within each of the other world religions, a task that is easier for some than for others and that can in each case only be undertaken from within the tradition itself.

This theological contribution, which has not surprisingly proved to be highly controversial, is presented most fully in my *The Metaphor of God Incarnate* (1993).

The broader hypothesis, within which this is a sub-theme, is developed in *An Interpretation of Religion* and defended from a variety of criticisms in (in the United States) *A Christian Theology of Religions* (1995) or (in Britain) *The Rainbow of Faiths* (1995). It exemplifies one, but of course by no means the only, way in which the philosophy of religion can respond to the epistemological problems created by the fact of religious diversity.

More generally, it seems to me that the philosopher of religion should be willing to embrace and reflect upon the great perennial human experiences of joy and suffering, life and death, and the sense of transcendence that is mediated through them and in many other ways, as well as the basic epistemological questions which determine one's response to the mysterious universe of which we are part.

## Notes

1. Richard Swinburne has named this the 'principle of credulity', *The Existence of God* (Oxford: Clarendon Press, 1979, pp. 254f); but I prefer to call it the 'principle of rational credulity'.
2. Indeed in *Perceiving God* (Ithaca and London: Cornell University Press, 1991) Alston says (p. xi) that his thinking was 'strongly influenced' by *Faith and Knowledge*, and he has written elsewhere that 'From the first edition the book made a profound impression on me' ('John Hick: *Faith and Knowledge*', in Arvind Sharma (ed.), *God, Truth and Reality: Essays in Honour of John Hick*, London: Macmillan, and New York: St. Martin's Press, 1993, p. 25).
3. This idea also occurs in the fourteenth-century English mystic, Julian of Norwich, in the longer text of her *Showings*, chapters 47 and 55.

## References

Alston, William. 1991. *Perceiving God* (Ithaca and London: Cornell University Press).

Feuerbach, Ludwig. 1957. *The Essence of Christianity* (trans. George Eliot) (New York: Harper Torchbooks).

Hick, John. 1973. *God and the Universe of Faiths* (London: Macmillan).

Hick, John. 1989. *An Interpretation of Religion* (London: Macmillan and New Haven: Yale University Press).

Hick, John. 1993. *Disputed Questions in Theology and the Philosophy of Religion* (London: Macmillan and New Haven: Yale University Press).

Horner, I.B. (trans.). 1957. *The Collection of the Middle Length Sayings* (London: Luzac).

Maimonides. 1904. *Guide for the Perplexed* (trans. M. Friedlander) (London: Routledge & Kegan Paul).

Padgett, Alan (ed.). 1994. *Reason and the Christian Religion: Essays in Honour of Richard Swinburne* (Oxford: Clarendon Press).

Plantinga, Alvin and Nicholas Wolterstorff (eds). 1983. *Faith and Rationality* (South Bend, IN and London: University of Notre Dame Press).

Wittgenstein, Ludwig. 1953. *Philosophical Investigations* (trans. G.E.M. Anscombe and R. Rhees) (Oxford: Blackwell).

# Part I

# In Dialogue with Contemporary Philosophers

# 1
# The Epistemological Challenge of Religious Pluralism

Many of us today who work in the philosophy of religion are in broad agreement with William Alston that the most viable defence of religious belief has to be a defence of the rationality of basing beliefs (with many qualifying provisos which Alston has carefully set forth) on religious experience. From the point of view of a Christian philosopher – as distinguished from a philosopher simply as such – there is, however, an obvious challenge to this in the fact that the same epistemological principle establishes the rationality of Jews, Muslims, Hindus, Buddhists, etc. in holding beliefs that are at least partly, and sometimes quite radically, incompatible with the Christian belief-system. Belief in the reality of Allah, Vishnu, Shiva and of the non-personal Brahman, Dharmakaya, Tao, seem to be as experientially well based as belief in the reality of the Holy Trinity. Alston himself acknowledges this as 'the most difficult problem for my position'[1] and this view is reflected in the fact that a third of the *Festschrift* recently published in his honour[2] is devoted to this topic.

Alston's solution to the problem is (in briefest summary) that since we have at present no neutral way of establishing which of the world religions is right, and since our own religion is both theoretically and practically satisfactory to us, it is much more reasonable for us to stay with it than to switch to another. On analogy with the rival doxastic practices – Aristotelian, Cartesian, Whiteheadian etc. – in terms of which we construe the physical world,

> In the absence of any external reason for supposing that one of the competing practices is more accurate than my own, the only rational course for me is to sit tight with the practice of which I am a master and which serves me so well in guiding my activity in the world . . .

Hence, by parity of reasoning, the rational thing for a practitioner of CP [Christian doxastic practice] to do is to continue to form Christian M-beliefs [beliefs about God's self-manifestation to us], and, more generally, to continue to accept, and operate in accordance with, the system of Christian belief.[3]

Alston is here assuming that there can be at most one 'true religion', so that the big question is, which of the competing religious belief-systems is the true one? But this widespread assumption is fatal to Alston's thesis that it is (with all the proper qualifications and safeguards) rational to base beliefs on religious experience. For if only *one* of the many belief-systems based upon religious experience can be true, it follows that *religious experience generally produces false beliefs*, and that it is thus a generally *unreliable* basis for belief-formation. This is a reversal of the principle, for which Alston has argued so persuasively, that religious experience constitutes as legitimate a ground for belief-formation as does sense experience. Further, whilst it is possible that the doxastic practice of one's own community constitutes the sole exception to a general rule, the claim that this is so can only appear arbitrary and unjustified unless it is supported by good arguments. And so William Wainwright, in his chapter in the *Festschrift*, holds that 'To be fully successful [Alston's defence of "sitting tight"] must form part of a persuasive cumulative case argument for the Christian world-view' (p. 188).

The arbitrariness of Alston's position is highlighted when we remember that if he had been born into a devout Muslim or Hindu or Buddhist family he would, using the same epistemology, be equally arbitrarily claiming that his Muslim, or Hindu, or Buddhist beliefs constitute the sole exception to the general rule that religious experience produces false beliefs! (Strictly speaking, of course, since it would not then be the same Bill Alston, one should say that when *someone* is born into a devout Muslim etc. family . . . But this does not affect the point.)

However, Alston might at this point retreat to a fall-back position prepared in *Perceiving God*, where he describes the absence of neutral grounds for preferring the Christian world-view as only a 'worst case scenario' (p. 270). A more desirable scenario would be one in which there are compelling metaphysical arguments for theism and in which in addition 'historical evidences give much stronger support to the claims of Christianity than to those of its theistic rivals – Judaism and Islam' (p. 270). However, Alston does not suggest that this better scenario actually obtains. 'Perhaps,' he says in the end, 'it is only in God's good time that a more thorough insight into the truth behind these divergent perspectives [i.e. of the different religions] will be revealed to us' (p. 278). His fall-back position is thus a hope rather than a reality.

However, even if it were a reality it would still undermine Alston's basic principle. For on his only-one-true-religion assumption the arguments and evidences establishing the truth of Christian beliefs would thereby establish the falsity of the beliefs of other religions, at least in so far as they are incompatible with Christian beliefs. And this incompatibility is clearly very considerable: God cannot be, for example, both personal and not personal, triune and not-triune, primarily self-revealed to the Jews, and to the Arabs, and so on. And yet religious experience within the different traditions has produced these incompatible beliefs. It thus follows as directly from Alston's best-case scenario as from his worst that religious experience is *not* generally a reliable ground for belief. On the contrary, it follows equally inescapably from either scenario that religious experience generally produces false beliefs, with Christian experience claiming to stand out as the sole exception.

It therefore does not seem to me that Alston has met, or can without a more radical adjustment meet, the challenge of religious diversity to his experience-based apologetic. On the other hand, his central argument that religious experience constitutes a valid basis for belief-formation still seems correct, and indeed (in my view) constitutes the most valuable current contribution to the epistemology of religion. But would this not be a much stronger contribution if the doxastic practices of the other world religions could be seen as further instances of it rather than as contradicting it?

Fortunately there is a fairly obvious way to reconcile the two desiderata: (a) that the principle that we properly form beliefs on the basis of our experience applies impartially to religious as well as to sensory experience (subject in each case to possible defeaters), and (b) that this principle holds impartially for non-Christian as well as for Christian forms of religious experience. This is by appealing to the distinction between God/the Ultimate/the Real/the Transcendent *an sich* and that ultimate reality as variously humanly conceived, and thus variously humanly experienced, and hence variously humanly responded to in historical forms of life. Such a recognition of variety in our human response to the Transcendent depends upon the epistemological principle propounded by St Thomas, 'Things known are in the knower according to the mode of the knower',[4] and developed in the modern world by Kant in a way that has affected nearly all western philosophy since. In the case of religion the mode of the knower, that is, the

conceptuality in terms of which the divine presence comes to consciousness, differs as between different religious cultures and epochs. I shall
not develop the pluralistic hypothesis further here, having done so
elsewhere.[5] Alston himself discusses this Kantian option, but rejects it
on the ground that it must be seen 'as a proposal for a reconception of
religious doxastic practices, rather than as a description and evaluation
of those practices as they are. It seems clear to me that most practitioners of one or another religion are pre-Kantian.... They think that [their]
beliefs embody true accounts of the Ultimate as it really is in itself...'[6] I
accept that this is so, but I suggest that the alternative to some kind of
religious pluralism is to leave unexplained the immensely significant
fact that the other great world faiths are as epistemically well based as
Christianity; and also that they seem, when judged by their fruits, to be
morally on a par with Christianity.

The next essay in the Alston *Festschrift*, Alvin Plantinga's 'Pluralism: A
Defense of Religious Exclusivism', affirms Christian exclusivism in
unqualified terms. His response to religious diversity is the straightforward claim that Christian beliefs are true and all beliefs inconsistent
with them are, therefore, false. He does not offer any positive reasons
for this but thinks it sufficient to argue, negatively, that it is not morally
reprehensible or epistemically out of order to adopt an exclusivist
stance. To be a religious exclusivist is, he argues, neither irrational,
unjustified, egotistical, intellectually arrogant, elitist, a manifestation of
harmful pride, self-servingly arbitrary, dishonest or oppressive and
imperialistic. His argument is characteristically thorough and elaborate,
involving among other matters the examination of four different senses
of rationality and three different conceptions of justification. But what
emerges at the end is simply that Christians are free to be (as throughout
Christian history Christians have nearly always been) exclusivists in
their attitude to non-Christians. One is not 'arrogant and egotistic just
by virtue of believing what I know others don't believe, where I can't
show them that I am right' (p. 200); and one who believes that Christians are right and non-Christians wrong has 'violated no intellectual or
cognitive duties or obligations in the formation and sustenance of the
belief in question' (p. 202). The scale of philosophical argumentation
leading to this conclusion suggests that Plantinga supposes himself to
be addressing the central issue between religious exclusivism and
religious pluralism. But in fact his argument has not even come within
sight of the central issue. Certainly, when people sincerely believe
(whether rightly or wrongly) that their own group has a monopoly of
the final religious truth, they are entitled to hold and propagate that

view, so long as their so doing does not harm others. And this applies impartially not only to evangelical Christians but also to evangelical Muslims, Hindus, etc., and likewise to much smaller and more recent religious communities such as Christian Scientists, or Kimbanguists, or the followers of the Reverend Sun Myung Moon, and so on. But to establish this principle is not to have addressed the epistemological challenge of religious diversity.

Instead, Plantinga is concerned to defend Christian exclusivism against the moral indignation that it has sometimes aroused, and which has sometimes been expressed in the contemporary philosophical and theological debates.[7] He deflects this by defining exclusivism so narrowly that only people who are 'rather fully aware of other religions' and aware also 'that there is much that at least look like genuine piety and devoutness' within them (p. 196) are to be counted as exclusivists. He thus ignores by stipulative definition the aspect of the Church's stance through the centuries that has been expressed in the persecution and murder of Jews, in violent crusades against Muslims, in the validation of European imperialism, and in the often ignorant denigration of other religions. As regards the latter, there are plenty of cases in Christian literature of theological exclusivism expressed in arrogant, proud, oppressive and/or unthinking and unfair ways. But it is of course also true that a knowledgeable, thoughtful and ethically sensitive Christian exclusivist, such as Plantinga himself, is morally as well as intellectually entitled to his exclusivist faith. But is this fact sufficient to dispose of the problem of religious diversity?

Plantinga does however, at one point, take up an issue in the debate. He refers to the fact, noted above, that religious allegiance depends in the great majority of cases on the accident of birth: someone born into a devout Muslim family in Pakistan is very likely to be a Muslim, someone born into a devout Hindu family in India to be a Hindu, someone born into a devout Christian family in Spain or Mexico to be a Catholic Christian; and so on. The conclusion that I have myself drawn from this is that a 'hermeneutic of suspicion' is appropriate in relation to beliefs that have been instilled into one by the surrounding religious culture.

> Having thus noted that Ptolemaic [i.e. exclusivist] theologies tend to posit their centers on the basis of the accidents of geography, one is likely to see one's own Ptolemaic [exclusivist] conviction in a new light. Can we be so entirely confident that to have been born in our particular part of the world carries with it the privilege of knowing

the full religious truth, whereas to have been born elsewhere involves the likelihood of having only partial and inferior truth?[8]

The relativity of religious belief to the circumstances of birth does not, of course, show that claims to a monopoly of religious truth are unjustified; but it does, I think, warn us to look critically at such claims. Plantinga's response is to point out that if he had been born elsewhere, such as in Madagascar, he would have had some different beliefs – for example, he would not have had the belief that he was born in Michigan. And, he says, 'the same goes for the pluralist. Pluralism isn't and hasn't been widely popular in the world at large; if the pluralist had been born in Madagascar, or medieval France, he probably wouldn't have been a pluralist' (p. 212); but, he points out, it does not follow that he is therefore not entitled to be a pluralist. This is true; but how relevant is it? One is not usually a religious pluralist as a result of having been raised from childhood to be one, as (in most cases) one is raised from childhood to be a Christian or a Muslim or a Hindu, etc. Surely the cases are so different that the analogy fails.

The next *Festschrift* essay is Peter van Inwagen's 'Non Est Hick'. Although this refers to Hick only in the title and the last sentence, van Inwagen's account of religious pluralism seems to be loosely based on my *An Interpretation of Religion*. He finds the whole idea offensive and even perhaps contemptible: 'the defense of religious pluralism,' he says, 'has always been entirely rhetorical' (p. 219). And so instead of engaging critically with it he presents his own understanding of religion, adding however that 'I do not expect this theory to recommend itself to anyone who is not a traditional, orthodox Christian' (p. 219).

van Inwagen outlines Western Augustinian–Calvinist orthodoxy: God, the primordial catastrophe of the Fall, redemption by the death of God's Son, the choice of Israel, the divine founding of the Christian Church. As to the world religions, 'they are the work of human beings, and their existence and properties are not a part of God's plan for the world' (p. 225) – although God may nevertheless make use of them, as He sometimes makes use of other human acts and products that He has not willed. van Inwagen makes much of the contention that whilst there are Christians, Buddhists, Muslims, etc., there are no such reified entities as Christianity or Buddhism or Islam, for these are 'compression' words naming abstractions. He holds that 'the concept of a "religion" is a piece of misdirection intended to advance what I shall call the "Enlightenment agenda" ' (p. 231), which he associates with religious pluralism. It is ironic that Wilfred Cantwell Smith's classic work *The*

*Meaning and End of Religion* (first published in 1962 and widely influential ever since[9]) deconstructed the concepts of 'religion' and of 'a religion' as modern Western creations, which distort the reality of human faith throughout the world, this deconstruction leading to Cantwell Smith's well-known pluralist conclusion!

van Inwagen also makes much of the 'uniqueness' of western Christian civilization. But of course, every civilization, including our own, is unique! And of course the Church has been a major factor throughout the history of the West. But some who speak of the uniqueness of Christian civilization do not merely mean to say, uncontroversially, that it is unique, but to make the substantial claim that it is morally superior to all other civilizations. van Inwagen wisely does not make this claim which is, as he says, highly controversial and 'could be argued interminably' (p. 233). He does, however, imply that but for Christianity science would never have come about. This is a highly debatable view that some (such as A.N. Whitehead) have suggested, but that others have rejected, seeing the origins of modern science in a confluence of cultures made possible by the Renaissance recovery of the spirit of free enquiry. But this is a big historical debate which van Inwagen does not pursue and which I shall not pursue here either.

van Inwagen holds that the church is 'the unique [meaning the one and only] instrument of salvation' (p. 237). He then takes up the obvious challenge, '"Well, isn't it fortunate for you that you just happen to be a member of this 'unique instrument of salvation'" ... Yes [he answers], it is fortunate for me, very fortunate indeed' (p. 238). He then, like Plantinga, seeks to dispose of the problem with an analogy. He points out that whilst 'one's adherence to a system of political thought and action is conditioned by one's upbringing', this is not 'a reason for doubting that the political system one favours is – if not the uniquely 'correct' one – clearly and markedly superior to its available rivals. And yet any argument to show that the Church's belief in her own uniqueness was arrogant would apply *a fortiori* to this universally held belief about politics' (p. 238). But has van Inwagen not here overlooked the crucial differences? The church *has* traditionally claimed to be 'the uniquely "correct" one', in the sense of being the sole instrument of salvation. The church's claim is not about the relative merits of different political systems but about the eternal fate of the entire human race. One can accept that a loving God leaves humans free to devise their own political systems, but can one suppose that the Heavenly Father, who loves all human beings with an equal and unlimited love, has ordained that only those who have the good fortune to be born in certain parts of the world shall have the opportunity of salvation? Is there not a major problem here that is merely concealed by the analogy with political systems?

That there is such a problem is implicitly acknowledged when van Inwagen goes on to say that 'It is not necessary for Christians to believe that there is no salvation outside the *visible* Church' (p. 239). Indeed, only one 'who has accepted Christian belief and rejects it and rejects it still at the moment of his death – and rejects it with a clear mind, and not when maddened by pain or grief or terror – is damned' (p. 239). Such people must, fortunately, form a very minute group. But 'What provision God makes for those who have never heard the Christian message, or who have heard it only in some distorted and falsifying form, I do not know. That is God's business and not ours' (p. 239).

This is a standard, indeed classic, evasion of the problem. It covers virtually everyone throughout the world and throughout history other than a soundly orthodox Christian minority. But if only God knows what provision God has made for the large majority of the human race, how does van Inwagen know that God has not caused the Buddhist *Sangha*, and the Muslim *Ummah*, and so on, as well as the Christian Church, to come into existence as 'instruments of salvation', and how does he know that each community's (including the Church's) affirm-ation of the unique religious superiority of its own faith is not an expression of our fallen human nature? How can he profess a genuine ignorance about God's ways with the hundreds of millions of people of other faiths, and at the same time be entitled to assert a dogmatic Christian exclusivism? Surely, if anyone knows that God is *not* working salvifically through other religions, as well as through Christianity, *non est* van Inwagen!

The next essay is Joseph Runzo's 'Perceiving God, World-Views, and Faith: Meeting the Problem of Religious Pluralism'. Since Runzo is an advocate of religious pluralism, though of a different version from my own, I shall not treat this as the place to discuss our intra-pluralist differences.

The final essay is George Mavrodes' 'Polytheism'. At the outset the reader is faced with what appears to be either an extravagant compliment or a splendid insult! Hick is, says Mavrodes, 'probably the most important philosophical defender of polytheism in the history of Western philosophy' (p. 262). He adds, 'I think that [Hick] does not much care for that description himself' (p. 262). He is right about this. But the appropriateness of the label in one limited sense and its inappropriateness in other senses is easily clarified and need not detain us long. One who accepts the distinction between, on the one hand, an ultimate and (in Kantian terms) noumenal Real *an sich*, and on the other hand its phenomenal appearances to human consciousness as the experienced god-figures (Jahweh, Allah, Holy Trinity, Shiva, etc.) and experienced non-personal absolutes (Brahman, the Dharmakaya, the Tao, etc.), is at one level a poly-something, though not precisely a polytheist, and at another level a mono-something, though not precisely a monotheist. So the 'polytheist' attribution requires a somewhat contrived hermeneutic, and I shall take Mavrodes' compliment/ insult as a friendly jest. It could even turn out, in view of Mavrodes' interesting and original discussion of polytheism in the ordinary sense of that word, and his qualified defence of it – he thinks that 'there are many beings who satisfy Swinburne's definition of a god' (p. 278) – that it is he who has become the main defender of polytheism in western philosophy!

But Mavrodes also has important things to say about the pluralist hypothesis. He is interested in a 'deep ambiguity in Hick's way of thinking about the relation of the Real to the gods' (p. 272). He describes two different and mutually incompatible models or analogies for this relationship. One is the disguise model. A prince, wishing to observe his people without their being aware of his presence, travels amongst them disguised in different ways, sometimes as a mendicant monk, sometimes as a journeyman stonemason, and so on. Thus the same person, the prince, appears to different groups in different ways, presenting himself to some as a monk, to others as a stonemason, and so on. The analogous possibility in relation to the Real is that the various gods and absolutes are each identical with the Real, which however takes these different forms in relation to different human groups. Here the diversity is all the work of the Real, with no special input on the part of the human perceivers. Mavrodes' alternative analogy is that of several artists painting the same landscape. But because they paint in abstract and non-representational styles one painting does not look much like another and none looks much like the landscape itself; for the artists' creative powers result in their producing very different aesthetic constructs. Analogously, the gods and absolutes are not identical with the Real, but each '*is a human creation* in reaction to some influence, input, or the like from the noumenon' (p. 272; italics original). And Mavrodes asks, which of these models am I using?

The answer is, neither. The disguise model, first, would be radically misleading. As Mavrodes points out, 'according to this model, there is just one god who appears in all the various religions' (p. 276). Presumably that one god, like the prince in the story, has his/her own definite, describable characteristics, including the intention to appear in a variety of ways. But such a god is not analogous to the postulated ineffable Real. This has no humanly conceivable intrinsic characteristics (other than purely formal, linguistically generated ones), and is accordingly not a person carrying out a revelatory plan. And the construct model is also radically misleading, though in one respect less so. It suggests that as the artists directly perceive the landscape, and then through their own creativity represent it in their different ways, so religious people directly experience the Real but respond to it by creating different concepts/images/mental pictures of it. But on the pluralistic hypothesis, as I have tried to formulate it, there can be no direct experience of the Real *an sich* which could then be imaged in a range of ways analogous to that in which the painters creatively represent the landscape. On the contrary, in religious awareness the organizing and form-giving activity of the mind operates at a pre-conscious level, so that religious (including mystical) experience already comes to consciousness as the awareness of a specific personal god or non-personal absolute. The Real is thus not experienced as it is in itself, but is postulated to satisfy (a) the basic faith that human religious experience is not purely projection, but is at the same time a response to a transcendent reality or realities; and (b) the observation that Christianity, Islam, Hinduism, Buddhism, etc., which are communal responses to these different gods and absolutes, seem to be more or less equally effective contexts of human transformation from self-centredness, with all the evils and miseries that flow from this, to a recentring in the Transcendent as experienced within one's own tradition.

But Mavrodes' two models do nevertheless each single out an aspect of the pluralistic hypothesis. The disguise model points to there being only one Real, whose impact upon us is experienced in different ways. And the construct model points to the positive contribution of the human mind in all awareness. The general truth that the form in which we perceive our environment, both natural and supernatural, depends upon the nature of our cognitive equipment and conceptual resources, suggests another analogy which, although still capable of misleading, is less so than Mavrodes'.

This is the difference between, say, the wooden table top that we experience as a solid, hard, brown, partly shiny, enduring three-dimensional object, and the account of it given by the physicists, as (very roughly) mostly empty space in which infinitesimal packages of discharging energy are moving about at a great pace, none of these having any of the properties of the table top that we perceive – neither colour nor weight nor extension nor density nor even fixed position. Let us now add other non-human observers – say angels, Martians and Alpha Centaurians – each species being equipped with quite different sensors and processing the input of those sensors through their own quite different conceptual systems. Let us suppose that as a result of this each species perceives something quite different, both from what the others perceive and also from the table top that we perceive. This now provides a partial analogy for the way in which different spiritual practices (I–Thou prayer, non-I–Thou meditation) and different sets of religious concepts lead to very different awarenesses of the Transcendent. But even this more far-fetched analogy would be only some degree less misleading than Mavrodes', for it still does not reach to the notion of the ineffable. There can indeed be no true analogy for the unique relationship between the postulated ultimate, ineffable, reality the universal presence of which gives rise, in collaboration with our human spiritual practices and conceptual schemes, to the range of forms of religious experience reported in the history of religions.

The purpose of this chapter, however, has not been to expound a particular version of religious pluralism, but to suggest that we do not yet have any adequate response from conservative Christian philosophers to the problem of religious diversity.[10]

## Notes

1.  William Alston, *Perceiving God* (Ithaca and London: Cornell University Press, 1991), p. 255.
2.  Thomas D. Senor (ed.), *The Rationality of Belief and the Plurality of Faith: Essays in Honor of William P. Alston* (Ithaca and London: Cornell University Press, 1995).
3.  Alston, *Perceiving God*, p. 274.
4.  Thomas Aquinas, *Summa Theologica*, II/II, Q. 1,art. 2.
5.  John Hick, *An Interpretation of Religion* (New Haven: Yale University Press, and London: Macmillan, 1989).
6.  Alston, *Perceiving God*, p. 265.
7.  Although in the case of those remarks of my own that Plantinga cites I think he has been a little oversensitive. That we should 'avoid the implausibly arbitrary dogma that religious experience is all delusory with the single exception of the particular form of the one speaking' (quoted, *Festschrift*, p. 197) is not a moral condemnation but an invitation to debate. And that 'The only reason for treating one's tradition differently from others is the very human but not very cogent reason that it is one's own' (quoted, p. 198) is not a charge that an exclusivist is 'arrogant or egotistical' but, again, a provocation to debate. And my *Interpretation*, p. 234, does not say what Plantinga

(p. 210) cites it as saying – though possibly the page number that he cites here is a misprint. He is however accurate in quoting me (p. 194) as saying that 'natural pride . . . becomes harmful when it is elevated to the level of dogma and is built into the belief system of a religious community . . . implying an exclusive or a decisively superior access to the truth or the power to save' – though this is not the same as saying that all exclusivist believing is an expression of human pride.

8. John Hick, *God Has Many Names* (Louisville: Westminster/John Knox, 1982), pp. 37–8.

9. Wilfred Cantwell Smith, *The Meaning and End of Religion* (Minneapolis: Fortress Press, 1962; 1991).

10. I am grateful to William Alston for his comments on an earlier draft of this chapter.

# 2
# Responses and Discussion

## 2(i)  William Alston[1]

This is a response to Hick's comments on my approach to the problem of religious diversity in *Perceiving God*. Before unearthing the bones I have to pick with him, let me fully acknowledge that I have not provided a fully satisfactory solution to the problem. At most I have done the best that can be done given the constraints within which I was working. But this best, if such it be, is not as bad as Hick makes it appear. To show this I need to make several corrections in Hick's depiction of the situation.

Hick says that on (my) assumption that at most one of the major world religious systems is true, 'religious experience generally produces false beliefs', and hence is not a reliable source of belief. But this is too fast in more than one way. First, it assumes that most of the beliefs in each system contradict most of the beliefs in the others. But that is by no means clear, and in the absence of any definite way of counting beliefs it could not be clear. Indeed, my impression is that it is false. Second, Hick unduly inflates the role of religious experience in grounding religious beliefs. Though I argue at length in *Perceiving God*[2] that it is one important ground of religious belief, I devote the last chapter to discussing the ways in which it interacts with other grounds – natural theology, revelation, etc. – each of which makes its own distinctive contribution. Thus, even if the major religious belief systems are mostly in contradiction, there is still the question of the extent to which this is to be laid at the door of religious experience. It could be that the differences are much more due to the other grounds and that, in so far as beliefs are based wholly or largely on religious experience, there is much less contradiction between the different religions.

But even if most beliefs based on religious experience were false, that would not contradict the epistemological claims (at least the most basic epistemological claim) I make for religious experience in the book. For that basic claim is that its seeming to one that some Ultimate Reality (UR) is presenting itself to one's experience as ø makes it *prima facie* justified that UR is ø. And this *prima facie* justification can be overridden by various contrary factors, including sufficient reasons for supposing that UR is not ø. Such an overrider might take the form of a predominance of (perhaps more strongly) justified beliefs that contradict the supposition that UR is ø. So even on my 'worst-case scenario', on which there are no sufficient reasons independent of religious experience to prefer one world religion to others, religious experience can still render the beliefs based on it *prima facie* justified, even if much or most of this justification is overridden.

One final note. Though I did not in the book try to show that there are extra-experiential reasons for preferring the Christian beliefs-system to its rivals, and though I have no intention of embarking on that here, I am not prepared to admit that it is 'a hope rather than a reality'. It is, indeed, a hope, but one that, I believe, can be given some substance.

### Notes

1.  William Alston is Professor of Philosophy at Syracuse University. N.Y., U.S.A.
2.  William Alston. *Perceiving God* (Ithaca and London: Cornell University Press, 1991).

### 2(i)(a)   Hick

William Alston's Response is the briefest, but is particularly important because it was his attempt, in *Perceiving God*, to deal with the epistemological problem posed by religious diversity that provoked this particular round of discussion, and because he takes the problem with full seriousness as 'the most difficult for my position' (*Perceiving God*, p. 255). I welcome his characteristically honest acknowledgement that he has not yet provided a fully satisfying solution to the problem, and I trust that he will continue to grapple with it.

He thinks I move too quickly from his belief that Christian religious experience justifies Christian belief, together with his belief that Christianity is the only fully true religion, to the conclusion that, according to him, since religious experience within other religions produces beliefs that are false in so far as they are incompatible with Christian belief, his implied principle is really that religious experience generally produces false beliefs, with Christianity as the sole exception. Thus his conviction of the unique superiority of his own religion undermines his philosophical argument for religious experience as a valid basis for belief-formation. He now offers two reasons for not accepting this conclusion.

The first is that 'it assumes that most of the beliefs in each system contradict most of the beliefs in the others', something that is by no means clear, since it depends in part upon how we choose to count beliefs. I agree with the latter point. But why should my argument be supposed to assume the contrary? (I was careful, when speaking of the beliefs of other religions as being, according to Alston, false to add 'at least in so far as they are incompatible with Christian beliefs', p. 279.) The argument only requires the incompatibility of the most central beliefs – that the ultimate reality is a personal God versus a non-personal Brahman, etc.; and within the monotheisms, that God is the triune God of Christianity versus the strictly unitary God of the Torah and the Qur'an; and equivalent differences within the non-theistic faiths. I don't think Alston would deny these central incompatibilities.

However, there is a possible way forward which some of Alston's remarks suggest might appeal to him. For in the case of the three great monotheisms it would be possible to restrict the perception-of-God argument to the experience of a personal divine presence, beliefs about whose further nature, purposes and activities are not experientially justified. This would place such specifically Christian ideas as the Trinity, Incarnation, atonement, the authority of Bible and Church, and indeed almost the whole of traditional Christian theology, in the category of non-experientially based beliefs – with corresponding distinctions for Judaism and Islam. Alston does, in fact, move in this direction when he points out that what is directly given in religious experience is very limited and does not include the expansion of a tradition's beliefs into its developed theological system. For example, 'One is aware of God's being *very* loving and powerful but not infinitely loving and powerful. One is aware of something sustaining one in being, but not aware of it as the creator of all' (*Perceiving God*, p. 293). As he adds, 'Christians regularly fill out these fragmentary epiphanies with what they have garnered from their tradition, taking what they perceive to go beyond what is revealed in experience in ways spelled out in the Christian tradition' (pp. 293–4).[1] When we follow the implications of this into Christian theology as a whole it becomes a very radical move. For it opens up the possibility that the traditional belief-system consists of human theories, which may therefore properly be criticized, and perhaps amended, or even rejected. Further, it might explain the theological differences between the great monotheisms – that is, they have the same kind of direct experience of God, but 'ramify' it (in Ninian Smart's phrase) in terms of their different religious conceptualities.

This would be a first step towards religious pluralism. But it would still not be radical enough to deal with the whole problem, since it could not be extended to the great non-theistic faiths. Corresponding distinctions between experience and theory can indeed be made within them, but not based on experience of the personal divine presence which is central to the monotheisms. So I do not think that Alston's first response deflects the criticism that it is intended to deflect. He has pointed out, correctly, that his position does not apply to *all* religious beliefs, but it does still apply to the most central ones.

Alston's second point is that my criticism 'unduly inflates the role of religious experience in grounding religious beliefs' (p. 37). Many will find this surprising. In *Perceiving God* Alston says that his thesis is 'that people sometimes do perceive God and thereby acquire justified beliefs about God' (p. 3). Again, 'The chief aim of this book is to defend the view that putative direct awareness of God can provide justification for certain kinds of belief about God' (p. 9). These are M[anifestation]-beliefs, that is, beliefs that God is now acting in some particular way in relation to oneself. And since God's acting clearly entails that God exists, belief in the reality of God is also thereby justified.

Alston adds that his thesis is the modest one that religious experience only *prima facie* justifies religious beliefs, since all cases of the experiential justification of belief are subject to the proviso that some overriding counter-evidence may nullify them (p. 38). But, whilst true, this is slightly disingenuous; for Alston does not believe that there are in fact any such defeaters. The situation, as he believes it to be, is that Christian religious experience does justify at least the central Christian beliefs; and this entails that the non-theistic forms of religious experience produce false central beliefs. So the original problem is still with him.

However, in the last chapter of *Perceiving God* Alston adds other grounds for a rational religious belief, namely natural theology, tradition (including belief in the Holy Spirit's guidance of individuals and the church), revelation, and also the good effects of Christian faith in many people's lives; and he shows how these, together with religious experience, all support one another in a mutual evidential network. As regards natural theology (which is not confined to any one tradition), he says, 'As for myself, I have no tendency to believe that the existence of God can be demonstratively proved from extrareligious premises', even though he finds 'certain of the arguments to be not wholly lacking in cogency' (p. 289). Here I agree with him, so long as the second statement is not allowed in any way to undermine the first. The good effects of religious faith in many people's lives are also not confined to any one tradition. And each religion has its own different 'revelations' and tradition. (In the case of Buddhism the revelation is not a verbal communication but the great initiating enlightenment of Gautama.) From the point of view of epistemological analysis, the fact of being internally supported by its own putative revelation and its own scriptures, and by saintliness within it, is thus not a ground for privileging one religion over others. Accordingly, it leaves the original problem intact. That is, each of the great world faiths, theistic and non-theistic, is epistemically equally well based, supported by religious experience, supposed revelation, revered scriptures, inspiring role models and a more general uplifting effect in people's lives; and natural theologies that would exclude the non-theistic faiths by proving a personal Creator do not succeed in doing so.

At the end of his Response Alston adds that he is not prepared to admit that, as I had claimed, the belief that there are good extra-experiential reasons for preferring the Christian beliefs-system to its rivals is a hope rather than a reality. 'It is, indeed, a hope,' he says, 'but one that, I believe, can be given some substance' (p. 38). But the only way to give it substance would be to produce good reasons for it, which Alston does not profess to do. Until he does, or points to someone else who has done it in a way that he is prepared to endorse, it does – surely – remain a hope for him rather than a reality.

So Alston's final position seems to be this: religious experience, supported by revelation, tradition, natural theology and the production of saintly individuals, justifies the conviction that Christian belief is true; and its truth entails the falsity of all other belief-systems in so far as they are incompatible with the Christian system. Thus the criticism still seems to me to stand that his implied conclusion is that Christianity is the sole exception to the general rule that religious belief-systems whose central core is experientially warranted are, in their essentials, false and that the grounds on which they are believed are therefore inadequate. This counts as a criticism, not in the sense that one could not hold such view, but in the sense that Alston does not want to; for if he did, he would not have treated it as a criticism.

Having referred to Buddhism several times I should like to add that Buddhism constitutes a crucial problem for any Christian theology of religions. For in its denial that the ultimate reality is a personal being it is as different from Christianity as it is possible to be, and yet in its teaching of universal compassion (*karuna*) and loving-kindness (*metta*) it is as close as it is possible to be. Buddhism has attracted a large number of western converts, partly because it rejects what it sees as Christianity's anthropomorphic conception of ultimate reality, and partly because of its very high ethic and the inner liberation that can be achieved through Buddhist meditation. And so it is incumbent upon the Christian theologian to explain how a religion that is, from a theistic point of view, so totally wrong, can have spiritual and moral fruits in human life that are not inferior to Christianity's.

### Note

1. Alston does, however, remind us that St Teresa of Avila, for example, believed that she had experienced God as three Persons in one Substance – a remarkably philosophical experience for anyone to have, and one obviously reflecting her theological beliefs. On the other hand, Julian of Norwich's experiences were, as she was uncomfortably aware, incompatible with the traditional Fall–Redemption model, which is equally integral to the tradition: for example, 'our Lord God cannot in his own judgment forgive, because he cannot be angry – that would be impossible' (*Showings*, Long Text, ch. 49, Colledge and Walsh trans., p. 263). For a discussion of Julian and her 'fruitful heresies', see my *The Fifth Dimension* (Oxford: One World, 1999), chs. 13–14.

### 2(i)(b)   Alston[1]

I must plead guilty to not having gone thoroughly into the relevant issues in my original response to Hick's article. I, no doubt ill-advisedly, limited myself to objecting to certain points and shirked the more important task of tackling at least some of the fundamental issues involved. Furthermore, as Hick recognizes, I have not worked through anything that I consider a completely adequate position on the questions raised by religious diversity for my position on the epistemology of religious belief. I am by no means insensible to the attractions of Hick's way of dealing with these questions, though, as I have made explicit in *Perceiving God* and elsewhere, I do feel that it gives away more than I am willing to. That leaves me with the task of working out a way of retaining more of the claims of traditional Christianity than are left standing by Hick's position, a way that also does justice to the sense that several religions that differ markedly, even if not wholly, in their belief-systems are all in effective contact with a supreme reality. As I say, I have not yet laid all this out in a satisfactory way. But *faute de mieux*, it may help to further the discussion if I lay out, as best I can, where I find myself in this enterprise at present.

I feel that my best strategy for this is to continue to focus on Hick's objections to my treatment in *Perceiving God* but to do so by way of going further into the relevant issues. Hick's main criticism remains the same – that 'his conviction of the unique superiority of his own religion undermines his philosophical argument for religious experience as a valid basis for belief-formation'. For, he says, since I hold that 'Christianity is the only fully true religion', I am thereby committed to holding that 'religious experience within other religions produces beliefs that are false in so far as they are incompatible with Christian belief'. Therefore, I am committed to the conclusion 'that religious experience generally produces false belief with Christianity as the sole exception', and this is incompatible with my thesis that religious experience is 'a valid basis for belief formation'.

The first step in a fuller response to this criticism is to clarify what the criticism does and does not depend on. As for the former, it requires (1) that there is a considerable degree of incompatibility between the beliefs of the major current world religions[2] and, moreover, (2) that a considerable proportion of beliefs that figure in such incompatibilities owe their epistemic credentials to religious experience, or, to switch to my favourite terminology, to 'mystical perception'. The first assumption is needed to ensure that a significant proportion of religious beliefs are false, and the second to ensure that a considerable number of mystical perception-based beliefs will be found in that class of false beliefs. To be sure, these are not assumptions that Hick himself accepts. He avoids the first (and hence the second) by construing religious beliefs as having to do with phenomena, the way in which the Ultimate appears to people in some particular religion, rather than with noumena, the Ultimate as it is in itself. Since all the major religions, or at least some considerable sub-set thereof, can each be correct in what it believes about the way the Ultimate appears to it, they need not contradict each other. What Hick needs for his criticism is merely that I accept these assumptions. And this is how his premise that I hold that 'Christianity is the only fully true religion' comes into his argument. For, as noted above, he derives from this that I am thereby committed to holding that 'religious experience within other religions produces beliefs that are false in so far as they are incompatible with Christian belief'. But it is very important to note that this consequence need not be so derived. Even if I did not hold that Christianity is (substantially) true and other religions (substantially) false where they contradict it, even if I did not believe this about any religion whatever, I could still, and undoubtedly would, hold that the major world religions are incompatible to some considerable extent. What is required for holding this is to disagree with Hick by holding that religious beliefs, at least the most important and central ones, are beliefs as to what the Ultimate is like (does, intends, etc.) in itself,[3] rather than how it is appearing to the devotees of the religion in question. So, whether I think that Christianity is the only (fully, mostly ...) true religion plays no essential role in the controversy. This correction has, of course, the result that my controversy with Hick is intimately connected with my most fundamental disagreement with him, the one over how to understand the force of religious beliefs.

Having identified the two features of my position that are deemed to imply that 'religious experience generally produces false beliefs', let us look more carefully at those features. We need to consider two questions concerning *extent*. How extensive are the incompatibilities (on my way of construing religious belief) between major world religions, and what proportion of those incompatibilities concern mystical perception-based beliefs? To attempt a precise answer to these questions would require a very extensive survey of religious belief-systems, their logical relationships, and a determination of which of their components are mystical perception-based. Obviously, I have not time for that here, and even if I had both the time and the qualifications for the task, I would have slight hope of arriving at a result that is both (even reasonably) uncontroversial and precise. What I can do is to identify a particular factor that, on my views (which are supposed to be what yields the *reductio*), has a crucial bearing on the questions. Let me begin by putting this into a certain context. I am prepared to acknowledge that, on my noumenal construal of religious beliefs, there is a considerable degree of incompatibility between central beliefs of different religions. But, as pointed out above, that will yield the conclusion that Hick thinks is fatal to my epistemology of mystical perception only if mystical perception-based beliefs figure prominently in a significant number of those incompatibilities. And that seems to me implausible. In *Perceiving God* I suggested that the kind of mystical perception open to people generally plays a restricted role as a source of religious belief. Its primary epistemic role is in producing and supporting *manifestation* beliefs, beliefs as to what perceivable features God has and as to what He is doing vis-à-vis the subject. Depending on how one delimits 'perceivable' divine features, this will presumably exclude most of the central beliefs of a religion from being directly supportable by religious experience of the sort available to people generally.[4] And it would seem that the main source of incompatibilities between religious belief-systems concerns the central beliefs about the Ultimate, its (his, her) nature, general activities, purposes, etc., rather than how it is related to this or that individual, or what its perceivable features are. This casts doubt on Hick's supposition that if different religions are, to a large extent, incompatible with each other, religious experience will mostly produce false beliefs.

But a more penetrating look at the situation will show that there is less to this than meets the eye, especially as concerns the viability of my position in the face of Hick's criticisms. For although in Chapter 8 of *Perceiving God* I stressed the fact that religious experience is only one of the major grounds of Christian belief (and the same goes for other major religions), it is also the case that I held that religious experience can provide significant justification for religious beliefs only if it is set in the context of an 'overrider system' for assessing the credentials of any particular belief based on that experience. My basic thesis about the epistemic efficacy of mystical perception is that the mere fact that a belief is formed on the basis of what one takes to be a direct experience (perception) of God (or other alleged supreme reality) is sufficient to render that belief *prima facie* justified. And that *prima facie* qualification presupposes a system of principles, background beliefs and tests by reference to which it can be determined, with respect to a particular belief, whether that *prima facie* status is upgraded to *justified unqualifiedly*, or whether it is 'overridden', negated, eliminated. And this background 'overrider' system will include all the major beliefs of the religion in question. And so in this way, the entire belief system of the religion is implicated in the support given to some beliefs by religious experience, even if only a small proportion of them are directly so supported. Thus, if a considerable proportion of the beliefs of a religion are false, mystical perception within that religion cannot be relied on to produce mostly true beliefs, since the overrider system employed, containing many false beliefs, cannot be depended on to separate the wheat from the chaff.

I need to spell out more explicitly than I did in *Perceiving God* the total position on the epistemology of religious beliefs that are based on mystical perception. The first component, to repeat the point, is that a belief formed on the basis of mystical perception is thereby *prima facie* justified, provided that this 'doxastic' (belief-forming) practice takes place in the context of a background system (overrider system) that provides resources for further evaluation of the epistemic status of each such belief when that is called for. Since different religious traditions employ (somewhat) different overrider systems, this implies that there are significantly different practices of forming beliefs on the basis of mystical perception in different religions. And, of course, this further implies (something not sufficiently underlined in *Perceiving God*) that a final, definitive evaluation of beliefs formed in one of these practices will also involve an epistemic assessment of the components of the overrider system of that practice.

Thus we have to envisage a two-stage process of further evaluation of *prima facie* justified beliefs: (1) Each can be critically scrutinized on the basis of the local overrider system;[5] but (2) the corpus of beliefs of a given religion that pass this local test are then subject to further challenge in terms of the credentials of the components of the relevant overrider system, which, as near as makes no difference, includes all the major beliefs of that religion. Needless to say, these critical evaluations, particularly the second, are only rarely carried out in any thorough or fully explicit way. But it is crucial that they be possible. It is important for the present discussion to emphasize (something I did make explicit in *Perceiving God*) that this epistemology applies equally to all directly experientially-based religious beliefs wherever an overrider system is available. And I recognize that these conditions are satisfied by all the major world religions.

What is implied by this is that the basic unit for a thoroughgoing epistemic assessment of religious belief, whether based on mystical perception or not, is the whole complex of belief-forming practices in the religion, including both specific bases in each case, *and also the background system in terms of which beliefs prima facie justified on such a basis can be further evaluated.* Mystical perception itself is not only simply one part of the total support for religious belief. It is not, even in that partial role, an *autonomous* support. In order to play that role it must receive cooperation from the total belief-system of the religion within which it is found.

Let me point out that although all the pieces of this system are present in *Perceiving God*, they are not explicitly put together in the way I have just done. And doing that is important for fully grasping my epistemology of mystical perception and its bearing on Hick's criticism. In *Perceiving God* I was primarily concerned to spell out and defend the first component of this system – the *prima facie* justification of beliefs by mystical perception. The extensive replies to criticisms of the claims to the epistemic efficacy of mystical perception in Chapters 5–7 were mostly narrowly focused on the initial *prima facie* justification claim.

My *apologia* is that in the present naturalistic climate of our intellectual culture, it is important to get at least a bridgehead for the epistemic importance of mystical perception. But the larger context in which this is set is also extremely important, and it needs more emphasis than it was given there.

To return to Hick's criticism, how does it stack up in the light of the above presentation of my position? In particular, is he justified in saying that I am committed to the conclusion that religious experience generally produces false beliefs, and if so, does that 'undermine my philosophical argument for religious experience as a valid basis for belief-formation'? Given the complexity of the position outlined above, the answer cannot take the form of a simple 'Yes' or 'No'.

First, are religious beliefs that I deem *prima facie* justified by being based on mystical perception mostly false? Before we can determine whether there are sufficient inter-religious contradictions between such beliefs to yield this result, we would have to consider the kind of content such beliefs have. As pointed out above, the vast majority concern perceivable features of God (the Ultimate) and what God is doing at the moment vis-à-vis the subject. As for the former it does seem plausible that quite different, allegedly perceivable features would be ascribed to God in theistic and non-theistic religions. However, it is not at all clear that these ascriptions are incompatible, in so far as their positive content is concerned (leaving aside any denials within the content). Why shouldn't the same ultimate reality have both personal and impersonal aspects? You and I do. We have both weight and size, and also thoughts and emotions. So although there may be incompatibilities across religions between such beliefs, it is by no means clear that this is frequently the case. But, on the other hand, there may be enough experientially-based beliefs within each religion that are overridden by the *internal* background system to ensure that a very considerable proportion of *prima facie* justified experientially-based beliefs are false. People do report all sorts of wild things about what God said to them, reports that are ruled out by the overrider system of the religion in question. So let's grant that enough such beliefs are false to imply that *prima facie* justification by itself is not enough for highly reliable belief formation.

Although this admission was just below the surface in *Perceiving God*, it did not actually make it to the surface, and this could well give the mistaken impression that I took *prima facie* justification itself to pass the test of truth-conducivity. I must plead guilty to not making it explicit in *Perceiving God* that it is only *unqualified justification* that satisfies the constraint of truth-conducivity. That, indeed, is the rationale of the insistence that a belief can only enjoy *prima facie* justification if it is subject to further assessment in terms of an overrider system. But the relation of the *prima facie*-unqualified distinction was not related with sufficient explicitness to the truth-conducivity requirement for justification in *Perceiving God*.

Thus I admit that Hick is substantially right in charging that most (at least a substantial proportion of) religious beliefs based on mystical perception are false, where all such beliefs that are *prima facie* justified are taken into account. But that fails to undermine my total epistemology of the doxastic practice of forming religious beliefs on the basis of mystical perception. For the claim of by-and-large truth is intended to apply only to the class of beliefs *prima facie* justified by mystical perception *that pass, or would pass, the further scrutiny by the local overrider system, where that overrider system itself is sufficiently justified in a truth-conducive manner.* This is a severe requirement, and there is no danger that the members of any class of beliefs that satisfies it would be mostly false, or even exhibit falsity in considerable numbers.

Note that this discussion has brought us to Hick's quotation from Wainwright: 'To be fully successful, however, I believe it [Alston's defence of Christian mystical perception] must form part of a persuasive cumulative case argument for the Christian world-view'. That, *pace* a few quibbles about 'world-view', is substantially what I have just been saying. This was meant by Wainwright as a criticism of *Perceiving God*, and since this final part of the project was not carried through there, it is a fair criticism to point this out. This I did explicitly recognize in *Perceiving God* (p. 270) – that the final stage of my programme was missing. I shied away from any attempt critically to evaluate the Christian belief system in general. I gave no explicit excuse for not doing so, but if I had I would have pointed out that I had done quite enough for one book and that this further task would take at least another (very large) volume. But I unreservedly confess that a full epistemic assessment of the output of Christian mystical perception, or any other practice of forming beliefs on the basis of mystical perception, requires this critical examination of the background overrider system. Perhaps some day I will have the opportunity to embark on the project.

In my first response, I wrote:

> Though I did not in the book try to show that there are extra-experiential reasons for preferring the Christian belief-system to its rivals, and though I have no intention of embarking on that here, I am not

prepared to admit that it is a 'hope rather than a reality', as Hick had charged. It is, indeed, a hope, but one that, I believe, can be given some substance.

Hick now chides me for remaining content with this promissory note and, in effect, asks me to put up or shut up. 'But the only way to give it substance would be to produce good reasons for it, which Alston does not profess to do.' In answer, I can only say, for the moment, that though I am by no means content with the unfulfilled promissory note, I cannot at present carry out what is promised. Here and now I can only throw Hick and the reader a crumb as an earnest of what I hope will be a full meal to follow at some future time, God willing. I envisage two main components to a full-dress defence of Christian belief, corresponding to the distinction Hick and many others draw between theistic and non-theistic religions. With respect to the latter, which I will think of in this sketch as impersonal absolute monisms, I would contrast them unfavourably in metaphysical terms with theism. I find that extreme monistic systems, such as we find in the Vedanta, run into far too much conflict with the massive evidence of experience and with critical common sense to be credible. Theistic metaphysics, on the other hand, runs into no such intractable problems, and has much to recommend it as a metaphysics.[6] The second component would be directed to the aspects of the Christian message that distinguish it from Judaism and Islam. Here the basic problems are historical. Can the Christian view of Jesus, his status, his mission, his death and resurrection, and of the status and history of the Church, be shown to be substantially accurate? This, of course, is not a task I would dream of undertaking on my own; it is a vast cooperative enterprise. But I would hope to contribute in the way open to a philosopher knowledgeable in the relevant literature. In any event, all this is the hope that, as Hick correctly says, is not yet a reality.

I will add one brief note to this programmatic sketch. There is an important distinction between showing that Christian belief is rational (in the sense of not irrational), and showing that it is superior to its most significant alternatives.[7] One might carry out the former task by showing that Christian belief constitutes one reasonable response to certain issues, while not yet touching the question of whether it is more reasonable than other responses. Hick is well known for being specially concerned with this second issue, although on his position it is dealt with in a very different way from arguing that one religious tradition is superior to the others. I certainly agree that if one, unlike Hick, construes religious belief 'noumenally' and adheres to a particular religious tradition, one is inescapably confronted with the question of the comparative claim to truth of different traditions. But this should not lead us to deny that the first task of showing Christian belief, for example, to be rational is worth while in itself, especially in the current intellectual dispensation, dominated as it is by various forms of naturalism.

In *Perceiving God*, just after my disavowal of any attempt to complete my programme there, I said that for the time being I would 'adopt a "worst-case scenario" and consider the prospects for the rationality of Christian mystical perception on the assumption that there are no significant independent reasons for preferring it to its rivals'[8] (p. 270). The position I defended was the following:

> In the absence of any external reason for supposing that one of the competing practices is more accurate than my own, the rational course for me is to sit tight with the practice of which I am a master and which serves me so well in guiding my activity in the world. (p. 274)

The argument involved imagining a diversity of sense-perceptual doxastic practices, analogous to the diversity we actually have with mystical-perceptual doxastic practices. For example, there could be a 'Whiteheadian' practice of seeing the environment as 'made up of momentary events growing out of each other in a continuous process', which would yield perceptual beliefs in conflict with our actual 'Aristotelian' practice of seeing the environment as made up of more or less discrete objects scattered about in space and retaining their identity through change over time (p. 273). I argued that just as it would be rational for us to continue to form perceptual beliefs in the same way even if in another culture people saw the environment in a 'Whiteheadian' way and we had no non-question-begging way of showing which one was correct, so it is with the actual diversity of mystical-perceptual doxastic practices. But we need not have recourse to such fanciful suppositions in order to support my 'worst-case' position. By bringing non-perceptual doxastic practices into the picture we can find plenty of analogues to the religious diversity case. Think of philosophy. Considering radically different philosophical orientations like current Continental forms of postmodernism vs. typical Anglo-American 'analytic philosophy', we get a nice analogue of religious diversity. Radically different methods are employed in the two camps, and the results are (often) incompatible, so far as one can tell. Even within, say, analytic philosophy radically opposed positions are held by thinkers employing pretty much the same procedures. And yet if we were to deny the rationality of David Lewis's continuing to hold his views on possible worlds because many able philosophers hold radically incompatible views and there is no neutral way of adjudicating the dispute, philosophy would come to a grinding halt. Assuming that this would be unfortunate and uncalled for, one is naturally led to think that something analogous should be said about the practitioner of one of the established mystical perceptual doxastic practices. Thus pending some solid results that show one of the religious competitors to be clearly superior to its rivals, considerations like these tend to show that it is rational for the practitioners of each of the competing mystical perceptual doxastic practices to continue the practice and to accept and guide one's life by the results.

Finally a half-loaf to 'pluralism'. I think that it can be persuasively argued that even where different religions hold incompatible beliefs about the nature of Ultimate Reality and the ways in which this impinges on human life, human destiny and the conditions of human flourishing, it is still reasonable to hold that they are all in effective contact with the same Ultimate Reality, however much they differ as to what this is like. In this I am at one with Hick, even though I take it – as he does not – that the different responses to this reality really are in disagreement with each other, so that the question as to which one (or ones) most nearly has it right, in my view, will not go away.

## Notes

1. Section 2(i)(b) © William Alston 2001.
2. This discussion will be restricted to the members of that (no doubt only vaguely demarcated) class. It at least includes Christianity, Judaism, Islam, Buddhism and Hinduism, with distinctions between different versions of each where that is called for.
3. This supposition has to be understood in such a way as to allow for beliefs about the Ultimate, even when as fully justified as possible, to fall short of a completely adequate account of the Ultimate.
4. I do not doubt that claims are sometimes made to establish basic theological doctrines by mystical perception. Teresa of Avila's report of having 'seen' how God is three in one is a notorious example. But sporadic claims of this sort certainly do not constitute the main support such doctrines receive in the Christian tradition generally. And I believe this is typical of the general situation.
5. Hick writes (pp. 40): 'Alston adds that his thesis is the modest one that religious experience only *prima facie* justifies religious beliefs, since all cases of the experiential justification of belief are subject to the proviso that some overriding counter-evidence may nullify them (*Perceiving God*, p. 295). But, whilst true, this is slightly disingenuous, for Alston does not believe that there are

in fact any such defeaters.' This ignores the difference between the two stages of evaluation spelled out here. (Hick has every excuse for not finding that in *Perceiving God*!) I certainly emphasize in *Perceiving God* that many experientially-based beliefs in the Christian mystical practice get thrown out on the basis of the Christian overrider system. It is only with respect to the second stage that one could reasonably suppose that I hold that 'there are no such defeaters' of the components of the overrider system. Even here I do not think that everything in traditional Christian doctrine survives criticism. But my point here is the importance of distinguishing these two stages of evaluation.

6.  Obviously, many thinkers hold that the problem of evil is such an intractable problem. In response I recommend the essays collected in Howard-Snyder (ed.) *The Evidential Argument from Evil* (1996).

7.  In Richard Swinburne *Faith and Reason* (1981: ch. 7) there is an illuminating discussion of the special problems that arise when we seek to show that a hypothesis is 'more probable' than certain alternatives.

8.  I should have called this only a 'worse'-case scenario. It could have been worse, if the beliefs in question were not *prima facie* justified and if there were no functioning overrider system.

*I am grateful for the half-loaf that Alston offers in his last paragraph but, like Oliver Twist, I still want to ask for more!*

## 2(ii)   Alvin Plantinga[1]

John Hick notes that I affirm Christian exclusivism: I accept classical Christianity (or C.S. Lewis's 'mere Christianity') and, naturally enough, reject as false any proposition incompatible with it. Now in the paper Hick criticizes, I argued that none of the moral and epistemic objections commonly urged against exclusivism is at all successful; they all fail. Hick seems to agree that these objections are not in fact compelling (although he points out that it is perfectly possible to accept Christian belief in an arrogant fashion, just as it is possible to be an arrogant pluralist). He claims, however, that I have altogether missed the central issue here: 'The scale of philosophical argumentation leading to this conclusion suggests that Plantinga supposes himself to be addressing the central issue between religious exclusivism and religious pluralism. But in fact his argument has not even come within sight of the central issue.' Well, I had thought that *was* the central issue here, or at any rate *a* central issue: many pluralists argue that there is something morally or epistemically wrong with Christian exclusivism – it is unjustified, or arbitrary, or irrational or arrogant or *something* – and I was trying to answer their criticisms. If there is nothing either morally or epistemically wrong with exclusivism, what's supposed to be the problem?

Hick doesn't say in the present piece what this central problem is, so I wrote him a letter and asked him. He graciously replied that the central problem, for the exclusivist, is 'how to make sense of the fact that there are other great world religions, belief in whose tenets is as epistemologically well based as belief in the Christian doctrinal system, and whose moral and spiritual fruits in human lives seem to be as valuable as those of Christian faith.' But then given that these beliefs incompatible with Christianity *are* 'as epistemologically well based' as Christian belief, it is *arbitrary* to insist, as I do, that Christian belief is true and beliefs incompatible with it are false; it is to treat relevantly similar things differently. He adds that 'The arbitrariness of this position is underlined by the consideration that in the vast majority of cases the religion to which a person adheres depends upon the accidents of birth.' The basic problem, then, is this: the fundamental tenets of the other great world religions are 'epistemologically as well based' as is Christian belief; but the exclusivist nevertheless accepts just one of these sets of beliefs, rejecting the others; and that is arbitrary.

But if *this* is supposed to be the problem for the exclusivist, then I *did* deal with it in the paper Hick refers to. I argued that the exclusivist is not in fact being merely arbitrary, because she doesn't believe that views incompatible with hers *are* 'as epistemologically well based' as her Christian beliefs. She may agree that the views of others seem just as true to them as hers do to her; they have all the same internal markers as her own. She may agree further that these others are *justified*, flouting no epistemic duty, in believing as they do. She may agree still further that she doesn't know of any arguments that would convince them that they are wrong and she is right. Nevertheless she thinks her own position is not only true, and thus alethically superior to views incompatible with her, but superior from an epistemic point of view as well: how then does she fall into arbitrariness?

Let me briefly look into this matter from a slightly different angle. First, it is not quite clear what Hick is claiming here. Is he claiming that the fact is there *isn't* any relevant epistemic difference between Christian belief and these other beliefs (whether the exclusivist knows this or not) and *therefore* the exclusivist's stance is arbitrary? Or is he claiming that the exclusivist *himself* agrees that there is no relevant epistemic difference between his views and those of the dissenters, but accepts his own anyway, thus falling into arbitrariness? If the first, then presumably Hick would need some *reason* or *argument* for the claim that in fact the exclusivist's beliefs are not epistemically superior to views incompatible with hers. The exclusivist is likely to think that he has been epistemically favoured in some way; he believes what he does on the basis of something like Calvin's *sensus divinitatis*; or perhaps the Internal Witness of the Holy Spirit; or perhaps he thinks the Holy Spirit preserves the Christian Church from serious error, at least with respect to the fundamentals of Christian belief; or perhaps he thinks that he has been converted by divine grace, so that he now sees what before was obscure to him – a blessing not so far bestowed upon the dissenters. If any of these beliefs is true, then Christian belief is not epistemically on a par with these other beliefs. And if Hick is to claim that Christian belief really is no better based, epistemically, than these other beliefs, he presumably owes us an argument for the conclusion that those claims of epistemic privilege are in fact false. Still further, it is very probable that if Christian belief is true, then Christians *are* in a better position, epistemically speaking, than those who reject Christian belief; so what Hick really owes us is a good argument with respect to whose conclusion it is very unlikely that Christian belief is true. I don't see how he could offer such an argument, and I'll bet he doesn't either.

Well, perhaps Hick means to embrace the other disjunct; his idea is that the exclusivist himself recognizes that views incompatible with his are 'as epistemologically well based' as his own, but accepts them anyway. But that is unfair to the exclusivist. If he did agree that these other views are as epistemically well based as his own, then perhaps he would indeed be arbitrary. But of course he doesn't. In the paper I considered the analogy with moral beliefs. I believe that it is utterly wrong to discriminate against people on the basis of their race or to advance my career by lying about my colleagues; I realize that there are those who disagree with me; I am prepared to concede that their views have for them the same internal marks mine have for me (they have that quality of seeming to be *true*); I am also prepared to concede that they are *justified* in holding these beliefs, in the sense that in holding them they are not flouting any epistemic duties. Do I therefore think their moral views are epistemologically as well based as my own?

Certainly not. Even though I grant that those beliefs are on an epistemic par with mine with respect to the properties just mentioned, I don't believe they are with respect to *other* epistemic properties. I think perhaps the racist is the victim of a bad upbringing that in some way blinds him to what he would otherwise see; or perhaps he suffers from a certain cognitive glitch that prevents him from seeing the truth here. I think the same goes for the person who thinks it proper to lie about his colleagues to advance his career: he too was brought up badly, or has been blinded by ambition, or doesn't have friends and confidants of the right sort, or suffers from a congenital moral blind spot. In either case I claim that they are not as well placed, epistemically speaking, as I; hence their contrary views are not as well based, epistemologically speaking, as mine. And because I think these things, I am not arbitrarily holding on to views I see are no better based, epistemically speaking, than others inconsistent with them. I am perhaps *mistaken*, but not arbitrary.

The same goes with respect to religious positions incompatible with my own. I believe (sometimes in fear and trembling) that they are not as well based, epistemically speaking, as my beliefs. (Something similar holds for philosophical views different from my own; I also believe – again, with fear and trembling, since those who disagree with me are sometimes philosophically more accomplished than I – that some blind spot or some other epistemic impediment prevents them from seeing the truth.) I believe that Christians are epistemically fortunate in a way in which those who disagree with them are not. But then of course I am not in the clearly arbitrary position of thinking non-Christian views are epistemologically just as well based as Christian beliefs, but self-indulgently prefer the latter anyway.

And I suppose something of the same must be true for Hick. He differs from the vast bulk of the world's population in thinking all of the great religions (and most of the non-great ones as well) are literally *false*. (No doubt he also exclusivistically thinks views incompatible with this one are false.) Now perhaps he thinks he has a *good reason* for this view of his: the fact that there *is* all this diversity, the best explanation for it being that they all have things literally wrong, even if many are salvifically effective. But of course, others have that same evidence and don't think it *is* a good reason for the view in question. Furthermore, chances are that Hick is prepared to concede that these others are flouting no epistemic duties in believing as they do, and that the internal markers of their views for them are like the internal markers for his own view; still further, he no doubt realizes he can't produce arguments that will convince those others that in fact what he takes to be a good reason for his pluralism really *is* a good reason for it.

Is he therefore being arbitrary in continuing to believe as he does? Not necessarily. He presumably thinks those who disagree with him just can't see something he does see; they suffer from a blind spot in an area where he doesn't; perhaps they aren't quite ready, psychologically speaking, for that cool and bracing air of scepticism with respect to the beliefs they have inherited from their elders. In any event, and whatever the explanation, he is somehow in a better epistemic position, he thinks, than those who disagree with him, even though he can't show them that he is. He might, therefore, be wrong (in my opinion he *is* wrong) but he's not being merely arbitrary; he's not treating differently things he sees to be the same.

But then the same goes for the Christian. He believes that those who disagree with him lack some epistemic benefit or grace he has; hence he isn't being merely arbitrary. He thinks those opposing opinions are less well founded, epistemologically, than his own.

Finally, just a word about Hick's suggestion that if I had been born elsewhere and elsewhen, I would have had different beliefs: he thinks this should give me pause about the beliefs I do in fact have. I pointed out in my paper that if Hick had been born elsewhere and elsewhen, he probably wouldn't have been a pluralist, so that by his own principle, he should think twice (or more) about his pluralism. He replies that he's thinking only of beliefs with which one is brought up, not just any beliefs one has. Well, I'm not sure that's a relevant difference, but let's go along with it for the moment. And once more let's consider moral beliefs. No doubt Hick, like me, was brought up to believe that racial intolerance is wrong. Now it is fairly likely that most relevant place-times are such that if he and I had been brought up there and then, we would have had quite different views on this topic. Does that mean that we should eye our tolerance with special suspicion? Maybe we should; but if, after careful, prayerful thought and consideration, it still seems to us that racial intolerance is wrong, unjust, and morally repugnant, there is nothing arbitrary in our continuing to reject racism. But then, why should it be different for Christian belief?

## Note

1.  Alvin Plantinga is John A. O'Brien Professor of Philosophy at the University of Notre Dame, Indiana, USA.

## 2(ii)(a)   Hick

It is difficult to argue with Alvin Plantinga's declaration of faith in the unique superiority of Christianity as the only true religion. How do you argue with someone who says, we Christians (or at least those who are theologically orthodox) are right and everyone else is wrong? He does not offer arguments for this, but simply asserts it, pointing out that in doing so he is not flouting any epistemic duties. I accept that he is not involved in any epistemological misdemeanour! And he would, I think, accept that precisely the same applies to dogmatists of any other faith, and not only members of the other world religions, but also of much smaller and more recent movements some of whose beliefs he (and I) would think bizarre. They all have an equal right to their dogmas, at least so long as these are not harmful to others.

This is evident in a more recent writing in which Plantinga, outlining his 'Reformed epistemology', ends by reducing it to a tautological If. He says that the Reformed epistemologist's belief in the existence of God 'has warrant if and only if it is true; hence whether one thinks it has warrant will depend upon whether one thinks it true'.[1] Presumably everyone thinks that she has warrant for believing what she believes to be true. But this fact is entirely tradition-neutral and in no way privileges Christianity over other religions. Is not the causal explanation of Plantinga using it in defence of specifically Christian beliefs that he was raised in the Calvinist Christian tradition, whereas someone raised in, say, the Islamic faith could equally well use it in defence of holding specifically Muslim beliefs?

It is worth pointing out that his *tu quoque*, that I might well not have advocated religious pluralism if I had been born in many other times or places, and that I affirm it in much the same way that others affirm traditional Christianity, misses the all-important difference that religious pluralism (presented in *An Interpretation of Religion* as 'The Pluralistic Hypothesis') is not another religious faith or dogma alongside others, but a second-order philosophical theory, or hypothesis, about the relationship between the world religions when these are understood religiously as distinguished from naturalistically.

### Note

1. Alvin Plantinga, 'Reformed Epistemology', in Philip Quinn and Charles Taliaferro (eds.), *A Companion to the Philosophy of Religion* (Cambridge, Mass., and Oxford: Blackwell, 1997), p. 389.

*Professor Plantinga did not wish to make a further response but was content to leave his position as in his original response to my chapter 1.*

## 2(iii)   Peter van Inwagen[1]

In my essay 'Non Est Hick'[2] I used a political analogy to show that there was nothing in principle more 'arrogant' about being a Christian than there was about being a Burkean conservative, a Rawlsian liberal or a Marxist. Commenting on the use I made of this analogy, Professor Hick says:

> But has van Inwagen not here overlooked the crucial differences? The Church has traditionally claimed to be 'the uniquely "correct" one', in the sense of being the sole instrument of salvation. The Church's claim is not about the relative merits of different political systems but about the eternal fate of the entire human race.[3]

This is a true statement about the church's claims,[4] but I don't see its relevance to my attempt to disarm the charge of arrogance. I have to figure out which political beliefs to have ('none' and anarchism being among the options). I have to figure out which religious beliefs to have ('none' and atheism being among the options).[5] In either case, if I do adopt a certain set of beliefs, I have to believe that I and those who agree with me are right and that the rest of the world is wrong. The argument that the 'religious exclusivist' is arrogant rests on the premise that it is arrogant to believe that one and those few who agree with one are right and that most of the world is wrong (or at least that such a belief is arrogant if it is not about one of those matters concerning which the truth is more or less demonstrable – a belief, say, about the population of North Dakota or the age of the earth). But it follows from this premise – and a few well-known facts about the diversity of political opinion – that 'political exclusivism' is arrogant. (By political exclusivism, I mean having a definite set of political beliefs not common to all or most of humanity – or that plus an adherence to the principle of non-contradiction.[6]) If, therefore, it is arrogant to be a religious exclusivist (to have a definite set of religious beliefs not common to all or most of humanity and to accept the principle of non-contradiction), it is arrogant to be a political exclusivist. What hangs on one's accepting a certain set of beliefs, or what follows from their truth, doesn't enter into the question whether it is arrogant to accept them.

It is, in any case, very hard to avoid being a religious exclusivist.[7] Professor Hick is himself a religious exclusivist. My religious beliefs are inconsistent with Islam, but so are his (and with popular Hindu polytheism and with ancestor-worship and with ... but practically everyone in the world believes something that is inconsistent with his Anglo-American academic religious pluralism). 'Religious pluralism' is not the contradictory of religious exclusivism, but one more case of it.

As I read the passage I have quoted from Professor Hick's paper (and the larger passage from which I have excerpted it), it is not an argument for the conclusion that I am being arrogant in holding the beliefs I hold. It is rather an argument for the conclusion that those beliefs are false. He argues, on moral grounds, that a loving God would not establish a geographically limited church that was the unique instrument of salvation. Hick is, of course, aware that in the essay he is criticizing, I attempted to reply to this very argument. My reply was not meant to be particularly original – it is, as Hick says, 'standard'. (He does not call what I say a reply. He calls it an evasion. I don't think that's right for if the statements my reply comprises are true, they do answer the 'moral' objection to God's having established a unique instrument of salvation that is geographically limited.) Hick's reasoning is essentially this: if, as I claim, I do not know what provision God has made for ('involuntary') non-Christians in His plan of salvation for humanity, I shouldn't claim to know that He has not established instruments of salvation outside the Church.

Why do I claim to know that there are no divinely ordained instruments of salvation (as opposed to things that arise in the world by chance and which God may use as instruments in securing the salvation of various individuals or classes of people) outside the Church? Let me lay aside the question of knowledge, and answer the question why I *believe* this. I believe it because it is a part of my religion, one of the articles of Christian faith. And not of my religion alone: it is a part of the religion of Paul and the Primitive Church and the Apostolic Fathers and the Fathers and the scholastics and Luther and Calvin and Cranmer and Trent and Wesley and Newman: it is 'mere Christianity'. I don't see how I could coherently give up this belief other than by ceasing to be a Christian.[8] I also believe that nothing concerning the particulars of the fate of 'involuntary' non-Christians is 'mere Christianity'. (Many Christians, of course, will dispute this. Some think that Universalism is implicit in the New Testament. Others think that the damnation of all non-Christians, even involuntary ones, is an essential element of the Christian faith. I think they're wrong. Well, this is an 'in-house' dispute, a dispute about one of those many theological questions concerning which a Christian can do no more than try, with fear and trembling, to figure out what to believe.) I do have some beliefs about this, but they're tentative and not parts of my faith.[9] What is a part of my faith is that God is a righteous Lord and a loving Father, and, therefore, whatever plans He has made for involuntary non-Christians, they will involve no injustice; and not only will they involve no injustice, but they will be the work of a love that surpasses human comprehension. Does Professor Hick think that, if the Church is the sole instrument of salvation, there is *no* plan that a being of unlimited power and knowledge could devise for involuntary non-Christians that would be consistent with His being a just Lord and a loving Father? If so, I must once again deplore 'the apriorism that is an endemic intellectual disease of philosophers and theologians'.

## Notes

1. Peter van Inwagen is Professor of Philosophy at the University of Notre Dame, Indiana, USA.
2. In T. Senor (ed.), *The Rationality of Belief and the Plurality of Faith* (Ithaca and London: Cornell University Press, 1995), pp. 216–41. The analogy is presented on p. 238.
3. 'The Epistemological Challenge of Religious Pluralism', p. 31 above.
4. But Professor Hick's syntax – his avoidance of a parallel construction where one was natural – makes the position of the Church and any given political party or system seem less alike than they are. This syntactical device could have been as easily deployed the other way round: 'The Party's claim is not about the relative merits of different theological systems but about the future of the entire human race.'
5. Or I might simply adopt the religious beliefs of my parents or my community without ever thinking about the matter. But the same is true of my political beliefs.
6. The qualification is perhaps not otiose. It was, I believe, Ronald Knox who identified the essence of Anglicanism as the belief that whenever two people accept mutually contradictory propositions, they're both right.
7. No religious belief is common to all or most of humanity. The only way to avoid being a religious exclusivist (other than denying the principle of non-contradiction) is therefore to have no religious beliefs. And this is not easy. Atheists, of course, have religious beliefs: that God does not exist, if no other. And every agnostic with whom I have discussed religious belief has the following religious belief: that agnosticism is epistemically preferable to theism.
8. One might, of course, ask why I am a Christian 'in the first place'. I do not propose to enter into this question in a brief note. The interested reader may consult my essay 'Quam Dilecta', in Thomas V. Morris (ed.), *God and the Philosophers* (New York: Oxford University Press, 1994), pp. 31–60.
9. Consider the story of Emeth, the young 'Calormene' nobleman who is a minor character in C.S. Lewis's 'Narnia' book, *The Last Battle*. ('Emeth' is a word of biblical Hebrew sometimes translated 'truth'; Lewis's choice of this name for his character should be understood in the light of his discussion of the word in *Reflections on the Psalms*.) If, on another shore, in a greater light, it should transpire that (within its limitations; it occurs in a work of imaginative fiction written for children) this story had presented a correct image of

the saving work of the Holy Spirit in the lives of involuntary non-Christians, I shouldn't be at all surprised. (The religion in which Emeth was brought up, the only religion he had ever known, was a religion in which evil things were worshipped. And that is the hard case; if one has admitted that the Holy Spirit might work in the way Lewis's story represents Him as working in the hearts of men and women brought up to believe in a religion that was, in all essentials, devil-worship, one should see no difficulty in the thesis that He might work in parallel or analogous ways in the hearts of Muslims and Buddhists.)

### 2(iii)(a)   Hick

Peter van Inwagen is centrally concerned 'to disarm the charge of arrogance' in holding that Christianity is the only true religion. This is clearly a big issue for him – he uses 'arrogance' and 'arrogant' eight times in the first page alone. However, I had not accused him of being arrogant – the term does not appear anywhere in my remarks about him except in a quotation from himself. But towards the end of his Response van Inwagen recognizes that

> Professor Hick's paper . . . is not an argument for the conclusion that I am being arrogant in holding the beliefs I hold. It is rather an argument for the conclusion that those beliefs are false. . . . Hick's reasoning is essentially this: if, as I claim, I do not know what provision God has made for ('involuntary') non-Christians in his plan of salvation for humanity, I shouldn't claim to know that he has not established instruments of salvation outside the Church. (p. 59)

And telling us why he believes that there are no divinely ordained instruments of salvation outside the Christian church, he says, 'I believe it because it is part of my religion . . . Does Professor Hick think that, if the Church is the sole instrument of salvation, there is *no* plan that a being of unlimited power and knowledge could devise for involuntary non-Christians that would be consistent with His being a just Lord and a loving Father?' (p. 60). Two comments on this. First, such a plan has in fact already been devised by such theologians as Karl Rahner, and today represents the main both Catholic and Protestant view. It is generally called 'inclusivism', and in its Catholic form it holds that non-culpable, or involuntary, non-Christians may be counted as 'anonymous Christians' who may accept Christ as their Lord at or after death. In its Protestant form it does not generally make a restriction to 'involuntary' non-believers. But van Inwagen's is of the Catholic, and it seems also of a strict Calvinist, variety. Inclusivism is a theological theory developed to solve a problem, and as such it should be considered on its merits. If you define salvation as being accepted by God because of the atoning death of Jesus, then it is by definition exclusively Christian salvation, and this can be generously extended to (some or all) non-Christians, who are then included within the sphere of Christian salvation – hence 'inclusivism'. This depends, of course, on the dogmatic assertion of the unique superiority of Christianity, which is the central matter at issue. But if salvation means something concrete, which can begin in this life, as an actual transformation from natural self-centredness to a re-centring in God, manifested in what St Paul called the fruit of the Spirit, 'love, joy, peace, patience, kindness, goodness, faithfulness, gentleness, self-control' (Galatians 5: 22), then we can see that it is taking place not only within the Church but equally outside it. Again, against van Inwagen's restricted inclusivism, why limit the divine generosity to 'involuntary' non-Christians? There are millions of adherents of other faiths who are well aware of the Christian claim but who do not accept it; and in many of them the salvific transformation is taking place as evidently as it is among many Christians. If we do not know what God's provision is for anyone other than Christians, how can we know that these will not also be included in the divine Kingdom?

*Professor van Inwagen did not wish to make a further response but was content to leave his position as in his original response to my chapter 1.*

## 2(iv)   George I. Mavrodes[1]

I suggested in my original paper that Professor John Hick may be the most important western philosophical defender of polytheism. Unfortunately, Hick himself takes vigorous exception to this, initially construing it as either an extravagant compliment or a splendid insult. Well, I certainly did not intend it as an insult of any sort. To some extent, I meant it as a compliment (though it was not, in my opinion at least, extravagant). Primarily, however, I intended it as a straightforward characterization of Hick's version of religious pluralism. In his paper here, Hick has in the end elected to take my characterization as a jest. And that, no doubt, is better than an insult.

Hick also returns the characterization 'polytheist' to me. I don't mind taking it as a compliment, but I have no desire at all to construe it as either an insult or a jest. For I do now think of myself as a descriptive (though not a cultic) polytheist. My polytheism is somewhat different from that which I attribute to Hick (but similar to that which I attribute to most Christian thinkers), and I have (I think) different reasons for it. But I discussed those points in the earlier paper, and I will not rehearse that discussion here.

But anyway, if Hick is not a polytheist then what is he? In his present paper he gives a curious answer, describing himself as 'at one level a poly-something, though not precisely a polytheist, and at another level a mono-something, though not precisely a monotheist'.[2] So, a poly-something. What is that?

In reading *An Interpretation of Religion*, I got the impression that Hick thought that Allah, the Holy Trinity, Shiva, etc., were the gods worshipped in some various religions. And in some other religions the roughly corresponding objects of adoration were 'impersonal ultimates' – e.g. Brahman, the Tao, etc. I also got the impression that all of these were distinct from one another. And finally, I had the impression that (on Hick's view) all of these were real beings.[3] That is what led me to the conclusion that Hick was really a serious (descriptive) polytheist.[4]

Of course, Hick also says that none of these gods is the really ultimate, 'the Real' as he calls it. In the book, as in his present paper, he repeatedly appeals to Kantian metaphysics – that is, to the distinction between the noumenal and the phenomenal. Given this distinction, the various gods, etc., would be phenomenal entities, and the Real would be the noumenon which lay behind them.

But in the Kantian scheme of things, as I understand it at least, a cantaloupe is a phenomenal entity. It is not a noumenon, it is not an ultimate reality, it is not the *Ding an sich*. Nevertheless, I did not imagine that a Kantian produce manager would feel insulted if he were described as believing that there were exactly 39 cantaloupes in the supermarket bin.[5] I suppose he would think that cantaloupes were just the sort of things of which it made sense to ask whether there were one or many or none at all, and that it was proper – indeed, commonplace – to believe and profess some answer to that question.

Hick, however, seems to be fierce in his repudiation of any analogous suggestion about himself and the gods. Why is that? Well, now I am rather more hesitant than before in professing to understand Hick's views. But my present conjecture is that I may have gone wrong in the third of the 'impressions' I noted above. I now suspect, that is, that Hick (despite what he sometimes says) does not think that the gods, etc., of the actual religions – Allah, Shiva, Brahman, the Holy Trinity, and so on – are real at all. Or, to put it more cautiously, they have at best a very tenuous and weak reality. They are much less real than, say, cantaloupes. And so no serious philosopher could be happy with the ascription to himself of a belief that there really are such beings, that they might have an impact on affairs in the ordinary world, and so on. It would be as though someone were to ascribe to him the belief that Santa Claus came from the North Pole on Christmas Eve to deliver toys through the various chimneys of the world. Despite his professed Kantianism, Hick may really think of the gods of *all* the religions as much more like fictional characters, illusions, etc., than like Kantian phenomena. And what he is poly about is this whole group of shadowy *insubstantia*.[6]

Well, so much for poly-something (here, at least). Hick also professes to be a mono-something. What is he mono about? Well, of course, it is the Real. Or is it? And what is the Real, after all? These questions react on one another, and the vagueness of the 'something' contributes to doubts about the 'mono'.

In this paper, as in the book, Hick is at least sometimes true to the Kantian framework in which he wants to cast his views. On these occasions he says that the Real is not an item in our experience, religious or otherwise. Not even a mystic could have an experience of the Real. And so he writes here, 'But on the pluralistic hypothesis, as I have tried to formulate it, there can be no direct experience of the Real *an sich* . . .'[7]

If the Real is not an item in our experience, then what is its epistemological status? How does it get into our discourse at all? Hick seems to give a straightforward answer to this question. The Real is *postulated*.

Now, I suppose that one may postulate whatever he or she wishes. But Hick pretty clearly wants to claim that the postulation of the Real is not arbitrary. It is grounded in some way. 'I want to say that the Real *an sich* is postulated by us as a pre-supposition, not of the moral life, but of religious experience and the religious life . . .'[8] And 'if from a religious point of view we are trying to think, not merely of what is logically possible (namely, anything that is conceivable), but of the simplest hypothesis to account for the plurality of forms of religious experience and thought, we are, I believe, led to postulate "the Real".'[9] And again, 'hence the postulation of the Real *an sich* as the simplest way of accounting for the data'.[10]

But just what is being postulated to account for the data of religious life, diversity, etc.? What is referred to by the expression 'the Real'? A person who experienced a certain entity might conceivably just give it a name, and later on use that name to refer to that entity again, perhaps in trying to account for some further data. And maybe other people could pick up the use of that name from him, and use it in the same way (roughly *à la* Kripke). But for a purely *postulated* entity, one which is not experienced, that procedure can hardly be supposed to work. It would seem that a purely postulated thing must be postulated via some *description* of the intended referent. What description is supposed to enable us to get a grip on what Hick is postulating to account for the facts of the religious world?

Maybe this question can also be formulated in this way. It does not take much effort to imagine a Christian who reads Hick, and then says something like the following.

> Why, I know just what Hick is talking about. It's the Holy Trinity! That's the most real thing there is, the ground of all reality, the creator of all things visible and invisible. So the expression, 'the Real', must be just Hick's name for the Holy Trinity. And maybe Hick is right in thinking that the Holy Trinity accounts for all the facts about the religious life of the world, and so on. But surely Hick must be mistaken in thinking that the Real has to be postulated. For the Holy Trinity has been revealed throughout the history of the world, and pre-eminently in Jesus Christ.[11]

But Hick himself seems to be committed to rejecting the advances of this apparent friend.

Why? Well, Hick apparently intends that the Real, as he postulates it, is in some way *incompatible* with the Holy Trinity, and so cannot be identical with it. In what way? In rejecting one of my 'models' Hick says (in the present paper),

> Presumably that one god, like the prince in the story, has his/her own definite, describable characteristics, including the intention to appear in a variety of ways. But such a god is not analogous to the postulated ineffable Real. This has no humanly conceivable intrinsic characteristics (other than purely formal, linguistically generated ones), and is accordingly not a person carrying out a revelatory plan.

So, the Holy Trinity presumably has some positive, describable, properties – being a trinity, for example, and carrying out a self-revelatory plan, etc – but the Real is ineffable and has no humanly conceivable, positive, properties at all.[12] Hence the Real is not identical with the Holy Trinity.

So here then we have a little stuffing to put into the expression, 'the Real'. Hick intends to postulate something which is characterized by the negative property of ineffability. OK. It seems plausible to say that *that* thing, whatever it is, is not identical with the Holy Trinity (and, I suppose, not identical with Shiva, or with Allah, etc.). But this stuffing, while it may secure the distinction of the Real from the gods of the actual religions, bristles with problems of its own.

Spelling out some of the consequences of the postulated ineffability, Hick says 'we cannot apply to the Real *an sich* the characteristics encountered in its *personae* and *impersonae*. Thus it cannot be said to be one or many, person or thing, substance or process, good or evil, purposive or non-purposive ... We cannot even speak of this as a thing or entity.'[13] And because Hick is so insistent on being known as a mono-something we naturally notice especially his recognition that the Real 'cannot be said to be one or many'.

For better or worse, that seems like a Kantian theme. Number belongs to the phenomenal world, and *one* is a number. The *Ding an sich* is not to be numbered, one or two or many. And so it would seem that Hick, if he is to be true to his professed convictions about ineffability, cannot consistently be mono about the Real. And of course he is not mono about the gods of the actual religions. It seems that in the end there is nothing at all about which Hick really is mono – nothing, that is, which is religiously relevant.

Now, Hick himself says a little about this problem. 'We then find that if we are going to speak of the Real at all, the exigencies of our language compel us to refer to it in either the singular or the plural. Since there cannot be a plurality of ultimates, we affirm the true ultimacy of the Real by referring to it in the singular.'[14] But this is a strangely weak argument, or so at least it seems to me. A mono-somethingism which is generated by a superficial exigency of English grammar hardly seems worth getting steamed up about. And anyway, could we not just as easily argue in the following way? 'English requires us to refer to the Real either in the singular or the plural. But since the ultimate cannot be one, we affirm the true ultimacy of the Real by referring to it in the plural.'

I said earlier that the ineffability of the postulated Real bristles with problems. Let me conclude this essay by mentioning two others briefly. One concerns Hick's attempt to ground this postulation by claiming that it provides us with 'the simplest way of accounting for the data'. But isn't it hard to see how something which is described *only* by the *via negativa* – 'not this, not that' – could provide any account at all, simple or otherwise, for any positive data? The religious life of the world is amazingly resistant and resilient. The religions of the world are surprisingly diverse. They are culturally fecund. They produce actual human characters of profound beauty and goodness. These are facts (or so, at least, it seems to me). What could account for such facts?

We might imagine people – or maybe we need not merely imagine them – who suggest that these facts may be accounted for by postulating the existence of a god with a beauty beyond that of the earth, with a goodness fiercer than that of the greatest saint and gentler than the humblest maidservant, and so on. That postulation might have a chance of accounting for some religious facts. But it is not Hick's way. He postulates something which is neither good nor evil, neither purposive nor non-purposive and of course Hick's Real is not loving, not powerful, not wise, not compassionate, not gentle, not forgiving. The Real does not know me (or anyone else), does not care about me (or anything else), and so on. The Real did not create the world, did not design the world, does not sustain the world, and will not bring the world to an end. What in the world does that Real have to do with anything which happens in the world? Why would anyone suppose that it 'accounts' for any fact at all, religious or otherwise?

Hick, I think, is himself unsatisfied with the ineffability which he professes. So he is continually drifting into causal, or quasi-causal, talk about the Real – that it is the 'noumenal ground' of certain experiences, that there is a 'transmission of information from a transcendent source to the human mind/brain', the Real has an 'impact upon us', and so on. But this talk is either empty (though with the appearance of content) or else it violates the prohibition of applying to the Real any humanly conceivable, positive, substantial characteristics.

The other problem concerns the claim of ineffability itself. Hick says that 'none of the concrete descriptions that apply within the realm of human experience can apply literally to the unexperiencable ground of that realm'.[15] Why not? How in the world could Hick discover a fact like that about the Real?

The line of reasoning to which Hick himself appeals is given in the succeeding sentence. 'For whereas the phenomenal world is structured by our own conceptual frameworks, its noumenal ground is not.' This does seem to be an authentically Kantian line of argument. But it does not, it seems to me, support the desired conclusion. Suppose that we are puzzled by the question of how there can be a genuine *synthetic a priori* knowledge of the world. And then we find ourselves attracted by the suggestion that the world is a phenomenal object – that is, it is somehow a human construct, 'structured by our own conceptual frameworks', built by us to match our own human categories of understanding, our forms of sensibility, and so on. And so now the problem of a *synthetic a priori* knowledge of the world seems manageable.

But, of course, the difference between the noumenal world and the phenomenal is supposed to be that the former, unlike the latter, is *not* a human construct. The noumenal is what is independent, prior, the ground, etc. And so it would be wrong to say that the categories of human understanding, humanly conceivable properties, etc., apply to the noumenal world because we constructed that world to order. For, on this Kantian–Hickian view, we did not construct the noumenal world at all.

Nevertheless, it does not follow that the humanly conceivable categories do not apply there. What does follow is that their application to the noumenal world is to be accounted for (if at all) in a way different from that which accounts for their fit with the phenomenal world. And indeed some religions, at least, have at hand a ready explanation. For in those religions it is held that human beings are themselves created by something (or better, Someone) noumenal. And so the categories of the human understanding, which structure the phenomenal, are themselves structured by the noumenal. And they are structured so as to provide for a genuine, though perhaps finite, knowledge of the noumenal. According to this suggestion, the human conceptual and cognitive apparatus, as a whole, is adapted to an understanding of *both* the phenomenal world and the noumenal world, although the 'direction of fit' is different in the two cases.

## Notes

1. George Mavrodes is Professor of Philosophy at the University of Michigan, USA.
2. This reply usefully calls attention to the fact that the big three theological 'isms' – polytheism, monotheism and atheism – are all quantifications on the concept of god, and so they require a concept of god. They all need to have an answer to the question, 'What sort of thing is it of which you say that there are many, or just one, or none at all?'
3. For example, 'Within each tradition we regard as real the object of our worship or contemplation.... It is also proper to regard as real the objects of worship or contemplation within the other traditions...' John Hick, *An Interpretation of Religion* (New Haven: Yale University Press, 1989), p. 249.
4. That, in fact, is the aspect of his work which stimulated my own philosophical interest in the topic of polytheism.
5. Maybe, though, he would laugh a little if he were described as a poly-cantaloupian? Surely he is a poly-something.
6. Many religious people think of the gods of *other* religions in this way. But hardly any such people think that way about the gods of their own religion.

Hick's view suggests that almost all of the world's religious believers are wildly mistaken about the objects of their worship and adoration.

7. But sometimes he talks in a substantially different way. For example, 'one can say that the Real is experienced by human beings, but experienced in a manner analogous to that in which, according to Kant we experience the world . . . ' (*ibid.*, p. 243). This is related to the 'deep ambiguity' which I discussed in my original paper.

8. Loc. cit.

9. *Ibid.*, p. 248.

10. *Ibid.*, p. 249. Perhaps in these latter two passages Hick means to shave the ineffable divine reality with Ockham's medieval razor?

11. I have discussed responses of this sort at greater length in 'The Gods above the Gods: Can the High Gods Survive?', in Eleonore Stump (ed.), *Reasoned Faith*: (Ithaca: Cornell University Press, 1993).

12. Unlike some aficionados of ineffability, Hick ascribes only a limited ineffability to the Real, and thus he avoids (initially, at least) the charge of self-referential incoherence. He allows that the Real may have some 'purely formal' properties, and that it may be properly characterized by *negative* properties such as *ineffability* itself. So he accepts the *via negativa*. He also apparently accepts that the Real may have substantial positive properties, just so long as they are not humanly conceivable. Cf. *ibid.*, pp. 236–49.

13. *Ibid.*, p. 246.

14. *Ibid.*, p. 249.

15. *Ibid.*, p. 246.

## 2(iv)(a)  Hick

George Mavrodes raises a number of issues clustering around the two central questions, 'What (according to my version of the pluralist hypothesis) is the ontological status of the *personae* and *impersonae* of the Real?' and 'Why postulate an ineffable Real; how does this help to explain the facts of religious life around the world?'

In *An Interpretation of Religion* I discussed a number of possible views of the status of the divine *personae* and metaphysical *impersonae*, and after rejecting several was left with two. Concerning these I said, 'the pluralistic hypothesis being propounded here could accommodate either of these models and does not require a decision between them. It therefore seems wise not to insist upon settling a difficult issue which, in logic, the hypothesis leaves open' (p. 275). I remain equally cautious at this point.

We can start with the fact that (as Alston notes – see p. 47 above) whilst religious experience may make us aware of, for example, an invisible loving personal presence, it does not tell us that this presence is infinite, or is the creator of everything other than itself, nor that it is triune or unitary, or is self-revealed in the Torah, or in the Christian

Bible, or in the Qur'an, or in the Bhagavad Gita, etc. These elaborations are supplied by the religious tradition within which the experience occurs and are often projected, in the mind's construction of the experience, onto the experienced presence. That is, the experiencer may report having experienced the presence of God, meaning by 'God' much more than is actually given in the experience itself.

One option, then, is to hold that the specific figure of the Heavenly Father, who is one person of a divine Trinity, and the specific figures of the Adonai (the Lord) of Jewish worship, and of the Allah of Muslim worship, and likewise of the Shiva and Vishnu of different strands of Hindu worship, are all human projections based (according to the pluralist hypothesis) on a genuine experience of a transcendent presence, this experience being a cognitive response, in a culturally conditioned form, to the universal presence of the Real. On this view, in religious experience we are aware of the Real as – in the case of the theistic religions – a specific deity; and this deity is, in the Kantian terms that I have used, a phenomenal appearance to us of the not directly experienceable noumenal Real-in-itself. The God-figures, in their tradition-specific particularities, are thus human projections, but are 'veridical projections' (analogous to 'veridical hallucinations', which express genuine information) in that they constitute an authentic cognitive response to a transcendent reality. Mavrodes says that such God-figures 'have at best a very tenuous and weak reality' (pp. 63–4). But this is certainly not the case for their worshippers. There is a genuine experience of a presented reality, and the fact that this experience is filled out in the process of perception by our human concepts is not unique to religious experience but occurs all the time in all our conscious experience. (This is something that I have argued at length in both *An Interpretation of Religion* and elsewhere, and which indeed many philosophers have argued ever since Kant, and the arguments need not be repeated here.)

The other option requires the idea of what in Buddhist thought are called the *devas*, usually translated as gods (as distinguished from God), or in Christian terms as angels and archangels. These are real personal beings with whom a real I–Thou relationship is possible; they are of a higher spiritual quality than us; they have some but limited power; and it may well be that they are specially concerned, as 'guardian angels', with particular human individuals and groups. Considered simply by themselves their existence does not require us to postulate the Real, or the Godhead. But considered in the context of the religions, both theistic and non-theistic, within which they are encountered, and in which they are experienced as agents of a more ultimate absolute reality, they are part of religious totalities for a religious understanding of which, I have argued, the Real has to be postulated.

However Mavrodes regards the concept of the Real as vacuous, empty, not the concept of anything. Presenting apparent difficulties in the concept he points out that 'Number belongs to the phenomenal world, and *one* is a number. The *Ding an sich* is not to be numbered, one or two or many. And so it would seem that Hick, if he is to be true to his professed convictions about ineffability, cannot consistently be mono about the Real' (p. 66). The problem here is one of language. We have to refer to the Real in either the singular or the plural, even though neither concept properly applies. But this is not only a problem in the English language, as Mavrodes suggests when he speaks of a 'mono-somethingism which is generated by a superficial exigency of English grammar' (p. 66). Maimonides, writing originally in Arabic, said, 'It would be extremely difficult for us to find, in any language whatsoever, words adequate to the subject, and we can only employ inadequate language. In our endeavour to show that God does not include a plurality, we can only say "He is one", although "one" and "many" are both terms which serve to distinguish quantity.'[1] The Upanishadic writers, using Sanskrit, faced the same problem in speaking of Brahman and used the deliberately paradoxical formula, 'the One without a second'.[2] These are ways of taking account of the limitations of language, something of which Wittgenstein reminded us but which later analytical philosophers have sometimes forgotten.

To see the function and value of the concept of the Real we need to see how it arises. If we hold that human religious experience, in its variety of forms, is not purely projection, but is at the same time a response to transcendent reality, it is clear that its validity does not consist in any one of its direct objects – the Christian or the Jewish or the Muslim or the Vaishnavite or the Shaivite or any other specifically characterized God – being the ultimate reality, since they cannot possibly all be. And so we are led to postulate a more ultimate reality, 'the Real', of which they are all manifestations to human consciousness, receiving their specific forms by different human religious mentalities integral to different cultural ways of being human.

But how does the Real 'impinge' upon us, 'impact' us, 'affect' us? Does not such language nullify its ineffability? There is a problem of language again. Our awareness of the Real depends upon the fact that there is an aspect of human nature which naturally responds to the Transcendent. This is variously referred to as the image of God within us, or as 'that of God in every man', or as the atman in the depth of our being, or as the Buddha nature present within us as our true nature, though now often overlaid by self-concern. The metaphorical language of impacting, impinging, etc. expresses the fact that when we are open to the universal presence of the Real we become aware of it – but always in terms of our necessarily inadequate human concepts.

In conclusion, I would like to draw attention to the fact that the great majority of critics of the pluralist hypothesis – including Alston, Plantinga, van Inwagen and Mavrodes – start from the presupposition that there can be at most only one true religion, and the fixed conviction that this is their own. A hermeneutic of suspicion cannot help wondering if their search for anti-pluralist arguments, usually philosophically very sophisticated arguments, is driven by a need to defend a highly conservative/evangelical/sometimes fundamentalist religious faith. For it is noticeable that thinkers, within both Christianity and other traditions, who are more progressive/liberal/ecumenical in outlook tend to have much less difficulty with the pluralist idea. They do not, of course, necessarily adopt my own particular philosophical version of it, but the basic idea that was poetically expressed, for example, by the Muslim Sufi, Jalaluldin Rumi, speaking of the plurality of religions, that 'The lamps are different, but the Light is the same', appeals intuitively to a great many people. Needless to say, and as the religiously conservative critics would probably be the first to point out, this does not show that they are mistaken in their beliefs. But, together with the fact that their holding conservative Christian, rather than conservative Muslim or Hindu or other, beliefs is precisely correlated with their having been raised in a Christian rather than a Muslim or Hindu or other society, it does 'make one think'.

### Notes

1. Maimonides, *Guide to the Perplexed,* trans. M. Friedlander (London: Routledge & Kegan Paul, 1904), p. 81.
2. *Chandogya Upanishad,* VI.2.4., trans. S. Radhakrishnan, *The Principal Upanishads* (London: Allen & Unwin and New York: Humanities Press, 1969), p. 449.

### 2(iv)(b)   Mavrodes[1]

Professor Hick has graciously invited me to add my own reaction to his response. My earlier paper was addressed to epistemological and metaphysical issues more directly than to the questions about religious pluralism. This response follows the same path.

Hick quotes Maimonides, 'In our endeavour to show that God does not include a plurality, we can only say "He is one", although "one" and "many" are both terms which serve to distinguish quantity.' And this seems to repeat (prospectively) Hick's claim that the difficulty here is simply that of an inadequate language. But that cannot be the whole story.

It is true that if God (or Hick's Real) is a noumenon in the Kantian sense, then God (or the Real) is not a plurality. And Maimonides apparently wants to 'show' (i.e. to express?) that fact. But why does Maimonides undertake that particular endeavour? Why does Hick undertake it? It cannot be merely for the sake of 'showing' a truth. For it is also a truth that if God is a noumenon in the Kantian sense, then God is not a singularity. And if we were to endeavour to show that God is not a singularity, using our inadequate language and availing ourselves of Maimonides' strategy, then we would refer to God (or Hick's Real) by saying 'They are many.'

Maimonides and Hick opt for 'one' instead of 'many', for singular nouns and pronouns rather than plurals. And that seems to be equivalent to picking one of these endeavours rather than the other. Why pick that one? *Both* these endeavours are equally related to the truth that Kantian noumena are not to be numbered.

Here we might (maybe if we are in a cynical mood?) appeal to another of Hick's strategies, one to which he often has recourse in discussing exclusivism. That is, we can appeal to the hermeneutics of suspicion. We might note that Maimonides belongs to a monotheistic religious tradition. Of course, it is not monotheistic about Kantian noumena; it is monotheistic about the LORD. Nevertheless, from childhood Maimonides no doubt heard and repeated the formula, 'The LORD is one.' Might not that 'make one think' that perhaps the childhood indoctrination disposed the mature philosopher to endeavour to show that God is not a plurality, rather than endeavouring to show that God is not a singularity? Or did Maimonides suggest some rational reason for preferring the one endeavour to the other?

Whatever may be the case with Maimonides, Hick (so far as I know) gives no reason for preferring the inadequate 'one' to the inadequate 'many', for preferring singular nouns (The Real) to plural nouns (The Reals). But Hick, like Maimonides, grew up in a monotheistic tradition. And so maybe the same suspicions arise over his preferences.

Whatever may be the psychological story behind Hick's preference for the language of singularity over the language of plurality, he has provided no rational justification for it. But that is just a special case of a more general difficulty in his approach, the problem of how to squeeze any philosophical blood out of an ineffable turnip. If it is really true, as Hick says, that 'the ineffable Real . . . has no humanly conceivable intrinsic characteristics', then there is nothing which we can know about the Real which has any bearing on any particular fact about the world of our experience. There is nothing there to which we can appeal in order to account for some element in the ordinary world. It is a fact about the world (or so, at least, it seems to me) that many religions include people whose lives are marked by a profound love, by compassion, etc. What might account for that fact? One might suggest that their religion has brought these people into contact with a Real which is itself overflowing with love. And maybe that would account for the love in the life of the religious devotee. At least it has some plausibility. But, of course, the Real which is overflowing with love cannot be Hick's Real. For Hick's Real has no humanly conceivable characteristic, and therefore it is not characterized by love.

Maybe Hick's Real is 'out there' somewhere. But what it has to do with love, with the plurality of religions, with mystical experience, or with anything else is anyone's guess. Since we know nothing positive about this postulated Real, we have no handle on how it might be related to any fact in the world. The postulation of a Real of this sort cannot be rationally justified by suggesting that it accounts for the religious phenomena in the world, or, for that matter, any other phenomena whatever.

Hick says that I regard the concept of the Real as vacuous, empty, etc. Well, that might indeed be what my critique comes to. But maybe not everyone would go that far. Imagine a speculative philosopher who thinks that Hick's concept is not empty. This philosopher professes to understand Hick's usage, and he agrees that Hick really does refer to something, maybe something very important, when he uses the term 'Real'. But he thinks that Hick is mistaken in one respect; he is mistaken about the relation of the Real to the religious life of the world. This philosopher thinks that the Real has practically nothing to do with religion. At best, he thinks, the Real is irrelevant to the religious phenomena.

This philosopher, however, recognizes the full range of religious phenomena. And like Hick, he thinks that something must account for this aspect of the world. So, how does he account for the religious facts? Like Hick, he does so by making a postulation. He postulates the Unreal.

We might think that he is making the same postulation as Hick, merely giving it a different name. But he strongly disputes this. He explains that the Unreal, just like the Real, is ineffable. That is, it has 'no humanly conceivable intrinsic characteristics'. But though it is ineffable, it can be described negatively, 'not this, not that'. And one of these 'nots' is that the Unreal is not identical with the Real. So there is the Real, and there is also the Unreal, and they are not identical. Furthermore, he postulates that the Unreal does not share a single ineffable property with the Real. Clearly, then, the Unreal is not the same postulate as the Real, and if both of these terms have any reference at all they do not have the same reference.

Finally, our philosopher says that the Unreal accounts for the religious phenomena of the world – that, after all, was the point of postulating it. How does the Unreal account for the saintly life of Francis of Assisi, for Sakyamuni's insights into human suffering, for the diversity of religions, and so on? That, of course, is mysterious, since (by definition, as it were) we know nothing positive about the Unreal. But it is no more mysterious than the corresponding questions about the Real. And what is the relation between the Unreal and the particular deities of the various religions? Our philosopher appeals, of course, to Kantian ideas, and says that the Unreal is the noumenon which is variously experienced and conceptualized as the particular gods of the diverse traditions.

This philosopher, of course, is not John Hick. But is either one of them worse off, philosophically, than the other?

### Note

1.  Section 2(iv)(b) © George I. Mavrodes 2001.

*Given the hypothesis that the God figures and their non-theistic counterparts are different phenomenal manifestations of a noumenal X, the way in which we refer to that X is a matter of linguistic preference. But 'the Unreal' would be confusing, and the plural would be more misleading than the singular, although in the nature of the case no language can be adequate.* (J. H.)

# 3
# Ineffability: A Response to William Rowe and Christopher Insole

## Transcategoriality in the world religions

The term 'ineffable', meaning inexpressible, transcending description, beyond the scope of our human concepts, is good semantic currency with a respectable Latin lineage. But today, because of such similar-sounding but very different-meaning words and phrases as 'effing' and 'the eff word', we may well be slightly uncomfortable with 'ineffable' and ready for an alternative. I suggest 'transcategorial', that is, outside or beyond the range of our categories of thought, and I shall use both terms in what follows.

We are concerned with transcategoriality as applied to God – using 'God' as our customary western term for the ultimate reality to which the religions point. Each of the great traditions says, in its own way, that God in God's ultimate nature is beyond characterization by the range of concepts available to human thought and embodied in our languages. But they balance this by also speaking of God in relation to ourselves as having, in the case of the monotheisms, humanly describable attributes such as personality, goodness, love, compassion, justice, and so on, in virtue of which prayer, worship and personal devotion are possible. The non-theistic faiths make corresponding distinctions, as we shall see presently.

Thus each of the world religions has a dual concept of God as both transcategorial in the ultimate divine nature and yet religiously available in virtue of qualities analogous to but limitlessly greater than our own. As a brief reminder, within Jewish mysticism a distinction is drawn between *Ein Sof*, the Limitless, and the God of the Torah – thus Gershom Scholem speaks of 'the difference between *deus absconditus*, God in Himself, and God in His appearance'.[1] The ultimate divine ineffability is also affirmed in the Qur'an: 'God is too glorious for what they ascribe to Him' (37: 159. Also 43: 82). This is developed by some of the Sufis in a two-level concept of the transcategorial Reality and the self-revealed Qur'anic Allah. For example, 'Abd al-Rahman Jami (d. 1492) writes, 'The unique Substance, viewed as absolute and void of all phenomena, all limitations and all multiplicity, is the Real (*al-Haqq*). On the other hand, viewed in His aspect of multiplicity and plurality, under which He displays Himself when clothed with phenomena, He is the whole created universe.'[2]

We shall come to the other great monotheism, Christianity, presently. But first we turn to the traditions originating in India. Within the streams of religious experience and thought collectively called Hinduism there is a pervasive distinction between *nirguna* Brahman, the ultimate transcategorial reality in itself, and *saguna* Brahman, that same reality humanly experienced as Ishwara, deity, expressed in the innumerable gods worshipped in different regions and areas of life. Sikhism, which has received much from Hinduism, also uses the *nirguna/saguna* distinction.[3]

Within the mahayana tradition of Buddhism an essentially similar distinction is drawn between the ultimate *Dharmakaya*, beyond human conceptuality, and its manifestation as the heavenly realm of the compassionate Buddhas, some of whom appear on earth in different historical periods. To quote a passage used by Shinran,

> Among Buddhas and bodhisattvas there are two aspects of dharmakaya: dharmakaya-as-suchness and dharmakaya-as-compassion. Dharma-kaya-as-compassion arises out of dharmakaya-as-suchness, and dhar-makaya-as-suchness emerges into human consciousness through dharmakaya-as-compassion. The two aspects of dharmakaya differ but are not separate, they are one but not identical.[4]

These distinctions between *Ein Sof* and the God of the Torah, between *al-Haqq* and the Quar'anic Allah, between *nirguna* and *saguna* Brahman, and between the *Dharmakaya* and the realm of the Buddhas, are clearly analogous to one another and also have their analogy in Christian thought.

Here virtually all the great church theologians from early times have affirmed the ultimately ineffable nature of God. This was laid down as a marker by the fourth-century Gregory of Nyssa, of whom Bernard McGinn, in his authoritative history of western mysticism, says that his theology is 'now recognized as one of the most powerful in the history of Christianity'.[5] Gregory said,

The simplicity of the True Faith assumes God to be that which He is, namely, incapable of being grasped by any term, or any idea, or any other device of our apprehension, remaining beyond the reach not only of the human but of the angelic and all supramundane intelligence, unthinkable, unutterable, above all expression in words, having but one name that can represent His proper nature, the single name being 'Above Every name'.[6]

In the fifth century the enormously influential Pseudo-Dionysius, about whom more later, wrote the definitive Christian affirmation of the absolute ineffability of God. Moving on through Christian history, Augustine treated it as an accepted fact that God 'transcends even the mind',[7] although this was not a central theme of his work. The ninth-century John Scottus Eriugena spoke of the God beyond God.[8] And Thomas Aquinas, deeply influenced by Pseudo-Dionysius (whom he cites some 1,700 times), said that 'by its immensity, the divine substance surpasses every form that our intellect reaches. Thus we are unable to apprehend it by knowing what it is.'[9] And the thirteenth/fourteenth-century Meister Eckhart completed the picture by distinguishing explicitly between the transcategorial Godhead (*Gottheit, deitas*) and the describable and worshipped God (*Gott, deus*). Later, in the fourteenth century, Margaret Porete, who was executed for heresy – paying the price of being a woman mystic in a male-dominated church – expressed the common theme of mystical theology that 'God [i.e. the Godhead] is totally incomprehensible and therefore "nothing" from the perspective of human categories.'[10] In the twentieth century Paul Tillich spoke of 'the God above the God of theism';[11] and Gordon Kaufman distinguished in his earlier work between the 'real God' and the 'available God', the former being an 'utterly unknowable X' and the latter 'essentially a mental or imaginative construction',[12] whilst Ninian Smart has spoken of 'the noumenal Focus of religion which so to say lies beyond the phenomenal Foci of religious experience and practice',[13] and I have myself based a hypothesis about the relationship between the world religions on the distinction between the noumenal Real and its phenomenal *personae* and *impersonae*.[14]

## Pseudo-Dionysius: ineffability versus religious availability

Let us now look more closely at one particular Christian writer, Pseudo-Dionysius, and at the way in which he faced the religious dilemma which the idea of divine ineffability brings with it. He was probably a fifth-century Syrian monk who pretended in his writings to be the biblical Dionysius the Areopagite (Acts 17: 34). His works remained immensely influential, with a 'Dionysian Renaissance' in the thirteenth century, at least up to the Reformation of the sixteenth century. Whether they would have been equally influential if it had not been believed that he was St Paul's convert, Dionysius, and thus close to Paul and so writing with a near-apostolic authority, we shall never know. But Denys (to use a more reader-friendly contraction of his name) is famous for his stress on the absolute and unqualified transcategoriality of God. He frequently uses non-personal terms, such as 'the Transcendent One', of which he says,

> It is not soul or mind, nor does it possess imagination, conviction, speech, or understanding. ... It cannot be spoken of and it cannot be grasped by understanding. ... It has no power, it is not power, nor is it light. It does not live nor is it life. It is not a substance, nor is it eternity or time .... It is neither one nor oneness, divinity nor goodness. ... It is not sonship or fatherhood and it is nothing known to us or to any other being. It falls neither within the predicate of nonbeing nor of being .... There is no speaking of it, nor name nor knowledge of it. ... It is beyond assertion and denial. We make assertions and denials of what is next to it, but never of it ... for it is ... free of every limitation, beyond every limitation: it is also beyond denial.[15]

Here and elsewhere Denys says, in as emphatic and unqualified a way as he can, that the Godhead, the ultimate One, is absolutely ineffable, eluding all our human categories of thought. He goes beyond a purely negative or apophatic theology, which confines itself to saying what God is not, by rejecting negative as well as positive statements about God. He says that 'we should not conclude that the negations are simply the opposites of the affirmations, but rather that the cause of all is considerably prior to this, beyond privations, beyond every denial, beyond every assertion.'[16] Thus the positive and negative statements jointly point beyond themselves to an absolutely transcategorial reality.

But Denys is then caught in the dilemma which faces everyone who affirms the ultimate divine ineffability but who is also required, by the practice of worship and the religious life generally, to think of God as a personal being with whom a personal relationship is possible. For how could we worship the totally transcategorial? And how could Denys, as a faithful Christian monk, allow the scriptures, liturgies and theologies of the church to be undercut by an unqualified divine ineffability? And so he says that God is the 'Source which has told us about itself in the holy words of scripture'.[17] He accepts fully the church's teaching that 'the Godhead is...one in three persons',[18] and affirms 'the most evident idea in theology, namely, the sacred incarnation of Jesus for our sakes'.[19] But clearly he has landed himself in a direct contradiction when he says (a) that the Godhead is absolutely ineffable, transcending all our human categories of thought, and (b) that the Godhead is self-revealed in the Bible as a trinity, one person of whom became incarnate as Jesus of Nazareth.

Denys was fully aware of the problem. He asks:

> How then can we speak of the divine names? How can we do this if the Transcendent surpasses all discourse and all knowledge, if it abides beyond the reach of mind and of being, if it encompasses and circumscribes, embraces and anticipates all things whilst itself eluding their grasp and escaping from any perception, imagination, opinion, name, discourse, apprehension, or understanding? How can we enter upon this undertaking if the Godhead is superior to being and is unspeakable and unnameable?[20]

His answer is that the language of scripture is metaphorical: 'the Word of God makes use of poetic imagery...as a concession to the nature of our own mind';[21] the divine Light makes truth known to us 'by way of representative symbols', so that 'this divine ray can enlighten us only by being upliftingly concealed in a variety of sacred veils which the Providence of the Father adapts to our nature as human beings'.[22] (Dionysius uses 'symbolic' with the same meaning as 'metaphorical'.[23]) He emphasizes the metaphorical character of the biblical language by pointing to the absurdity of taking it literally. In the Bible, he says, 'God is clothed in feminine adornments or in the armour of barbarians. He is given the attributes of an artisan, be he potter or refiner. He is put on horses, on chariots, on thrones. Well-laid feasts are put on for him. He is represented as drinking, as inebriated, as sleeping, as someone hung-over.'[24] Clearly such imagery and language must not be understood literally.

Denys adds that the function of this metaphorical language is to draw us onwards in our spiritual journey. He says that the Godhead 'generously reveals a firm, transcendent beam, granting enlightenments proportionate to each being, and thereby draws sacred minds upward to its permitted contemplation, to participation and to the state of becoming like it',[25] and he speaks of 'what scripture has revealed to us in symbolic and uplifting fashion',[26] saying that the divine Word 'uses scriptural passages in an uplifting fashion as a way... to uplift our mind in a manner suitable to our nature'.[27] This is interestingly analogous to the Buddhist concept of 'skilful means' (*upaya*), according to which religious teachings are not eternal truths but are ideas adapted to our present state in order to lead us towards Enlightenment, and they are to be left behind when they have served their purpose.[28]

Denys thus deals satisfactorily with the question of religious language. But he says nothing about ordinary religious experience, such as the sense of the presence of God. The next step was taken centuries later by Meister Eckhart when he identified the object of Christian worship and devotion as God in distinction from the ineffable Godhead. 'God and the Godhead,' he says, 'are as different from one another as heaven and earth .... God acts. The Godhead does not.'[29] He even took the next, even more daring step of recognizing that because the worshipped God is partly a human construction, he (or she) exists only in relation to the worshipping community. Thus 'before there were creatures,' he says, 'God was not god, but, rather, he was what he was. When creatures came to be and took on creaturely being, then God was no longer God as he is in himself, but God as he is with creatures.'[30] He thus points to the idea that the God of the Bible and of the religious life is a manifestation in human terms of the ultimate divine reality, and that as manifest he (for he was nearly always spoken of as male) exists only in relation to his worshippers. The same theme occurs in the twelfth/thirteenth-century Sufi, Ibn al-Arabi, who says, 'The Essence, as being beyond all these relationships, is not a divinity ... it is we who make Him a divinity by being that through which He knows Himself as divine. Thus, He is not known [as 'Allah'] until we are known.'[31] These are daring ideas, pregnant with important future developments.

## Transcategoriality and religious pluralism

All this is consonant with the contemporary pluralist hypothesis that the ultimate transcategorial reality, the Godhead or the Real, is universally present and that our awareness of it in religious experience is a joint product of that presence and our own conceptual systems and their associated spiritual practices. Thus, as worshipped, the different God-figures exist only in relation to their worshippers. For example, the development of the God of the Torah from a violent tribal deity into the Lord, blessed be he, of contemporary Jewish worship, reflects the historical development of Hebrew society and culture. He is part of Israelite history, and that history is in turn integral to his divine biography.[32] The same is true of the Gods of India, some of whom have undergone major transformations through the centuries, even amalgamating in celestial takeovers which mirror historical movements in Indian society. Again, the Christian God was, during much of the medieval period, a terrible judge threatening eternal hell for sinners, an object of intense dread, but later, beginning around the fourteenth century, became for many a God whose limitless love is expressed in the sacrificial death of his son Jesus. These developments do not mean that the ultimate divine reality itself has changed through the centuries, but that our varying human conceptions of it have changed, producing new and sometimes very different forms of religious experience.

All this is easily understood from a naturalistic point of view as the variety of projections of imaginary gods. But how is it to be understood from the point of view of a faith that religious experience is not purely imaginative projection but is also, at the same time, in varying degrees a cognitive response to transcendent reality? The hypothesis that seems to me most promising is based on the epistemological principle enunciated by Thomas Aquinas: 'Things known are in the knower according to the mode of the knower.'[33] It was not within Thomas's sphere of interest to apply this principle to the relation between religions. However this had already been done, in poetic form, by the ninth-century Sufi, al-Junayd, in his saying that 'the colour of the water is that of its container', on which Ibn al-Arabi commented, 'If [one] knew Junayd's saying, "The water takes its colour from the vessel containing it", he would not interfere with other men's beliefs, but would perceive God in every form of belief.'[34] For the different traditions are the containers that give its recognizable colour (that is, character) to our human awareness of the Real.

To build on the application of this principle to religion we need a distinction analogous to Kant's, but in this case between the noumenal Real *an sich* and its phenomenal appearances to human perceivers.[35] For 'the mode of the knower' varies from religion to religion, so that the ultimate Godhead, the Real, can only be humanly experienced in terms of our varying religious conceptualities and spiritual practices. In the intriguing words of an ancient Hindu text, 'Thou art formless. Thy only form is our knowledge of thee.'[36] We cannot attribute to the unexperienceable reality in itself the attributes of its experienceable personae, the God-figures, or its impersonae, the non-personal 'absolutes'. The Real in itself is thus, from our human point of view, totally transcategorial. But the principle of equal validity, that is, the basic faith that human religious experience is a range of responses to a transcendent reality, taken together with the observation that the moral and spiritual fruits of the different world faiths are, so far as we can tell, equally valuable, helps to render the global religious situation intelligible. For it becomes intelligible when we postulate the ineffable Real as the necessary condition, not of the moral life, as Kant proposed, but of the religious life as described in the history of religions.

## Objections and responses

(a) Three logical objections have been made to this use of the concept of ineffability. The first is that when we say that God is absolutely transcategorial, we are saying something about God, namely that God is absolutely transcategorial. And indeed in referring to anything, including God, we are attributing to it the characteristic of being able to be referred to. It cannot therefore be *absolutely* transcategorial.

This is true, but it is in itself a trivial truth in that nothing significant follows from it. It does however prompt us to distinguish between at least two kinds of attributes. There are what we can call substantial attributes, which would tell us something about what the Godhead in itself is like – for example, that it is personal or that it is impersonal. And there are what I have called formal attributes, which do not tell us anything about what the Godhead in itself is like. Thus, for example, that it can be referred to does not give us any information about its nature. Formal attributes are thus trivial or inconsequential in that nothing significant follows from them concerning the intrinsic nature of the Godhead.

It is worth adding at this point that the divine transcategoriality does not entail that the Godhead has no nature, but only that this nature cannot be grasped in human thought and language. For ineffability is relative to the cognitive capacity of the knower. The Godhead is what it is; and the religions have always presumed it to be infinitely rich in nature. But this nature does not fall within the range of our human categories of thought – except, again, purely 'formal' ones.

(b) The second, much more substantial, logical objection is presented by William Rowe. His 'chief difficulty with Hick's Real' is that 'I cannot see how the Real can avoid having one or the other of two contradictory properties'.[37] I had argued that the transcategorial Real cannot be said to be either personal or impersonal, good or evil, purposive or non-purposive, etc., because it is not the sort of thing that could be any of these – as the number two cannot be said to be either green or non-green. Rowe says,

> According to Hick's argument, to ask whether the number two is green or non-green would be misleading, for the question presupposes that the number two is an entity of the kind that *could* be green or non-green.... My response to this argument is that even though to ask whether the number two is green or non-green may be to presuppose that it's an entity of the kind that could be green or non-green, and would thus be an inappropriate or senseless question if asked by someone who knows that no number can be green, it hardly follows that the proposition that the number two is non-green is false or in some way meaningless. Indeed, the proposition that the number two is non-green is necessarily true. And it is precisely because every number must be non-green that it would make no sense for someone who is aware of that fact to ask whether the number two is green or non-green.[38]

Applying this to the postulated Real, Rowe insists that if the Real cannot possibly be personal, because it is not the sort of thing that *could* be personal, then clearly it is non-personal.

I do not disagree with this as a purely formal truth from which nothing significant follows concerning the nature of the Real. However, Rowe claims that something significant does follow. He says that 'if Hick were to agree that the Real is non-personal, this could create a serious difficulty for the assessment of religions favouring personal deities as opposed to religions favouring non-personal absolutes'.[39] For if God is non-personal it follows that the theistic religions are fundamentally in error; and this would indeed be a very significant implication. But if, on the other hand, the Real is not personal simply because the concepts of personality and impersonality do not apply to it, then, surely, nothing significant follows concerning its nature. One can say that the Real is non-round, non-green, non-large, non-intelligent, non-French and so on *ad infinitum*, as well as non-personal, simply because it is not the kind of reality that could have any of these attributes. But none of this tells us anything significant about the nature of the Real in itself.

However, Rowe still insists that it is logically necessary that if the attribute of being personal does not apply to the Real, then the Real has the attribute of being non-personal. For 'personal' and 'non-personal' are logically interdependent, in that if X is not personal, it is necessarily non-personal. But the inference from 'X is not personal' to therefore 'X is a non-personal, or impersonal, reality' only holds within the domain of things to which the concepts 'personal' and 'non-personal' apply. The transcategorial Real is not in that domain. Indeed, the concept of the ineffable is precisely the concept of that which is, by definition, outside that realm. To deny – as in effect Rowe does – that there can be a reality beyond the scope of human conceptuality seems to me to be a dogma that we are under no obligation to accept.[40]

(c) Christopher Insole, in his article 'Why John Hick Cannot, and Should Not, Stay out of the Jampot',[41] raises issues in the same area. In response I shall try to show why I can and should stay out of the jampot. The 'jampot' in question – which first appeared in William Alston's larder[42] – contains all the religiously significant qualities that the ultimate reality has been said by religious thinkers to have. These include, in Christian theology, goodness, power, knowledge and being three-persons-in-one, the second of whom became incarnate as Jesus Christ; in Jewish theology, being unitary (not triune) and having adopted the children of Israel as his chosen people; in Muslim theology, being strictly unitary and being self-revealed in the Qur'an; in advaitic Hindu thought, being the non-personal Brahman; in different schools of Buddhist thought, being the non-personal *Dharmakaya* or the non-personal *nirvana*. These instances are enough to remind us that there is not just one but a whole row of jampots, many of whose ingredients are mutually incompatible. How then should we proceed?

Insole is not unsympathetic to the idea of the ultimate reality being differently known within different religious traditions, so that within them people are brought from self-centredness to a re-centring in the transcendent Real. 'This,' he says, 'is a substantial doctrine of God for which Hick has compelling and serious reasons' (p. 9). But he objects strongly to the distinction between formal and substantial attributes being brought into the picture.

The pluralist hypothesis that I wish to defend is not, however, that formulated by Insole when he says, 'Hick believes that the Real *an sich* is a transcendent divine reality which reveals itself partially ... in different faiths, but never fully in one faith' (p. 8), or that it is 'authentically self-revealing in not one but many faiths' (p. 6), or when he speaks of the Real's 'partial and aspectual self-revelation in different world faiths' (p. 1). That would indeed require the Real in itself to have the various qualities that it reveals within the different religions. But this is ruled out by the fact that many of these attributes are non-compossible.

Indeed, the language of revelation, and of the Real as 'self-revealing', which Insole frequently uses, suggests a theistic presupposition which is misleading in this context.

However, Insole's main argument does not depend on that misunderstanding. The principle of equal validity requires us to say that the Real is such that it is authentically responded to from within the different world religions. But is not this 'being such that . . . ' an attribute of the Real? And if so, is it a substantial or a formal attribute? Or is it perhaps an attribute of some third kind?

Insole is clearly right in pointing out that 'being authentically responded to within different religions' is not the same purely formal kind of property as 'being able to be referred to'. But the question remains, How can the noumenal Real be phenomenally experienced as the gods and absolutes of the different religions without itself having any of the attributes of those gods and absolutes, since many of these are mutually incompatible? Philip Quinn, in his proposal for 'thinner theologies',[43] has suggested that we might attribute to the Real only those qualities on which the major traditions agree. He does not specify these, but they cannot include personality or impersonality, or any properties that presuppose either of these. But it could well be argued – and I have myself argued – that all the major religions report that their object of worship or focus of meditation is ultimately benign in relation to humankind. Can we not then at least make the religiously significant affirmation that the ultimate reality, the Real or the Godhead, is benign – an attribute which does not necessarily imply personality (we speak, for example, of a benign climate)? For this is a very important ingredient common to all the jampots.

The answer, I suggest, does not lie in the nature of the Real itself but in our own human nature. 'Benign' and also 'good' – together with our other value terms – are human conceptions. They apply within human life, and they apply to the range of divine phenomena which we have ourselves partially constructed; but not to the ultimate noumenal reality in itself. Our human nature, with its range of concepts and languages, is such that *from our point of view* the Real, experienced in a variety of divine phenomena, is benign, good. But there may possibly be other kinds of creature which also make a benign/malign distinction in relation to themselves, but by whom the Real is experienced as hostile, not good but evil; and others again by whom it is experienced as morally neutral.

But, again, is not 'being capable of being experienced as benign by humans, as malign by others – perhaps devils – and as morally neutral by yet others' (let us call this, not very elegantly, multi-perceptibility), an attribute of the Real? It seems to me preferable to hold that this is not an intrinsic attribute of the Real in itself, but an attribute of human (and possibly some non-human) nature. Is it an intrinsic attribute of a mountain that it looks smaller to an observer the more distant the observer is from it, or is it not rather an attribute of we observers that objects look smaller to us the further we are from them? Is it an attribute of objects that they appear coloured to some, but not to the colour-blind, or are these not rather attributes of the different per-ceivers? For there could be mountains but no observers, and the same objects but no perceivers, but there is eternally (according to the religions) the ultimate transcategorial reality whether or not there are humans or others to respond to it – and, of course, a million years ago there were no humans. It therefore seems to me reasonable to treat the multi-perceptibility of the Real as inhering, not in the Real *an sich*, but in the different finite perceivers with their different cognitive capacities and interpretative frameworks.

And so my conclusion is that these suggested logical difficulties are by no means insuperable. The concept of ineffability is viable, and it can contribute to a viable religious understanding of religion in its variety of forms.

## Notes

1. Gershom Scholem, 'General Characteristics of Jewish Mysticism', in Richard Woods (ed.), *Understanding Mysticism* (New York: Doubleday, 1980), p. 148.
2. Reynold Nicholson, *The Mystics of Islam* (London and Boston: Routledge & Kegan Paul, 1963), pp. 81–2.
3. Trilochan Singh, 'Theological Concepts of Sikhism', *Sikhism* (Patiala: Punjabi University, 1969), p. 53.
4. Shinran, *Notes on 'Essentials of Faith Alone'*, trans. Dennis Hirota and others (Kyoto: Hongwanji International Center, 1979), p. 5.
5. Bernard McGinn, *The Foundations of Mysticism* (London: SCM Press, 1991), p. 140.
6. Gregory of Nyssa, *Against Eunomius*, Book 1, ch. 43, trans. William Moore and Henry Austin Wilson, *The Nicene and Post-Nicene Fathers*, Series II, Vol. V, 1957, p. 99.
7. St Augustine, *Of True Religion*, para. 67, trans. John Burleigh, *Augustine: Earlier Writings* (Philadelphia: Westminster Press, 1953), p. 259.
8. See Bernard McGinn, *The Growth of Mysticism* (London: SCM Press, 1994), p. 117.
9. Thomas Aquinas, *Summa contra Gentiles*, Book 1, ch. 14, para. 2, trans. Anton Pegis, *On the Truth of the Catholic Faith*, Book 1 (New York: Image Books, 1955), p. 96.

10. Bernard McGinn, *The Flowering of Mysticism* (New York: Crossroad, 1998), p. 257.

11. Paul Tillich, *The Courage to Be* (New Haven: Yale University Press, 1959), p. 190.

12. Gordon Kaufman, *God the Problem* (Cambridge, MA: Harvard University Press, 1972), pp. 85–6.

13. Ninian Smart, 'Our Experience of the Ultimate', *Religious Studies*, Vol. 20, no. 1 (1984), p. 24.

14. John Hick, *God Has Many Names*, ch. 5 (Philadelphia: Westminster Press, 1980); *Problems of Religious Pluralism*, ch. 3 (London: Macmillan and New York: St Martin's Press, 1985); *An Interpretation of Religion* (London: Macmillan and New Haven: Yale University Press, 1989); *Disputed Questions in Theology and the Philosophy of Religion*, ch. 10 (London: Macmillan and New Haven: Yale University Press, 1993); *The Rainbow of Faiths* (London: SCM Press = *A Christian Theology of Religions*, Louisville: Westminster/John Knox, 1995).

15. Pseudo-Dionysius, *The Mystical Theology*, ch. 5, in *The Complete Works of Pseudo-Dionysius*, trans. Colm Lubheid (New York: Paulist Press, 1987), p. 141.

16. Dionysius, *The Mystical Theology*, ch. 1. Lubheid, p. 136.

17. Dionysius, *The Divine Names*, ch. 1, para. 2. Lubheid, p. 51.

18. Dionysius, *The Celestial Hierarchy*, ch. 7. Lubheid, p. 166.

19. Dionysius, *The Divine Names*, ch. 2, para. 9. Lubheid, p. 65.

20. Dionysius, *The Divine Names*, ch. 1, para. 5. Lubheid, p. 53.

21. Dionysius, *The Celestial Hierarchy*, 2:1. Lubheid, p. 148.

22. Dionysius, *The Celestial Hierarchy*, ch. 1:2–3. Lubheid, p. 146.

23. Cf. Denys Turner, *The Darkness of God* (Cambridge: Cambridge University Press, 1995), pp. 35–8.

24. Dionysius, *Letters*, 9. Lubheid, p. 282.

25. Dionysius, *The Divine Names*, ch. 1. Lubheid, p. 50.

26. Dionysius, *The Celestial Hierarchy*, ch. 1. Lubheid, p. 145.

27. Dionysius, *The Celestial Hierarchy*, ch. 2. Lubheid, p. 148.

28. *Majjhima Nikaya*, I, 135. *The Middle Length Sayings*, trans. I.B. Horner (London: Luzac, 1954), p. 173.

29. Eckhart, Sermon 27. *Meister Eckhart*, trans. Raymond Blakney (New York and London: Harper & Row, 1941), pp. 225–6.

30. Sermon 28. Blakney, p. 228.

31. Ibn al-Arabi, *The Books of Bezels* (Mahweh, N.J., and London: Paulist Press, 1990), p. 92.

32. For the divine biography see, for example, Karen Armstrong, *A History of God* (London: Heinemann, 1993).

33. Thomas Aquinas, *Summa Theologica*, II/II, Q. 1, art 2.

34. R.A. Nicholson, *The Mystics of Islam* (London and Boston: Routledge & Kegan Paul, 1963), p. 88.

35. Some critics have made heavy weather of this use of Kant, and have assumed that I have been engaged in a controversial exercise in Kantian exegesis – recently, for example, Chris Firestone in 'Kant and Religion: Conflict or Compromise?', *Religious Studies*, Vol. 35, no. 2 (1999). Christopher Insole also, in his article in the present volume, at some points makes the

same assumption. But I have only borrowed from Kant his basic noumenal/ phenomenal distinction, and am well aware that his own epistemology of religion is very different from that which I am recommending. This is something that I have pointed out in the book which Firestone and Insole discuss – *An Interpretation of Religion*, pp. 242–3.

36. *Yogava'sistha*, I, 28.
37. William Rowe, 'Religious Pluralism', *Religious Studies*, Vol. 35, no. 2 (1999), p. 146. (William Rowe is Professor of Philosophy at Purdue University, Indiana.)
38. *Ibid.*, pp. 147–8.
39. *Ibid.*, p. 149.
40. Rowe says that he does not reject the concept of the ineffable, provided being ineffable just precludes the possession of positive, substantial attributes conceivable by us. He does not allow that 'non-personal' is such an attribute. But it seems to me that if we know that the Real is a non-personal reality, we do know something positive and significant about it – for we know that it is such that the theistic religions are basically mistaken in their account of it.
41. *Religious Studies*, March 2000.
42. William Alston, 'Realism and the Christian Faith', *International Journal for Philosophy of Religion*, Vol. 38, nos. 1–3 (1995).
43. Philip Quinn, 'Towards Thinner Theologies: Hick and Alston on Religious Diversity', *International Journal for Philosophy of Religion*, Vol. 38, nos. 1–3 (1995).

# 4
# Religious Pluralism and the Divine: A Response to Paul Eddy[1]

Paul Eddy's careful critique ('Religious Pluralism and the Divine: Another Look at John Hick's Neo-Kantian Proposal', *Religious Studies*, xxx, 1994) requires a response. The religious pluralism in question is a hypothesis about the relationship between the world's religions. It is a form of *religious* pluralism in that it is conceived from within the basic faith that religious experience is not *in toto* human imaginative projection but, whilst involving human conceptuality and imagination, is also a cognitive response to what Eddy calls the Divine and I (to avoid the theistic connotation of 'divine') generally prefer to speak of as the Real. The hypothesis is that the great world faiths are different contexts of the salvific transformation of men and women from natural self-centredness to a new orientation centred in the Real or the Divine. They constitute different ways of conceiving and therefore of experiencing the Real, expressed in correspondingly different historical forms of life. The Kantian, or neo-Kantian, or Kantian-like distinction between the Real in itself, which lies beyond the scope of our human religious concepts, and the Real as humanly thought and experienced in terms of those concepts, is central to this hypothesis.

Eddy objects to the idea of the ultimate ineffability of the Real. He points out that whilst Christian thought has affirmed ineffability ('by its immensity, the divine substance surpasses every form that our intellect reaches',[2] 'The first cause surpasses human understanding and speech',[3] and so on) it has not intended this to exclude the affirmation of 'some positive characterizations of the divine' (p. 470). And it is true that, whilst acknowledging theologically that God is beyond our conceptual grasp, Christians have always also talked devotionally and liturgically of God as our divine heavenly Father, with magnified human-like attributes. In traditional theology the relation between, on the one hand, the inference to infinity and ineffability and, on the other hand, the experience of a specific personal divine presence with determinate characteristics, is left as a cloudy mystery. But I suggest that the cloud can be dispelled and the two desiderata reconciled by distinguishing between the-Real-in-itself and the-Real-as-humanly-thought-and-experienced.

On this view the attributes of the objects of worship and the foci of religious meditation for the different traditions are not attributes of the Real as it is in itself, but of one or other of its manifestations or appearances to human consciousness. These attributes include many that are mutually incompatible – such as a being personal and being non-personal, being a substance and being a non-substantial process, being an agent who intervenes in human history and not being such an agent, becoming incarnate as a human being and not becoming incarnate as a human being, being three-in-one and being strictly unitary, and so on. Therefore, this range of characteristics cannot be attributed to the Real in itself. We have instead to suppose that the Real *an sich* does not come within our spectrum of categories. It is in other words, from our human point of view, ineffable or, in eastern terms, formless.

I accept the traditional argument, which Eddy rejects, for the ineffability of the Divine, namely that the infinite cannot be thought to have finite and limiting qualities, such as being personal, purposive, etc. But I add this other argument above, on which I place the greater weight.

The distinction between purely formal and logically generated attributes such as 'being able to be referred to', and substantial attributes such as 'being personal, good, etc.', seems to me, despite Eddy's disagreement, to be entirely sound.[4] But I accept Paul Eddy's (and Keith Ward's[5]) point that Anselm's formula, 'that than which no greater can be conceived', is not a good example of a purely formal statement about God, in that Anselm thought of 'greatness' as including 'whatever it is better to be than not to be'[6] – although he did add that God is not only that than which a greater cannot be thought but also 'something greater than can be thought'.[7]

The ineffability of the Real is not, however, the religious impoverishment that Eddy takes it to be. For the religious traditions always centre upon the Real as humanly thought and experienced in some particular form – as the Adonai of Judaism, or as the Holy Trinity of Christianity, or as the Allah of Islam, or as the Vishnu or the Shiva of theistic Hinduism, or as the Brahman of advaitic Hinduism, or as the Dharma or Nirvana or Sunyata of Buddhism, or as the Tao, and so on. But if we grant the rough parity of the great traditions as contexts of a salvific human transformation from self-centredness to reality-centredness (which is another of the legs on which religious pluralism stands), we are led to see them as responding to different phenomenal manifest-ations of the ultimate noumenal Real. This hypothesis is not, however, part of the first-order religious language of the particular traditions, but of the second-order philosophical attempt to understand the relation between those traditions.

Eddy's other main criticism concerns Kant. As he notes, the pluralistic hypothesis could be presented without mentioning Kant. But it was Kant, above all, who has drawn attention to the importance of the distinction between a reality as it is in itself and as it appears to us with our distinctive cognitive capacities; and it seems to me proper to recognize this. But I do not have to be committed to every aspect of Kant's use of the distinction; and indeed whether what I want to say is or is not properly Kantian is not a question of concern here – though I have often pointed out that Kant's own epistemology of religion is quite different from the one that I am recommending. However, I cannot accept Eddy's suggestion that I ought, having appealed to the noumenal/phenomenal distinction, to hold that the entirety of religious experience is supplied by the experiencer. The pluralist hypothesis is that the universal presence of the Real is affecting us all the time and that when we allow this impingement upon us to come to conscious-ness it takes the varied forms of what we call religious experience. The 'givenness' of the experience is thus the impact upon the human spirit of the Divine, whilst the 'form' that the experience takes is supplied by our own religious concepts and imagery.[8]

It is, of course, true that, as Eddy says, it is possible to regard the entire phenomenon of religious experience as being 'accounted for by those religious concepts and sentiments found in the religio-cultural systems and/or in the individuals themselves' (p. 477), and thus to fall in line with Feuerbach. But this consideration is double-edged. For the naturalistic option can be invoked against non-pluralist as easily as against pluralist religious views. It is not an argument that an exclusiv-ist believer in the reality of the Divine can use against a pluralist believer in the reality of the Divine.[9] If one displays the different forms of religious experience, including that of one's own tradition, and then considers a Feuerbachian account of them, this account will apply as much to religious experience within one's own tradition as in others.

Paul Eddy's basic error then, in my view, is his failure to keep clear the distinction between grounds for believing that there is a transcendent divine reality, and reasons for thinking that such a reality is differently conceived, experienced and responded to from within the different religious traditions. He and I agree in denying that religious experience, as such, is purely an imaginative projection of our human concepts and sentiments. My own argument for the rationality of basing beliefs on religious as well as on sensory experience is given in another chapter of the book that Eddy was mainly discussing.[10] If this argument (along basically the same lines as William Alston's in *Perceiving God*) is correct, it entitles the religious experiencer to believe in the reality of the Divine as he or she experiences it to be. But we then have, as philosophers concerned with the entire field of religious experience, to notice that this argument provides precisely the same rational entitlement to people within different religious traditions to hold mutually incompatible beliefs – for example, the belief that the divine is the Qur'anic Allah and the belief that the Divine is Brahman. In order, then, to make sense of the religious situation (and not merely of our own local bit of it) we have, as it seems to me, to complicate our understanding by distinguishing between the Real as it is in itself, independently of human cognizers, and the Real as humanly experienced in a range of different ways. To acknowledge this variety is called by Eddy 'radical subjectivism'. But it is more accurately described as a critical realist epistemology of religion, that is, a realism that takes full account of the perceiver's contribution to all human awareness. It is thus a middle way between the non-realism of Feuerbach (and his contemporary echoes), and the naive realism of evangelical theology. It is this moderate, rational, balanced, Anglican-style middle way that I have recommended.

## Notes

1. Paul Eddy is Assistant Professor at Bethel College, Minnesota, USA.
2. St Thomas, *Summa contra Gentiles,* I, 14, 2.
3. St Thomas, *In librum de Causis,* 6.
4. Though possibly William Alston's terminology is to be preferred when he distinguishes between extrinsic and intrinsic attributes (*Divine Nature and Human Language*, Ithaca and London: Cornell University Press, 1989, p. 40).
5. Keith Ward, 'Truth and the Diversity of Religions', *Religious Studies*, XXVI (1990), p. 10.
6. *St. Anselm's Proslogion*, trans. M.J. Charlesworth (Oxford: Clarendon Press, 1965), p. 121 (ch. 5).
7. *Ibid.*, p. 137 (ch. 15).
8. One of Eddy's sub-arguments should be noticed at this point. He asks (p. 478) what 'information' the transcendent input to religious experience supplies or could supply. But I have used the term 'information', not in the

sense of 'items of information', but in its cybernetic sense, as any impact of our environment upon us. In the case of religious experience the 'impact' is the universal presence to us of the Real, or the Divine, as the ground of our being, and this comes to consciousness in the ways shown to us in the history of religions. (John Bowker was, so far as I know, the first to apply the cybernetic concept of information to religious awareness in *The Sense of God* [Oxford: Clarendon Press, 1973].)

9.  That Paul Eddy counts himself as an exclusivist believer is evident from his contribution to 'a much needed evangelical critique of John Hick's religious pluralism' in *The Challenge of Religious Pluralism: An Evangelical Analysis and Response*, being the Proceedings of the Wheaton Theology Conference, Wheaton College, Wheaton, Illinois, 1992, p. 36.

10. John Hick, *An Interpretation of Religion* (London: Macmillan, and New Haven: Yale University Press, 1989).

# 5
# Transcendence and Truth:
# A Response to D.Z. Phillips

Dewi Phillips[1] has asked me to write about Transcendence and Truth. 'Transcendence', as indicating beyondness, is a very general idea which waits to be given specific meanings in specific contexts. It is perhaps most commonly used in contrast to immanence. However, I am not here focusing upon that polarity but am using the term to refer to the characteristic in virtue of which the divine, the ultimate reality, is said to be other and 'greater' (in an Anselmic rather than a spatial sense) than the physical universe. The area of discourse is thus that occupied by the debate between naturalistic and what we can, for want of a better term, call transcendental understandings of the universe. The medievals used the term 'supernatural' here, but that word has today shrivelled in meaning to indicate the occult, ghosts, spirits, magic spells and the like. And so I shall speak of transcendence, and of the Transcendent as that which, according to the religions, transcends the multiple forms of discharging energy constituting the natural or physical universe.

The natural or physical universe includes this earth and the human and other forms of life on it, and thus includes the multitude of human brains and their functioning, which in turn includes the production of thought, language, feeling, emotion and action. Thought, feeling, emotion and volition may or may not be identical with physical brain processes – there is disagreement among naturalistic thinkers about this – but on a naturalistic view there can be no mental life that does not continuously depend for its existence upon brain activity, so that if there were no brains there would be no sentient life, and in particular no human life – no thought, feeling, emotion, language, personality, imagination, culture, social interaction, artistic production, religion. And so if by 'nature' or 'the natural' we mean the physical universe, including human cerebral activity and the entire realm of mental life that depends upon it, then by the Transcendent I mean the putative dimension or range of reality that transcends this and that cannot be accommodated within a naturalistic understanding of the universe. We can say that the Transcendent is that which there must be if the various forms of religious experience are not purely projection but at the same time also response. The Transcendent is thus the necessary postulate of the validity, not (as Kant proposed) of morality, but of religion.

## Naturalistic (= without transcendence) conceptions of religion

The most straightforward naturalistic view of religion is that it consists in individual and communal self-delusion. Ideas of the Transcendent – in the forms of God, or Brahman, or the Dharmakaya, or the Tao, and so on – are all products of the activity of human thinking, so that if there were no human brains there would be no God, Brahman, Tao, Dharmakaya, etc. If in imagination we compress the 15 or so billion-year history of the universe into 24 hours, human life has only emerged during the last millisecond. Before that, on a naturalistic view, there was no God, Brahman, Tao, etc. And again, after either the heat or the cold extinction of life on this earth the Gods, Brahman, the Tao, etc. that we create in our imaginations will have ceased to exist. According to naturalism, then, our planet is the locus of a momentary flash of conscious life within an otherwise unconscious universe; and we are in the extraordinary position of being part of this in some ways wonderful and in other ways appalling moment. As conscious individuals we may live for some 70–80 or so years and then simply cease to exist – like a word deleted from the computer screen! And one day, in its endless expansion or its 'big crunch', the universe will be as if the entire episode of human existence had never occurred.

The harsh implications of this view for our human self-understanding have probably never been so fully and honestly faced as by Bertrand Russell. In an early essay, 'A Free Man's Worship', written in 1902, he said:

> That Man is the Product of causes which had no prevision of the end they were achieving; that his origin, his growth, his hopes and fears, his loves and his beliefs, are but the outcome of accidental collo-cations of atoms; that no fire, no heroism, no intensity of thought and feeling, can preserve an individual life beyond the grave; that all the labours of the ages, all the devotion, all the inspiration, all the

noonday brightness of human genius, are destined to extinction in the vast death of the solar system, and that the whole Temple of Man's achievement must inevitably be buried beneath the debris of a universe in ruins – all these things, if not quite beyond dispute, are yet so nearly certain, that no philosophy which rejects them can hope to stand. Only within the scaffolding of these truths, only on the firm foundation of unyielding despair, can our soul's habitation henceforth be squarely built.[2]

And in the third volume of his *Autobiography* Russell reprints a letter, written in 1962, in which he says, by way of self-criticism, that the language of this passage is 'florid and rhetorical', but adds: 'However, my outlook on the cosmos and on human life is substantially unchanged.'[3]

Russell's picture constitutes an unflinchingly honest acceptance of the implications of a naturalistic understanding of the universe and our place in it. This world-view is, according to the Nobel prize-winning physicist Steven Weinberg, who also espouses it, 'chilling and impersonal'.[4] Within such a naturalistic framework we can opt, with Russell, for a noble Stoicism. We can accept our mortality and concentrate upon the immediate sources of happiness, including the attempt to reduce pain and misery in others, and can thus find meaning and satisfaction within our short existence. We can, with Russell, reject all notions of the Transcendent but nevertheless accept love, freedom, the search for truth, a commitment to reducing misery and promoting happiness, as intrinsically valuable (in the sense of being valued by us for no reason beyond themselves) despite their brief and insecure tenure of existence. We can recognize that human life has no ultimate purpose or meaning, that it is not a project aiming at any goal, and then proceed to make the best we can of it. Although I do not accept this outlook I nevertheless find that I can imaginatively identify with it and respect it.

In addition to this straightforward rejection of religion as illusion there is a school of thought which likewise presupposes a naturalistic understanding of the universe, but nevertheless uses religious language to express certain important aspects of human experience. This is religion without transcendence. Ludwig Feuerbach was the first major thinker to formulate a version of it. He is often depicted as having a purely negative attitude to religion, whereas in fact he was advocating a positive appreciation of it, but only of religion without transcendence. This does not veto talk of God, Brahman, the Tao, the Dharmakaya, etc., but it denies that these concepts have any referent that transcends the purely natural. They refer to aspects of the natural world, and more specifically to ideas and ideals and speech-acts produced by the human brain, and to consequent modes of individual and communal behaviour.

Religion without transcendence has room for the most exalted conceptions of divinity and for the highest moral and spiritual ideals and attitudes and forms of life. It can value the renunciation of the ego point of view, making no claim upon life but seeing it as (metaphorically) a gift and receiving its hardships and tragedies, as well as its delights, in a spirit of humble acceptance. Whilst still presupposing that human life is, in Russell's words, 'the product of causes which had no prevision of the end they were achieving' and that 'all the labours of the ages, all the devotion, all the inspiration, all the noonday brightness of human genius' are destined to be as though they had never occurred, religion without transcendence can nevertheless endorse the moral dispositions that have been so eloquently extolled in recent times by such writers as Tolstoy, Kierkegaard, Wittgenstein, Simone Weil and others. Putting it in terms close to those of Theravada Buddhism, one should live in the present moment, as the world being conscious of itself from one point of view within it, without being specially concerned about the particular point in the world process that is momentarily 'me', and so valuing equally oneself and others and delighting in all that is good in our human experience. Thus religion without transcendence can accept most of the moral teachings of the traditional religions, and can retain virtually the whole realm of religious language, although evacuating it of its metaphysical content. Among contemporary philosophers this strategy is advocated, for example, by Dewi Phillips, and among contemporary theologians by, for example, Don Cupitt.

## The unconscious elitism of this form of religion

I now want to point to a feature of this position which is not usually recognized by its advocates. I have acknowledged that we can find positive meaning and fulfilment within a naturalistic interpretation of life. But who are the 'we' for whom this is true? We are the fortunate minority who have a reasonably secure sufficiency of food and shelter, of personal safety and freedom, of educational opportunities and cultural resources. We are the fortunate ones who are not chronically undernourished and living in fear of starvation, not oppressed or persecuted or enslaved, not refugees, not trapped in abject poverty and desperately anxious for our own and our family's and community's short-term future. We can, if we choose, recognize that we can do very little to end the injustices and sufferings of those who have been less lucky than ourselves in life's lottery, and proceed to enjoy our own lives as best we can, accepting the fleeting insignificance of the entire episode of human existence. But to think that *all* men and women are free to join in this positive response would be like saying that the desperately poor and starving in, say, the deprived and dangerous slums of Calcutta, or for that matter of Los Angeles or Glasgow, are free to rise into serenity and inner peace. This would be true only in a cruelly ironic sense. In principle they can do so, but not in reality. And so we must recognize that the 'we' for whom a religion without transcendence can be positively challenging, and even inspiring, consists in a minority who have been highly privileged by the accident of birth and other circumstances. In other words, to extol the value of religion without transcendence as other than the luxury of a fortunate minority is to ignore the immense fact of evil in the forms of physical pain and mental and emotional suffering caused by 'man's inhumanity to man' and by the structure of the physical environment.

I do not want to overstate this fact of evil, immense though it is, or to forget the many marvellous and enjoyable aspects of human existence. When we look back along the axis of history we must not be misled by the contrast between the comforts and cultural possibilities provided by modern wealth and technology, and the lack of these in previous centuries. There have been large tracts of history in which many people have lived in small tribal societies that were stable, largely egalitarian, generally internally peaceful, and with a sufficiency of food and fuel. In comparison with life in modern industrialized cities, life was then very simple and was lived at subsistence level, and with none of our modern medical remedies; but nevertheless there was quite possibly more contentment, a stronger communal feeling and sense of mutual support, and a readier acceptance of mortality, than in our affluent but fragmented and anxious western world today.

But that having been said, the larger truth is still that the life of the majority of human beings has been, in the words of Barbara Ward and René Dubos, 'cramped with back-breaking labour, exposed to deadly or debilitating disease, prey to wars and famines, haunted by the loss of children, filled with fear and the ignorance that breeds fear'.[5] Restricting attention to our world today, the broad picture is that there are hundreds of millions of men, women and children who are suffering from one or more of the following calamities: being refugees with no fixed home, being physically or mentally ill and having no access to the kind of medical aid that is available to ourselves, being hungry, being chronically undernourished and lacking the protein necessary for full physical development, being desperately anxious for their own and their family's future, being caught in famines, earth-quakes, floods, storms and other natural disasters, lacking even ele-mentary education, being ruthlessly exploited by uncaring financial and political powers.

What I am suggesting, then, is that in the light of the massive reality of evil – that is, the pain, suffering and deprivation caused both by fellow humans and by the environment – a naturalistic philosophy can only be accepted with equanimity by a privileged minority. For human-ity as a whole, the naturalistic picture is very bad news. It means not only that evil has always been a massive reality, but that past evil is irreparable, in that those who have suffered from it have ceased to exist; and it must be expected that this will be true also of present and future evil. There can be no question of the universe being, as the religions teach, such that good is ultimately brought out of evil. I am not of course implying that naturalism is therefore false. It may be true. But I am arguing that forms of religion that presuppose naturalism – forms, in other words, of religion without transcendence – which present themselves as liberating and ennobling, are highly elitist. Further, this is something of which their proponents have seldom shown themselves to be aware.

## The project of human existence

Let me at this point introduce the idea of what I shall call the project of human existence. According to naturalism, human existence is not a project aiming at any fulfilment. It is just something that has been thrown up for a brief moment in the evolution of the universe. But for the religions, human existence as we know it is an unfinished project. All the great world religions teach that our present life is only a small part of our total existence, and that within that existence as a whole there is a realistic possibility for all human beings to attain, or receive, or realize what the religious traditions conceptualize as union with God, or with Brahman, or as *nirvana*, or as awakening to the universal Buddha-nature, and in yet other ways. The structure of reality, whereby this fulfilment is eventually possible for everyone, is very variously con-ceived. But the basic truth of the belief in a good outcome of the project of human existence does not depend upon the fulfilment of the specific expectations of any one of the religious traditions. We are talking about a mode of existence that is outside our range of experience and that may well take a form or forms that lie beyond our present conceptual and imaginative capacities.

Feuerbach, the patron saint of religion without transcendence, perceptively noted that the idea of immortality is essentially involved in the idea of a benign God.[6] Let me spell out why this is so. Human nature includes wonderful potentialities which we see realized in the remarkable men and women whom we regard, in our customary western term, as saints, or, in one of the eastern terms, as *mahatmas,* great souls. I am not speaking here of those who have been officially canonized by the Catholic Church, although some of these are certainly among them. I am speaking of those whose lives show us, always of course in culturally specific ways, something of the heights of which human nature is capable. These include the great spiritual leaders whose impact has launched new religious movements – such as Moses, Gautama, Jesus, Mahomed; and great renewers or reformers of existing traditions, such as Shankara, Guru Nanak, Shinran, St Francis; and again innumerable individuals within every tradition who have been transformed by their response to Adonai, or the Heavenly Father, or Allah, or Vishnu, or Shiva, or to the Dharma or the Tao or the require-ments of Heaven. In the modern period, with new possibilities opened up by the spread both of democracy and of a pervasive 'sociological consciousness', sainthood has increasingly taken political forms in such people as Mahatma Gandhi in India, Martin Luther King in the United States, Archbishop Romero in El Salvador, Dom Helda Camera in Brazil, Nelson Mandela in South Africa. As these examples show, the saints of the modern world are not perfect human beings – there can be no such thing – but people who, in response to a transcendent claim, have risen above self-concern to serve their fellows in very significant ways. In such people we are made aware of a human potentiality that is only very slightly developed in most people in each generation. It follows that if individual human existence ceases at death, the full human potentiality is only realized by those few who are able to realize it in this present life. But in the great majority of men and women those potentialities must remain forever unfulfilled. Such a situation is clearly incompatible not only with a Christian belief in the limitless love of God but equally with Jewish or Muslim or Hindu theistic belief in the divine love and mercy, and with Advaitic Hindu or Buddhist belief in a universal destiny in union with Brahman or in the attain-ment of Buddhahood. There can be no loving God, and more generally no ultimate reality that is benign from our human point of view, if there is no continuation of human spiritual growth beyond the point reached at the time of bodily death. In a slogan: No theodicy without eschatology.

## Cosmic optimism and cosmic pessimism

Naturalism, then, including naturalistic religion – religion without transcendence – is a form of cosmic pessimism, whilst the great world religions are, in contrast, forms of cosmic optimism. Needless to say, I am not arguing that because the naturalistic possibility would be such bad news for the human race as a whole it must therefore be mistaken! I am concerned, rather, to try to see clearly what the two possibilities are, and wherein lies the difference between them. The difference is so great and all-encompassing that alternative versions of a given religion, one affirming and the other denying transcendence, amount to two radically different forms of religion; and this is so even though they use a common stock of religious language. Thus traditional Christianity is much closer to traditional Islam or Judaism or Hinduism or Sikhism or Jainism or most forms of Buddhism than it is to a form of Christianity without transcendence. For the traditional religions all affirm that the physical universe is the partial expression or manifestation or creation or emanation – all of these different concepts are used – of an ultimate reality which neither begins nor ends with the history of the physical universe and which transcends its ever-changing character as a temporal process. The basic religious faith is that this reality, which I am calling the Transcendent, impinges upon distinctively human consciousness in the many forms of what we call religious experience. On the basis of this the religions declare – and this is their character as gospel, or good news – that the Transcendent is benign in relation to humanity in that the project of human spiritual growth continues to what in our various belief systems we refer to as the Vision of God, union with Brahman, moksha, Nirvana, awakening to the universal Buddha-nature, etc.

## Truth for religion without transcendence

Now my remit is to consider the notion of truth in religion without transcendence, and this is best done in contrast to the notion of truth in transcendental religion.

Let us consider first a Christianity without transcendence. All the statements that are regarded as true in traditional Christianity can still be accepted as true, but the religiously central ones in a radically different sense. Historical beliefs, such as that Jesus of Nazareth lived in the first third of the first century CE, remain unaffected. But theological and religious statements – for example the statement that 'God loves us' – become true only in a totally different sense.

However, before looking at such beliefs as this we need to clear out of the way a complication which might seem to, but does not, affect the real issue. This is that a great deal of religious language is metaphorical. That God is great is not intended to mean that God occupies a large volume of space. That God is high above us is not intended to mean that God is further from the centre of the earth than we are. That God is our Heavenly Father is not intended to mean that God is our biological father. And so on. And it is important, even though elementary, to see that the issue between religion with and religion without transcendence is not whether such statements should be understood literally or metaphorically. All sensible persons in both camps will agree that they are metaphors.

Turning, then, to the belief that God loves us, this means in the naive realism of traditional Christian belief that there is a personal Being who has created the universe, who is unlimited in knowledge and power, who intervenes from time to time in the course of history, and who loves his human creation in a manner analogous to that of an ideal human father. This belief entails that in addition to all the human consciousnesses that currently exist there is another consciousness which is the consciousness of God. But for Christianity without transcendence there is no such Being. There is the *idea* of such a Being, and there is the *language* in which the term 'God' plays a central role, and there are *forms of life* and *outlooks on life* which use the word 'God' and theistic language generally. But there is nevertheless no God in the sense that I spelled out above, involving (minimally) a divine consciousness in addition to the millions of human consciousnesses.

The same principle of interpretation applies to other central traditional Christian beliefs, such as the belief in a life after death. Here the non-realist (or 'without transcendence') understanding has been very clearly set forth by Dewi Phillips in his book *Death and Immortality*. It would, he says, 'be foolish to speak of eternal life as some kind of appendage to human existence, something which happens *after* human life on earth is over. Eternal life is the reality of goodness, that in terms of which human life is to be assessed ... Eternity is not *more* life, but this life seen under certain moral and religious modes of thought.'[7] Again, he says that from his point of view, 'Questions about the immortality of the soul are seen not to be questions concerning the extent of a man's life, and in particular concerning whether that life can extend beyond the grave, but questions concerning the kind of life a man is living.'[8] Now it is a good Fourth Gospel metaphor to say that 'this is eternal life, that they know thee the only true God, and Jesus Christ whom thou hast sent' (John 17: 3). But it is, surely, obvious that this is not intended to be inconsistent with the belief, present throughout the New Testament, in a continuation of eternal life in this sense beyond the present life. Heaven is described in the New Testament, particularly in the Book of Revelation, in what some understand in a naively realistic way and others regard as imaginative imagery. Either way, it is surely clear that the reality of an 'eternal' quality of life now does not preclude its continuation, or its attainment, after death. But Phillips apparently assumes at this point an exclusive either/or. The contrast, then, between a realist and a non-realist interpretation of Christian eschatological language is stark. According to Phillips there is no continuation of consciousness after bodily death, although the traditional language about it can be used to refer instead to a quality of our present living. According to the traditional Christian understanding, on the other hand, it is true both that a present right relationship to God has 'eternal' value, and also that life embodying that value continues beyond death, and indeed that life continues after death *in order that* this value may be more fully and more widely realized.

## A critical realist understanding of transcendental religion

I have referred to Phillips' unwarranted either/or. More generally, many advocates of religion without transcendence make the mistake of assuming that the only options are, on the one hand, a naive realist understanding of the Transcendent, and on the other hand a total rejection of transcendence. The third option that they miss is a form of critical realism which holds that there is a transcendent reality that is limitlessly important to us, but that this reality is only known to us in limited human ways. We cannot know it as it is in itself, but only as it affects us. In Kantian terms, we do not experience the divine noumenon, but a range of divine phenomena to the formation of which our human religious concepts have contributed. But rather than risk getting distracted by Kantian exegesis I shall take as my text for critical realism in religion the extraordinarily fertile statement of St Thomas Aquinas that 'Things known are in the knower according to the mode of the knower.'[9]

I shall develop a critical realist understanding of religion, and of truth in religion, in terms of the concept of meaning: not semantic meaning, the meaning of words and sentences, but what I shall call pragmatic meaning. In order to get at this we can start from Wittgenstein's concept of 'seeing as' in the *Philosophical Investigations*, where he refers to ambiguous pictures such as Jastrow's duck–rabbit. We can see it *as* the picture of a duck's head facing left and *as* the picture of a rabbit's head facing right – though not of course as both at the same time. And we can see it in these two different ways because we possess the two different concepts of duck and rabbit, in terms of which we interpret the marks on paper. As Wittgenstein says, 'we see it as we interpret it'.[10] Now Wittgenstein thought that seeing-as is peculiar to puzzle pictures and other appearances, such as facial expressions, which are easily mistaken. So he said that '"seeing as..." is not part of perception'.[11] He denied, in other words, that *all* seeing is seeing-as, pointing out that it would not be natural to say of the knife and fork on the table, 'Now I am seeing this as a knife and fork.' And indeed it would not. But I think he was mistaken in the conclusion that he drew. For the reason why this would not be for us a natural way of speaking is that we are so accustomed to knives and forks, as part of the familiar furniture of our culture, that we automatically identify them as such. There is for *us* no ambiguity. But it does not follow that what *we* know as a knife and fork could not be seen as something quite different by people of another culture in which knives and forks are completely unknown. Imagine Stone Age persons suddenly transported here in a time machine. They would see the items on the table, but might see them as small weapons, or as wonderful shining ornaments, or as sacred objects full of *mana*, too dangerous to be touched – and no doubt in various other ways. What the things are seen *as* depends on the concepts in terms of which the observer recognizes them. In other words, the activity of seeing-as, or recognizing, is relative to the perceiver's system of sortal concepts.

This is true not only of the recognition of objects but also of the more complex situations which objects jointly form. Let us at this point expand the concept of seeing-as to that of experiencing-as, of which seeing-as is the visual component. Thus I am experiencing our present situation as a meeting of a philosophy of religion conference – that is, as a gathering at which it is expected that this paper, having been circulated in advance, will be discussed. I am taking for granted certain aspects of the pragmatic meaning of the situation as I am experiencing it, such as the convention that critical remarks will be in order; that when you disagree with me or point out errors in my reasoning this is socially acceptable and I am not required to challenge you to a duel; that we shall not go on discussing indefinitely but will end at approximately the stated time, and so on. All this presupposes a vast cultural background, including a more or less civilized society in which people can meet at a specified time in a prearranged place and in a peaceful environment, and the existence of universities, the study of philosophy, the use of the English language, and so on and so on. But if Stone Age persons were dropped in among us at this meeting they would not experience the situation as we are experiencing it, because they would not have these concepts that are elements of our culture but not of theirs.

This suggests a way in which, taking a hint from Wittgenstein, we can formulate a critical realist epistemology. We live in a real environment, which we experience as having meaning for us, the kind of meaning (or the sense of 'meaning') in question being practical or pragmatic meaning. To experience the things on the table as a knife and fork is to be in a dispositional state in relation to them such that I shall use them in the ways in which in our culture we normally do use them. I shall not worship them or fight with them but shall use them as instruments with which to eat. To recognize them by means of our concepts of knife and fork is, in part, to be in this dispositional state. And for me to experience our present situation as a session of a philosophical conference is, again, to be in a dispositional state to behave within it in ways that are appropriate to that. The physical configurations of matter, simply as such, do not have meaning, but we endow them with meaning through what for other animals are recognitional capacities and for us are systems of concepts fixed and embodied in language. In general, then, to be conscious is to be discriminatingly aware of various selected features of our environment, recognized by means of our operative conceptual or recognitional system, so that we can act within it in ways that we take to be appropriate. So the meaning for us of our phenomenal world is its character as rendering appropriate some rather than other behavioural dispositions.

We can now apply to religion the complementary notions of experiencing-as and pragmatic meaning. Each religion trains its adherents to experience the universe as having a distinctive meaning which is reflected dispositionally in a distinctive form of life. This includes the experiencing of specific objects and places and events, and also of life as a whole. Thus in the context of the eucharist Christians experience the bread and wine, not simply as the natural objects that they know them to be, but as mediating the presence of Christ. Or a Hindu, bowing to an image of one of the gods who are manifestations of Brahman, and laying flowers or fruit before it, experiences the image not as just the piece of clay that she knows it to be, but as mediating and focusing a universal divine presence. And more generally, the Christian, for example, experiences the world – at any rate in consciously religious moments – as a divine creation, life as a gift of divine love, and its varied experiences, bad as well as good, as episodes in a pilgrimage through time towards the Kingdom of God, which in its fullness lies beyond this life. The difference between living and not living by a religious faith is a difference between living in the world experienced as having two different meanings, evoking different total dispositional states; and faith is the free interpretative activity in virtue of which we make (usually unconsciously) the cognitive choice between a naturalistic and a transcendental interpretation of the universe.

Let us now fantasize for a moment. If the different species all had their own conceptual systems and languages, these would be as different as the phenomenal worlds which they inhabit. And, to fantasize further, if the species had their own religions, these would also be built out of concepts peculiar to each species, which would accordingly think of the Transcendent in terms of concepts derived from their own forms of experience. As Rupert Brooke reminds us, the fish might believe that

> somewhere, beyond Space and Time,
> Is wetter water, slimier slime!
> And there (they trust) there swimmeth One
> Who swam ere rivers were begun,
> Immense, of fishy form and mind,
> Squamous, omnipotent, and kind;
> And under that Almighty Fin,
> The littlest fish may enter in.[12]

And returning to human life, a critical realist would expect us to conceive and therefore to experience the Transcendent in distinctively human ways – ways in the plural because there are different ways of being human, constituting the different cultures of the earth, which include different ways of thinking and experiencing the Transcendent. For critical realism in the epistemology of religion is the view that there is a transcendent Reality to which religious experience is a cognitive response, but that the forms that this takes within the different traditions depend upon their different sets of religious concepts together with their correspondingly different spiritual practices. The most predictable such concept is that of a limitlessly greater and higher Person – God. But there are also non-personal concepts, and hence non-personal modes of religious experience, of the Transcendent as Brahman, the Tao, Nirvana, the Dharmakaya, and so on. These different conceptualities, linked with appropriately different spiritual practices – for example, I–Thou prayer and non-personalistic meditation – give rise to both the experienced God-figures and the non-personal foci of religious contemplation.

I am thus appealing to the distinction between the Transcendent as it is in itself, beyond the scope of our conceptual systems, and the Transcendent as variously constructed within human religious experience. There is an analogy here with the physicists' language about the unobservable but inferred structure of the physical or natural universe. It is now a commonplace that advanced theories in physics have to be expressed either in mathematical or in metaphorical language. In contemporary works on physics we read of bundles of energy, of gluons and glueballs, of charm, of cosmic dust, of universes as bubbles within a mega-universe, of quantum tunnelling, of glitches and strings (which latter 'can be visualized as tiny one-dimensional rips in the smooth fabric of space'),[13] and so on in a riot of poetic metaphor. In religion, the analogous use of language is customarily described as mythological. In religious mythology we speak of the Transcendent in terms derived from the natural. And the truth of myth is a practical or pragmatic truthfulness consisting in its capacity to evoke (or tend to evoke) an appropriate dispositional response in the hearer. Thus the image of the Transcendent as a loving Heavenly Father tends to evoke a dispositional state which expresses itself in love for one's neighbours as fellow children of God. In so far, then, as the Heavenly Father is an authentic manifestation of the Transcendent to human consciousness, what is literally true of the heavenly Father – that he is good, loving, wise, etc. – is mythologically true of the Transcendent in itself. Again, in so far as the story of the Heavenly Father sending his Son to be born as a human being and to die for the sins of the world tends to evoke in us a trust and love that can illuminate and elevate our lives, to that extent the story is mythologically true. The same principle applies, of course, to the stories and mental pictures of the other great religious systems. Our language cannot be literally true of the Transcendent as it is an itself, but can be mythologically true of it in virtue of evoking an appropriate dispositional state in response to religious phenomena (the God-figures, etc.) which are manifestations or 'appearances' to human consciousness of the Transcendent.

Such a view of the function of religious language is rather close to the Buddhist concept of *upaya*, 'skilful means'. This is the idea that religious teachings, including the Buddhist dharma itself, cannot be literally true, because they refer to the Ultimate Reality which is empty (*sunya*) of our human conceptual projections. But the dharma can nevertheless be useful, indeed indispensable, as a means to draw people towards the final experience of liberation, enlightenment, awakening, *satori*. Different teachings may be effective for different people, and also for the same people at different periods of their life. But we should not cling to these teachings once they have served their purpose of helping us to move on to another stage of cognition. And so the Buddha told the parable of the man who crosses a river to safety by means of a raft and then, because the raft has been so useful, is tempted to lift it onto his shoulders and carry it with him. But he should go on, leaving the raft behind; and likewise, the Buddha said, the dharma 'is for carrying over, not for retaining ... You, monks, by understanding the parable of the raft, should get rid even of (right) mental objects, all the more of wrong ones'.[14] One is reminded of course of Wittgenstein's 'My propositions are elucidatory in this way: he who understands me finally recognizes them as senseless, when he has climbed out through them, on them, over them. (He must so to speak throw away the ladder, after he has climbed up on it).'[15]

The thought that our concepts apply to reality as humanly experienced, but not to reality as it is in itself, translates in religious terms into the idea of the ineffability, or in Eastern terms the formlessness, of the Transcendent. In the words of a fascinating saying in one of the Hindu holy books, 'Thou art formless: thy only form is our knowledge of thee.'[16] The Transcendent is not literally personal or impersonal, good or evil, purposive or non-purposive, active or passive, substance or process, even one or many; for these dualisms are aspects of our human conceptual systems. But in denying that the Transcendent is personal one is not affirming that it is impersonal, but rather that the personal–impersonal polarity does not apply to it. And the same with all the other dualisms. The Transcendent, as it is in itself independently of human awareness of it, is postulated as lying beyond the scope of human conceptuality. That is to say, it has no humanly conceivable intrinsic attributes, although its 'impact' upon us can of course only be described in terms of our human conceptualities.

There is however an obvious qualification to be made to this last statement. To say that X is ineffable is to say that X's nature cannot be described in terms of our human concepts. But of course to say that is already to describe it – namely, as being humanly indescribable. And so we have to distinguish between substantial attributes, such as goodness, power, personality, and purely formal and logically generated attributes, such as being such that our substantial attribute concepts do not apply to it. Ineffability must be defined in terms of the former, not the latter; and also in terms of the intrinsic nature of the Real, as distinguished from the effects of its presence upon ourselves.

The critical realist religious picture that I am proposing is, then, as follows. Using (perforce!) our human conceptuality, we can say that there is an ultimate source and ground of the universe in both its physical and its non-physical aspects – 'all things visible and invisible'. I have been referring to this as the Transcendent. The Transcendent is universally present, and affects human consciousness in many forms of what we call religious experience – within which I include the pervasive sense of living in the presence of God, and of being part of the samsaric process that leads towards unity with Brahman, and of oneness with the living universe that is an expression of the universal Buddha-nature, and as the sense of living in response to the Tao, or to the requirements of Heaven, as well as 'peak experiences' of enlightenment, awakening, visions and auditions and photisms and other such moments. These examples suffice to remind us that the impact of the Real comes to human consciousness in a variety of ways due to the different conceptual systems and spiritual practices of the religious traditions. The ultimate noumenal reality is thought, and therefore experienced, and therefore responded to in forms of human life in a range of ways, all formed by our different conceptual systems. The key concept of deity, or of the Transcendent as personal, presides over the theistic religions, whilst the key concept of the Absolute, or of the Transcendent as non-personal, presides over the non-theistic traditions. In each case the concept is made more concrete in terms of human history and culture. And so deity is thought and experienced, within Judaism specifically as Adonai, the God of Abraham, Isaac and Jacob; within Christianity as the Blessed Trinity of Father, Son and Holy Spirit; within Islam as the strictly unitary Allah; within theistic Hinduism as Vishnu, who became incarnate as Krishna, or as Shiva, whose cosmic dance is the ongoing life of the universe; and so on. And likewise the ultimate as non-personal is thought and experienced within Advaitic Hinduism as the Atman which is identical with the eternal Brahman; within the different streams of Buddhism as *Nirvana*, or as the universal Buddha-nature of the universe; within Taoism as the eternal transcendent reality whose nature cannot be expressed in words; and so on.

What is the epistemological status of this suggestion? It is a theory, or hypothesis, offered as a 'best explanation' of the data provided by religious experience as reported in its plurality of forms by the history of religions. It is however offered as a (transcendental) *religious* interpretation of religion, that is, one that accepts human religious experience not as purely projection and imagination but as at the same time a response to the Transcendent. And in so far as it is correct it will be progressively confirmed in future experience beyond this life.

## Conclusion

What I hope to have done in this chapter is to draw out the contrast between religion with and without transcendence, showing in each case the sense in which religious beliefs can be true or false. The difference hinges upon different conceptions of the nature of reality as making or not making possible the ultimate fulfilment of the human project. And I have pointed out that we are not confined to a choice between a naive realist interpretation of religious language and the non-realist interpretation which issues in religion without transcendence. The third possibility is a critical realism which postulates an ultimate reality which is the ground of everything, including the possibility of the realization of the highest potentialities of human nature; which is in itself beyond the network of human concepts, but which is humanly thought and experienced and responded to in the range of ways described in the history of religions.

## Notes

1. Dewi Phillips is Danforth Professor of the Philosophy of Religion at the Claremont Graduate University, California, and Rush Rhees Research Professor at the University of Wales, Swansea.
2. Bertrand Russell, *Mysticism and Logic and Other Essays* (London: Edward Arnold, 1918), pp. 47–8.
3. Bertrand Russell, *Autobiography*, vol. 3 (London: Allen & Unwin, 1969), pp. 172–3.
4. Steven Weinberg, *Dreams of a Final Theory* (London: Hutchinson Radius, 1993), p. 41.
5. Barbara Ward and René Dubos, *Only One Earth*, Report on the Stockholm Conference on the Human Environment (Harmondsworth and New York: Penguin Books, 1972), p. 35.
6. Ludwig Feuerbach, *The Essence of Christianity*, trans. George Eliot (New York: Harper Torchbooks, 1957), p. 175.
7. D.Z. Phillips, *Death and Immortality* (London: Macmillan, and New York: St Martin's Press, 1970), pp. 48–9. See also his *Religion Without Explanation* (Oxford: Blackwell, 1976), chapters 8–9.
8. *Ibid.*, p. 49.

9. St Thomas Aquinas, *Summa Theologica*, II/II, Q. 1, art. 2.
10. Ludwig Wittgenstein, *Philosophical Investigations*, trans. G.E.M. Anscombe (Oxford: Blackwell, 1953), p. 193.
11. *Ibid.*, p. 197.
12. Rupert Brooke, 'Heaven', in *1914 and Other Poems* (Solihull: Helion Books, 1993), pp. 19–20.
13. Weinberg, *Dreams of a Final Theory*, p. 170.
14. *The Middle Length Sayings*, Vol. 1, trans. I.B. Horner (London: Pali Text Society, 1954–9), pp. 173–4.
15. Ludwig Wittgenstein, *Tractatus Logico-Philosophicus*, trans. C.K. Ogden (London: Routledge & Kegan Paul, 1922), 6.54.
16. *Yogava'sistha*, 1:28.

# Part II
# In Dialogue with Evangelicals

# 6
# Religious Pluralism for Evangelicals

## My conversion experience and spiritual pilgrimage

I began my Christian life as a fundamentalist. I was baptized as a baby in the Church of England and was taken as a child and teenager to its services, which were to me a matter of infinite boredom. The whole Christian 'thing' seemed to me utterly lifeless and uninteresting. But I was nevertheless conscious of being in some kind of long-term state of spiritual dissatisfaction and search. My unformed world-view was broadly humanist. At the age of 16 I was thrilled by the writings of Nietzsche and greatly enjoyed reading Bertrand Russell.

But as a law student at University College, Hull, at the age of eighteen, I underwent a powerful evangelical conversion under the impact of the New Testament figure of Jesus. For several days I was in a state of intense mental and emotional turmoil, during which I became increasingly aware of a higher truth and greater reality pressing in upon me and claiming my recognition and response. At first this was highly unwelcome, a disturbing and challenging demand for nothing less than a revolution in personal identity. But then the disturbing claim became a liberating invitation. The reality that was pressing in upon me was not only awesomely demanding but also irresistibly attractive, and I entered with great joy and excitement into the world of Christian faith. Some of my fellow students were members of the InterVarsity Fellowship, the evangelical campus organization; and throwing in my lot with them, I accepted as a whole and without question the entire evangelical package of theology – the verbal inspiration of the Bible; Creation and Fall; Jesus as God the Son incarnate, born of a virgin, conscious of his divine nature, and performing miracles of divine power; redemption by his blood from sin and guilt; Jesus' bodily resurrection, ascension and future return in glory; heaven and hell.

Intending now to enter the ministry of the Presbyterian Church of England, mainly because my InterVarsity friends were Presbyterians, I moved to Edinburgh University to study philosophy, with which I was already fascinated, before going to seminary. The regular meetings, prayer meetings and Bible study groups of the Evangelical Union at Edinburgh occupied a good deal of my time, and I also engaged in its other activities, such as conducting ward services in the Edinburgh Royal Infirmary.

However, this was 1941, with World War II, of course, having already begun in Europe. Previously in Hull I had taken part along with other students in 'fire watching' and was on duty during the three nights when almost the entire centre of Hull was destroyed by bombing. In the summer of 1942, I was due for military service. Although nearly all my fellow students joined the forces, I felt called to be a conscientious objector on Christian grounds. The way I thought about it then was simply that the teachings of Jesus were utterly incompatible with the mass violence of war. I would now add that, regardless of the justification at the time for any particular conflict – and World War II was, in the circumstances of the Nazi threat to Europe, probably as well justified on the Allied side as almost any war could be – war between nations is a collective insanity of killing, maiming and destroying our common human assets. An observer from outer space would say that in a 'world war' the human race goes temporarily mad, kills off much of the best of its present generation, undermines the degree of civilization it has achieved and may even eventually destroy itself. The only way to communicate this as other than an unheard bleat was actually to refuse to take part in war. I saw this refusal as a vocation for some of us, while others had a vocation to take part in what was to them the lesser of two evils. However, I could not opt out of the war itself, but only out of the willingness to kill; thus, I joined the Friends' (i.e. Quakers') Ambulance Unit, and this option was endorsed by a Conscientious Objectors' Tribunal. I served in the F.A.U. for the last three years of the war – first in hospitals in London and Edinburgh, then in Egypt, Italy and Greece.

## Intellectual doubts

After the war I returned to Edinburgh University for the remaining three years of my philosophy course. I rejoined the Evangelical Union, but soon found that I was no longer fully in tune with it. My philosophical training was leading me to ask awkward questions. How, for example, could one understand the sun standing still for about a day as recounted in Joshua 10: 13? In the light of our modern knowledge of astronomy, we would have to say that the earth, which rotates at a speed of about a thousand miles an hour, suddenly ceased to rotate; but taken seriously, this is mind-boggling. Again, can biological evolution responsibly be rejected just because it is contrary to the book of Genesis? Are there not numerous contradictions between this biblical text and that? And could it really be an expression of infinite love to send the majority of the human race to eternal torment in hell? And so on. But instead of such questions being honestly confronted, there seemed to me to be a distinct reluctance on the part of the student and faculty leadership to face them, a feeling that they were dangerous and ought not to be raised, and that they constituted a temptation to back-sliding. Thus I drifted away from the conservative evangelical student movement, though continuing for many years to be what I would now describe as theologically fairly conservative.

The year I graduated a new scholarship came into existence to support an Edinburgh philosophy graduate to do research at Oxford. I received this award and became the first Campbell Fraser scholar at Oriel College, Oxford, working for the D.Phil. degree under Professor H.H. Price and writing my thesis on 'Faith and Belief', later revised as *Faith and Knowledge*.[1] After Oxford I studied for three years at the Presbyterian seminary, Westminster College, Cambridge. There I remember being profoundly shocked by a graduate student who argued that Jesus was not God incarnate but a remarkable human being. At the end of the seminary course I was ordained to the ministry of the Presbyterian Church of England (subsequently, after union with the Congregationalists, the United Reformed Church). At the same time I was married and for the next three years served a rural congregation just south of the Scottish border. I greatly enjoyed the work, the congregation flourished, and our first child was born.

However, one day a totally unexpected letter arrived from the Philosophy Department at Cornell University, asking if I would be interested in going there as an assistant professor teaching philosophy of religion. We went there and enjoyed Cornell enormously. While there, I published my first article, in the *Scottish Journal of Theology* (March 1958), criticizing D.M. Baillie's 'paradox of grace' Christology for departing, more than he seemed to recognize, from Chalcedonian orthodoxy. In other words, I had not yet proceeded very far from the conservative theology with which I started. The first noticeable departure occurred in 1961, while teaching at Princeton Theological Seminary, when I questioned whether belief in the Incarnation required one to believe in the literal historicity of the Virgin Birth.

## The necessity for an intellectual appropriation of the Christian faith

I have recounted this piece of autobiography to help conservative readers to appreciate that I have some understanding of their position, because it was once my own. My departure from it was gradual and was partly the result of further reflection prompted by a philosophical training, partly of reading the works of the New Testament scholars, and partly of trying to preach the gospel in a way that made sense to ordinary twentieth-century men and women, both young and old. My conversion experience, with its powerful awareness of a divine presence that was both profoundly challenging and at the same time profoundly creative and life-giving, remains basic; but the particular fundamentalist intellectual package that came with it has long since crumbled and disappeared. I can, however, recognize – as some liberal Christians do not – that the conservative evangelical wing of Christianity sometimes serves a vital purpose in challenging young people and jolting them out of the pervasive secular humanism of our culture. It can in many cases be good to undergo a 'fundamentalist' conversion, so long as one later sorts out the intellectually acceptable and unacceptable and is able eventually to discard the latter.

## The religious way of experiencing-as and revelation

Having done that sorting out, I ought at this point to make clear to a conservative readership how I differ from them on the questions of revelation and the authority of Scripture. I do not think that it is possible to settle theological issues with 'The Bible says ... '. The Bible is a collection of documents written during a period of about a thousand years by different people in different historical and cultural situations. The writings are of a variety of kinds, including court records, heavily edited and slanted history, prophetic utterances, hymns, letters, diary fragments, memories of the historical Jesus, faith-created pictures of his religious significance, apocalyptic visions, etc. The human authorship and historical setting must always be taken into account in using the Scriptures. We do not, for example, need today to take over the pre-scientific beliefs and cultural assumptions of people living in the remote past in a very different human world. If they thought that the earth is flat and that physical diseases are caused by demons, we do not have to follow them in that. It is their religious experience that is important. God is always and everywhere present to us – above, beneath, around and within us. And when a human being is exceptionally open to the divine presence, he or she has a vivid awareness of God, which is then called revelation.

Usually within our Judaeo-Christian tradition, this awareness takes the form of experiencing some event in one's own life, or in the wider history of which one is part, as mediating or revealing the presence and activity of God. Thus the Old Testament prophets characteristically experienced events in the history of Israel as occasions of God's presence in the form of guidance, aid, warning, or punishment. For example, Jeremiah saw the Chaldean army, advancing on Jerusalem, as God's instrument to punish faithless Israel. This was not, I believe, a retrospective theological interpretation, but an expression of the way in which the prophet actually experienced the event at the time. No doubt others experienced the same event as having a purely political or economic significance. The religious way of experiencing-as does not negate these secular ways but adds another layer of meaning to it. Thus the Chaldeans had their own purely human purposes; but Jeremiah experienced this moment of history, including those human purposes, as serving a divine purpose. The difference between the religious and secular modes of experiencing-as occurs in the interpretive element within the formation of the experience. Religious faith is this uncompelled interpretive element within religious experience.[2]

## The New Testament's confession of Jesus

And what of the New Testament? This is a selection of Christian documents from the first century, which takes us as far back to the historical Jesus and the origins of Christianity as we can get. The earliest document, Paul's first letter to the Thessalonians, is probably dated about A.D. 50, and the earliest Gospel, that of Mark, about A.D. 70 We should not think of the four Gospels as if they were eyewitness accounts by reporters on the spot. They were written between 40 and 70 years after Jesus' death by people who were not personally present at the events they describe; for all are dependent on sources in a way in which an eyewitness would not be. Furthermore, intensive developments had taken place within the Christian community during those formative decades.

These documents are all documents of faith. They all see Jesus as one who mediated God's presence and God's call to live now as citizens of the coming kingdom. The earliest conceptualization of this faith response to Jesus seems to have been as a Spirit-filled prophet and healer; in the words attributed to Peter in Acts, 'a man attested to you by God with mighty works and wonders and signs which God did through him in your midst' (Acts 2: 22).[3] This God-inspired man seems to have understood his own role as that of the final prophet, proclaiming the imminent coming of the kingdom on earth. And the early church lived in the fervent expectation of his return as God's agent to inaugurate the kingdom. As this expectation gradually faded, Jesus was exalted in communal memory from the eschatological prophet to a divine status. The New Testament documents were written during the early stages of this development and contain both flashbacks to the human Jesus of history and anticipations of the divine Christ of later official church doctrine.

I am not sure whether it is generally known to students in the evangelical world that many human beings were called 'son of God' in the ancient world. At least, I did not know this myself when I was a student in that world. Today, in our science-dominated secular society it would take earth-shaking miracles to cause us to regard a man or a woman as being also divine. But in the ancient world, the concept and language of divinity was much looser. Emperors, pharaohs and great philosophers and religious figures were sometimes called 'son of God' and regarded as divine in the broad sense that 'divine' then had. Further, the 'son of God' designation was familiar within Judaism. Israel as a whole was called God's son (Hos. 11: 1); angels were called 'sons of God' (Job 38: 7); kings were enthroned as sons of God (2 Sam. 7: 14; Ps. 2: 7). The Messiah, being of the royal line of David, would be in this sense a son of God. Indeed, any outstandingly pious Jew could be called a son of God, meaning one who was close to God, served God and acted in the spirit of God. In terms of our modern distinction, this was clearly intended as metaphor. No one thought that King David, to whom God said at his coronation, 'You are my son; today I have begotten you' (Ps. 2: 7), was literally God's son. And it would be entirely natural that Jesus, as a great charismatic preacher and healer, should be thought of as a son of God.

However, this idea was sometimes less clearly metaphorical in the Gentile world. And when Paul took the gospel into that world, this 'son of God' metaphor began to change. As Jesus was gradually deified in the minds of Christians, he became the semi-metaphorical, semi-literal Son of God, and then finally, after several centuries, the literal God the Son, the Second Person of a divine Trinity. All this was the work of the church as it lived through new situations, and particularly as it became in the fourth century the official religion of the Roman empire.

I thus see theology as a human creation. I do not believe that God reveals propositions to us, whether in Hebrew, Greek, English or any other language. I hold that the formulation of theology is a human activity that always, and necessarily, employs the concepts and reflects the cultural assumptions and biases of the theologians in question. As a clear example, the successive atonement doctrines that have become prominent during the history of Christian doctrine have reflected the states of society within which they were produced.[4]

## The challenge of other religions

Returning to the personal story that I was recounting, there is at least one major difference between my own experience, now more than half a century ago, and that of the present younger generation. Whereas the question of other religions and the challenge that their existence poses to a conservative Christian faith were hardly on the agenda at that time, both aspects have today become prominent and unavoidable. At seminary I learned little about other faiths, though I did take one course from H.H. Farmer along the lines of his subsequent book *Revelation and Religion*, in which he saw Christianity as fulfilling what was partially available in the other world religions. And apart from an occasional Jew, I did not meet anyone who was not at least nominally a Christian. I shared the general Christian assumption that it was God's will that the whole world be evangelized and that humanity was in fact slowly but surely becoming Christian. At that time this belief was not problematic to me, and I remember being shocked when Reinhold Niebuhr declared that the mission to the Jews was a mistake.

How, then, have I come to adopt a 'pluralist' understanding of the relation between Christianity and the other great world faiths? And what is this 'pluralist' understanding? I can answer these questions by continuing the narrative. After teaching at Cornell, then at the fairly conservative Princeton Theological Seminary, and then at Cambridge University, I moved to the H.G. Wood Chair in the Theology Department of the University of Birmingham. This city, in the middle of England, is an industrial centre which was one of the main receivers of immigration during the 1950s and 1960s from the Caribbean islands and from the Indian subcontinent. There was thus a sizeable presence of several non-Christian traditions, consisting of the new Muslim, Sikh and Hindu communities, as well as a small but long-established Jewish community; subsequently there have come to be several Buddhist groups. Immigration was then a hotly debated issue, and the neo-Nazi National Front was active in the area, generating prejudice and hatred and promoting violence against black and brown people and against Jews. It was a challenging time and place in which to find oneself.

During my fifteen years at Birmingham I became deeply involved in a variety of 'community relations' organizations. I was one of the founders and the first chair of the activist AFFOR (All Faiths for One Race), based in the largely black area of Handsworth, and chair of the Birmingham Inter-Faiths Council, chair of the Religious and Cultural Panel of the governmentally sponsored Birmingham Community Relations Committee, and chair of the coordinating committee of the Statutory Conference convened under the 1944 Education Act to create a new Agreed Syllabus of religious education in the city's schools. The latter operation lasted two years and produced a new multi-faith curriculum to replace the previous exclusively Christian one.

This was a busy and sometimes exciting period. The first director of AFFOR was violently assaulted several times by National Front thugs; the Jewish investigative journalist with whom I collaborated in a published exposure of the records of the National Front leaders – many of whom had been in prison for violent offences – was knifed; and others of us received threats. In all this I found myself in active comradeship with Muslims, Jews, Hindus, Sikhs, Marxists and humanists, as well as with fellow Christians. It has to be said that in the 1970s – the situation is happily very different today – the British churches, so far from leading the opposition to racial prejudice and discrimination, were largely uninterested in the issue and also unready to face the theological questions raised by the fact of religious plurality.

In the course of this work I went frequently to Jewish synagogues, Muslim mosques, Sikh gurudwaras, Hindu temples and, of course, a variety of churches. In these places of worship I soon realized something that is obvious enough once noticed, yet momentous in its implications. This is that although the language, concepts, liturgical actions and cultural ethos differ widely from one another, yet from a religious point of view basically the same thing is going on in all of them, namely, human beings coming together within the framework of an ancient and highly developed tradition to open their hearts and minds to God, whom they believe makes a total claim on their lives and demands of them, in the words of one of the prophets, 'to do justice, and to love kindness, and to walk humbly with your God' (Mic. 6: 8). God is known in the synagogues as *Adonai*, the Lord God of Abraham, Isaac and Jacob; in the mosques as *Allah rahman rahim*, God beneficent and merciful; in the Sikh gurudwaras as God, who is Father, Lover, Master and the Great Giver, referred to as *war guru*; and in the Hindu temples as Vishnu, Krishna (an incarnation of Vishnu), Rama, Shiva, and many other gods and goddesses, all of whom, however, are seen as manifestations of the ultimate reality of Brahman; and in the Christian churches as the triune God, Father, Son and Holy Spirit. And yet all these communities agree that there can ultimately only be one God!

If there is indeed only one God, maker of heaven and earth, two obvious possibilities present themselves. One is that God as known within one particular religion, namely one's own, is the real God and that all the others are unreal. The other is that God as known to Christians, Jews, Muslims, Hindus, Sikhs and others represents different manifestations in relation to humanity, different 'faces' or 'masks' or *personae* of God, the Ultimate Reality. But there is also a third, intermediate position, adopted today by the majority of mainline theologians, that God as known within Judaism, Islam, Hinduism and Sikhism are partial or distorted glimpses of the real God, who is fully known within Christianity. This range of options seems to cover the field.

Why, then, do I opt for the pluralistic view that the God-figures of the great theistic religions are different human awarenesses of the Ultimate, rather than for the traditional Christian view that we alone have a true knowledge of God, the others having at best pale reflections of it? The answer still lies in the realm of personal experience and observation, though expanding beyond multi-faith Birmingham to visits to Hindu, Muslim, Sikh India, Buddhist Sri Lanka and Japan, and with involvement in Jewish-Christian-Muslim and Buddhist–Christian dialogues.

## Morality in the major world religions

Coming to know both ordinary families, and some extraordinary individuals, whose spirituality has been formed by these different traditions and whose lives are lived within them, I have not found that the people of the other world religions are, in general, on a different moral and spiritual level from Christians. They seem on average to be neither better nor worse than are Christians. Clearly in saying this, I am presupposing a common criterion, a general sense of what we mean by the human goodness that reflects a right relationship to God. This is the universally recognized sense of goodness as consisting in concern for others, kindness, love, compassion, honesty and truthfulness.

The basic ideal of love and concern for others and of treating them as you would wish them to treat you is, in fact, taught by all the great religious traditions. Jesus said, 'As you wish that men would do to you, do so to them' (Luke 6: 31). Confucius said, 'Do not do to others what you would not like yourself' (*Analects*, XII: 2). Taoism says that the good man will 'regard [others'] gains as if they were his own, and their losses in the same way' (*Thai Shang*, 3). Zorastrianism declares, 'That nature only is good when it shall not do to another whatever is not good for its own self' (*Dadistan-i-dinik*, 94: 5). In the Hindu *Mahabharata* we read, 'One should never do that to another which one regards as injurious to one's own self. This, in brief, is the rule of Dharma' (*Anushana parva*, 113: 7). The Jain scriptures tells us that one should go about 'treating all creatures in the world as he himself would be treated' (*Katanga Sutra*, Bk. I, lect. 11: 33). The Buddhist scriptures contain many injunctions to compassion and loving-kindness, such as this: 'As a mother cares for her son, all her days, so towards all living things a man's mind should be all-embracing' (*Sutta Nipata*, 149). The Jewish Talmud tells us that 'what is hateful to yourself do not do to your fellow man. That is the whole of the Torah' (*Babylonian Talmud, Shabbath* 31a). And in the Hadith of Islam we read the prophet Muhammad's words, 'No man is a true believer unless he desires for his brother that which he desires for himself' (*Ibn Madja*, Introduction 9; cf. other hadiths).

In each case, for both Christian and non-Christian, this is of course an ideal. The important question is the extent to which the ideal is put into practice. The honest answer, in each case, is that it has been practised very imperfectly. Each tradition has its great saints and great sinners, and in the lives of ordinary believers a wavering attempt to live up to the ideal, but with human behaviour all too often sliding into a loveless and selfish treatment of others. We have no way of accurately recording the individual actions of hundreds of millions of people within the great world religions over the centuries or today. It is, of course, easy to pick out some manifest example of gross injustice or cruelty within some non-Christian community and contrast it with some manifest example of true goodness within a Christian community. But such a procedure could easily be reversed, and in each case it is manifestly unfair. We can only go on personal observation and the reports of others, both contemporary and historical, and on this basis form a global impression, though one that we cannot claim to prove. My own global impression, based inevitably on having known a limited number of families and individuals and having read a limited amount of history and travellers' accounts, is that the virtues and vices seem to be spread more or less evenly among human beings, regardless of whether they are Christians or – to confine ourselves for the moment to the 'great world religions' – Jews, Muslims, Hindus, Sikhs or Buddhists.

But is this what we would expect if Christians have a more complete and direct access to God than anyone else and live in a closer relationship to him, being indwelt by the Holy Spirit? Should not the fruit of the Spirit, which according to Paul is 'love, joy, peace, patience, kindness, goodness, faithfulness, gentleness, self-control' (Gal. 5. 22–23), be more evident in Christian than in non-Christian lives? It would not, of course, be fair to expect that any randomly selected Christian be morally superior to any randomly selected non-Christian. But surely the *average* level of these virtues should be noticeably higher among Christians than among non-Christians. Yet it does not seem to me that in fact Christians are on average noticeably morally superior to Jews, Muslims, Hindus, Sikhs or Buddhists. But rather than suggest a comparative quantification of a kind that is not in fact possible, I propose the more modest and negative conclusion, that it is not possible to establish the moral superiority of the adherents of any one of the great traditions over the rest.

And when we turn to the large-scale expressions of religion in human societies and civilizations over the centuries, I find that we are led to a similar conclusion. Christian, Muslim, Hindu, Buddhist, Chinese, African and other 'primal' cultures have each been a mixture of good and evil. But the goods and the evils are often incommensurate. How does one weigh the evil of the Indian caste system – which, incidentally, operates in the Christian as well as in the Hindu communities in India – over the centuries against the evil of the European class system over the same centuries? How does one weigh the poverty of many Muslim, Hindu and Buddhist countries against the greedy use of the earth's non-renewable resources and the heedless destruction of the environment by the western Christian countries? How does one weigh the social problems of Calcutta or Bangkok or Cairo against those of some of our own inner cities, with their daily murders, violent crimes, destructive drug use, poverty, deprivation and despair? Or how do we weigh the cruelties of some eastern regimes against the virulent anti-Semitism of Christian Europe, culminating in the Holocaust of the 1940s? It is, of course, once again easy to pick out some manifestly good aspect of our own civilization and compare it with some manifestly evil aspect of another. But as before, this is not a just way of proceeding. Again I conclude that it seems appropriate to come to the modest and negative conclusion that one cannot establish the unique moral superiority of any one of the great religious civilizations.

Some will disagree with this estimate. Unfortunately, any debate about it is likely to be inconclusive. But it is worth at this point to pose the question whether the position of Christian conservatives requires that the moral fruits of Christian faith are superior to those of any other faith, and if so, whether this is an *a priori* claim or one they believe can be substantiated?

## The phenomenon of salvation

Assuming, however, that my negative conclusion is correct – namely, that it cannot properly be claimed that the fruits of Christian faith in human life, both individual and corporate, are superior to those of the other major world religions – what then? A conservative might be tempted to reply that morality is something different from salvation. To see Jesus as God incarnate – more precisely, as God the Son, the second Person of the Holy Trinity, incarnate – and to take him as one's Lord and Saviour, pleading his atoning death to cover one's sins, is to be justified in God's sight; this is what it means to be saved. The sanctification that follows is a long process. We are not immediately perfected, and Christians can be found in all stages of sanctification, from miserable sinners to devout saints. Thus it is not fair to expect Christians generally to be morally superior to non-Christians generally.

But is such a reply adequate? Surely the work of the Holy Spirit within us should have the effect of raising the general moral level of the Christian community above that of the surrounding world. Jesus called men and women to turn round in their lives and to begin to live the life of the coming kingdom. He called them to love their neighbours, to turn the other cheek, to overcome evil with good, to trust wholly in God rather than secure themselves by power or possessions, and to give without expecting any reward. And the criterion of judgment in his parable of the sheep and the goats was not a theological but a practical one: Have they given food and drink to the hungry, welcomed strangers, clothed the naked, and visited the sick and those in prison (Matt. 25: 31–46)? Such behaviour is the natural fruit of true religion: 'Are grapes gathered from thorns, or figs from thistles? So, every sound tree bears good fruit' (Matt. 7: 16–17). But if the fruit of Christian faith seems in general to be neither better nor worse than the fruit of Jewish,

Muslim, Hindu or Buddhist faiths, should this not lead us to think more positively about those other great Ways?

This path of thought, reflecting both personal observation and a fair amount of reading, suggests to me that we should think of salvation in more universal terms than has been customary in Christian theology. This in turn leads to a new understanding of the function of the world religions, including Christianity. If we define salvation as being for-given and accepted by God because of Jesus' death on the cross, then it becomes a tautology that Christianity alone knows and is able to preach the source of salvation. But if we define salvation as an actual human change, a gradual transformation from natural self-centredness (with all the human evils that flow from this) to a radically new orientation centred in God and manifested in the 'fruit of the Spirit', then it seems clear that salvation is taking place within all of the world religions – and taking place, so far as we can tell, to more or less the same extent. On this view, which is not based on theological theory but on the observable realities of human life, salvation is not a juridical transaction inscribed in heaven, nor is it a future hope beyond this life (although it is this too), but it is a spiritual, moral and political change that can begin now and whose present possibility is grounded in the structure of reality.

This salvific transformation is conceived in different sets of terms within the different religions. *Salvation* is primarily a Christian term. *Redemption* is common to Christians and Jews. Muslims think in terms of a *total submission to God*, who is the giver of life and who is ever gracious and merciful to humankind. The eastern religions do not always experience the ultimate reality we call God as a personal being and do not think primarily in terms of guilt and forgiveness. Rather, this transformation is experienced as *liberation* or *enlightenment*, that is, the dispelling of the spiritual blindness of *avidya* and the discovery of ultimate oneness with Brahman, the eternally real. Another character-istic eastern term is *awakening*, that is, awakening to the true nature of reality when experienced from a universal rather than an ego-centred point of view; this transformed consciousness, whose expression is compassion for all of life, is *nirvana*. These are very different experi-ences, formed by very different conceptualities and integral to very different religious totalities. But they are all forms of the same funda-mental human transformation from self-centredness to a recentring in the ultimately Real as variously thought and experienced within the different ways of being human that constitute the great religious cultures of the earth. When trying to think on the global scale, I have therefore become accustomed to using the hybrid term *salvation/ liberation*.

The process of reasoning in which I find myself engaged is thus inductive, in the sense of proceeding upwards from observable data, rather than being deductive, in the sense of starting with *a priori* premises and deducing conclusions from them. I start from within the circle of Christian faith, committed to the fundamental conviction that Christian religious experience is not, as the sceptics believe, purely imaginative projection, but is our response to the ultimate transcendent reality that we call God. The Christian totality, by which my own religious experience is shaped, is a complex historical process covering now 20 centuries, and it includes both great goods and great evils; but the tradition as a whole, 'warts and all', constitutes my spiritual home. I then notice that there are also in the world other more or less equally ancient, vast and complex streams of religious thought and experience, each likewise including both great goods and great evils. But looking at them all, including my own, I see them as imperfect contexts of salvation/liberation. They are contexts within which men and women have been transformed, in varying degrees, from self-centredness to Reality-centredness. Their soteriological power can only be humanly judged by their human fruits, and, as indicated above, these fruits seem to me to be found more or less equally within each of the great traditions.

It therefore seems logical to me to conclude that not only Christianity, but also these other world faiths, are human responses to the Ultimate. They see the Divine/Sacred/Ultimate through different human conceptual 'lenses', and they experience the divine/sacred/ultimate presence through their different spiritual practices in correspondingly different forms of religious experience. But they seem to constitute more or less equally authentic human awarenesses of and response to the Ultimate, the Real, the final ground and source of everything.

Let me now relate this to the central focus of the book, namely, the fate of non-Christians. For a traditionally orthodox theology, this is a grave problem, for the eternal destiny of the large majority of the human race is at stake. The unacceptable aspect of the old exclusivist view that non-Christians are eternally lost, or eternally tormented in hell, is its dire implication concerning the nature of God. Is it compatible with the limitless divine love that God should have decreed that only a minority of human beings, those who have happened to be born in a Christian part of the world, should have the opportunity of eternal life?

Taking up this issue elsewhere, I have argued on Christian grounds for a doctrine of universal salvation.[5] But from the point of view of religious pluralism the issue takes a different form. It is no longer specifically a question of the fate of non-Christians, but of the fate of Christians and everyone else alike. Will all, or some, or none of the human race – whether they be Christian, Buddhist, Muslim or humanist – eventually reach their final fulfilment in relation to the divine Reality? In my view, the cosmic optimism of the great traditions – their proclamation that a limitlessly better existence is available to all because it is rooted in the ultimate structure of reality – strongly suggests that all will in the end, perhaps after many lives in many worlds, attain to this. But the point to stress is that this is distinct from the issue of religious pluralism as such. Pluralism maintains that the question of limited or universal salvation/liberation applies equally to the people of all religions and even to those without one. It is not, as traditional orthodoxy holds, a different question for Christians as opposed to others.

## Pluralism as a philosophical explanation of religious phenomena

This raises immense questions. How can we understand the situation of a plurality of great religious traditions that conceive and experience the Ultimate, the Real, in such different ways, with such different and incompatible belief systems, but nevertheless seeming to be more or less equally effective contexts of human salvation/liberation?

Some will be content just to acknowledge that this is apparently how things are, without seeking to make intellectual sense of it. But the philosophically minded will want to understand the situation. And I suggest that philosophically the answer lies in an epistemological principle that was propounded long ago by Thomas Aquinas when he wrote, 'Things known are in the knower according to the mode of the knower.'[6] That is to say, the human mind is not a passive screen on which the world imprints itself. On the contrary, it is continuously involved in interpreting the data of perception in terms of the intellectual systems within which we live. In other words, the perceived world is partly, but only partly, constructed by the activity of perception. There is a reality there, but the form in which we are conscious of it comes from ourselves. This is the critical realist epistemology.

Thus, we must distinguish between the world as it is in itself, unperceived, and that same world as humanly perceived. For example, what I am conscious of as the continuous, brown, hard, heavy surface of my desk, which makes a sound when I bang it, is, according to the physicists, a region of mostly empty space within which infinitesimally minute packets of discharging energy are moving about at immense speed. These 'particles' – currently identified as 'quarks' – do not have colour, weight, hardness, sound or fixed position. But for a human perceiver, located where we are on the macro–micro scale and endowed with our particular kind of perceptual machinery and conceptual systems, the physical world appears as it does. It must be something very different for a microbe, or a horse, or a bird, or a fish. We therefore have to distinguish, as Immanuel Kant proposed, between a thing as it is in itself and that thing as humanly perceived – that is, as phenomenon. This understanding of our cognitive situation is well supported today not only by strong epistemological considerations, but also by research in cognitive psychology and the sociology of knowledge.

If, then, it is a general truth about the human mind that we become aware of our environment, and are able to act and react appropriately within it, through a continuous interpretive activity, this will also be true of religious awareness. We must expect there to be a human contribution to the forms in which we are aware of our ultimate environment, the universal presence of the Divine. To apply Aquinas's insight, the ultimate Reality is known in accordance with the cognitive mode/ nature/state of the knower; and this varies, in the case of religious awareness, from one religio-cultural totality to another. If, then, we distinguish between the Real/Ultimate/Divine in itself and that Reality as humanly perceived, recognizing that there is a range of modes of human cognition, we can at once see how there is a plurality of religious traditions constituting different, but apparently more or less equally salvific, human responses to the Ultimate. These are the great world faiths.

## The Real in itself and as experienced by humans

I have been using a variety of terms – the Ultimate, the Real, the Transcendent, Ultimate Reality – where normally in Christian discourse we would simply say God. From this point on I will use the term 'the Real', partly because it conforms to our Christian way of thinking of God as that which alone is fully and absolutely real, but also because it corresponds sufficiently to the Sanskrit *sat* and the Arabic *al Haqq*. For when we acknowledge the other great world religions as different but, so far as we can tell, more or less equally effective contexts of salvation/

liberation, we have to think beyond the anthropomorphic God-figure of theistic piety. We have to recognize, with virtually all the greatest Christian thinkers, that the reality we call God exceeds the scope of human thought. Thus one of the Church Fathers, Gregory of Nyssa, insisted that no human words or ideas can grasp the divine nature. He wrote:

> The simplicity of the True Faith assumes God to be that which He is, namely, incapable of being grasped by any term, or any idea, or any other device of our apprehension, remaining beyond the reach not only of human but of angelic and all supramundane intelligence, unthinkable, unutterable, above all expression in words, having but one name that can represent His proper nature, the single name being 'Above Every Name'.[7]

Augustine declared that 'God transcends even the mind'.[8] Anselm defined God as that than which no greater can be thought, adding that God is even 'something greater than can be thought'.[9] If we think we know what God is, then what we are thinking of is not God! Thomas Aquinas echoed this when he wrote that 'then only do we know God truly when we believe him to be above everything that it is possible to think about him', and 'by its immensity the divine substance surpasses every form that our intellect reaches'.[10]

Other classic Christian thinkers who have said essentially the same include Lactantius, Pseudo-Dionysius, John Scotus Erigena, St. John of the Cross and the writer of the *Theologia Germanica*. Martin Luther, who once said that he owed more to the *Theologia Germanica* than to any other book apart from the Bible and Augustine's works, rejected attempts to know God's essence in distinction from God's purpose, that is, God in relation to us. God is *deus absconditus*, the hidden God, in the infinite divine nature. Karl Barth, in the twentieth century, likewise stressed the absoluteness and transcendence of God when he spoke of God as the 'Wholly Other'. And Paul Tillich spoke of 'the God above the God of theism', echoing Meister Eckhart's distinction between the Godhead (*deitas*) and God (*deus*).

This apophatic strand running through Christianity from the earliest times is the basis within our own tradition for a distinction that also occurs in all of the other great world faiths. In its Christian form it is the distinction between God *a se*, God in God's eternal self-existent reality, 'prior to' and independent of the creation, and God *pro nobis*, God in relation to humankind as our creator, redeemer and inspirer. Our Christian theologies are perforce concerned with God as known to us, acknowledging that God in God's own infinite being lies beyond the range of our finite thought. Nicholas of Cusa in the fifteenth century developed some of the implications of this when he wrote:

> As creator, God is three and one; as infinite, he is neither three nor one nor any of the things which can be spoken. For the names which are attributed to God are taken from creatures, since he in himself is ineffable and beyond everything that can be named or spoken.[11]

I mentioned that this distinction between, on the one hand, the Real *a se* – or in Kant's German *an sich*, or, using the neuter, 'in itself' (which the English language requires if we are to avoid speaking of the Real as either male or female) – and, on the other hand, the Real as humanly known, occurs within all the major traditions. The great Jewish philosopher Maimonides distinguished between the essence and the manifestations of God; and both Jewish and Muslim mystics have distinguished between *Ein Sof* (the Infinite) in Jewish Kabbalah or *al Haqq* (the Real) in Islamic Sufism, and the self-revealing God of the Hebrew Bible or the Qur'an. The Taoist scripture, the *Tao Te Ching*, begins by declaring that 'the Tao that can be expressed is not the eternal Tao'. In Hindu thought the distinction is between *nirguna* Brahman (that is, Brahman without attributes as beyond the range of human conceptuality) and *saguna* Brahman (Brahman as humanly experienced as a personal God). And in the Mahayana Buddhist tradition there is the distinction in the Trikaya doctrine between the Dharmakaya, the ultimate, absolute, ineffable reality that cannot be expressed in human thought forms, and its manifestation as the heavenly Buddha figures (the Sambhogakaya), some of whom become incarnate as earthly Buddhas (the Nirmanakaya). In its generic form the distinction is between the Real as it is in itself and the Real as variously humanly conceived and experienced as the personal God-figures and the non-personal 'absolutes' of the world religions.

The pluralistic hypothesis, offered as a religious understanding of religion around the world and across the centuries, is based on this distinction, together with the epistemological principle that there is an interpretive contribution to all human cognition. The hypothesis is that in order to account for the existence of the different religio-cultural totalities that we call, in rough historical order, Hinduism, Judaism, Buddhism, Taoism, Confucianism, African primal religion, Christianity, Islam, Sikhism and the Baha'i faith, as apparently more or less equally effective contexts of salvation/liberation, we have to postulate an ultimate transcendent reality, the source and ground of everything, that is in itself beyond the scope of human conceptuality but is variously conceived, therefore variously experienced, and therefore variously responded to in life, from within these different religious totalities.

A qualification has to be made to the idea of the Real *an sich* as the ultimate reality that is ineffable in that it transcends our human thought forms. This is that purely formal statements can be made even about the ineffable – such as, for example, that it is ineffable! But this is a logical triviality. We cannot attribute to the Real *a se* any intrinsic attributes, such as being personal or non-personal, good or evil, purposive or non-purposive, substance or process, even one or many, though the limitations of our language compel us to speak of it in the singular rather than the plural. For example, we are not affirming that the Real is impersonal by denying that it is in itself personal. This polarity of concepts simply does not apply to it, and likewise with the other polarities. Our systems of human concepts cannot encompass the ultimately Real. It is only as humanly thought and experienced that the Real fits into our human categories.

How then can we worship the Real, if it is beyond all human characterization? The answer is that we do not worship the Real in itself but always one or other of its manifestations to humanity – as the heavenly Parent of Jesus' teaching, or as the Qur'anic Allah, or as the *Adonai* (the Lord) of rabbinic Judaism, or as Vishnu, or as Shiva, or we orient ourselves to it in religious meditation as *pratitya samutpada*, or as the universal Buddha nature (*sunyata*), or as the Tao. Or again in non-theistic advaitic Hinduism one orients oneself in meditation to the universal reality of Brahman, which in the depths of our being we all are. These are all ways of referring to the ultimate reality, to awaken to which is peace and joy and compassionate kindness towards all life. In other words, the pluralistic hypothesis is not a new religion seeking to supplant the existing religions. It is a philosophical interpretation of the global religious situation. Acceptance of some form of the pluralistic view does, however, make a difference that is more important to some traditions than others; for it prompts each to de-emphasize and eventually winnow out that aspect of its self-understanding that entails a claim to unique superiority among the religions of the world.

## Implications of pluralism for Christianity

What does this pluralistic hypothesis involve for Christianity? It is here, and also in Islam, that the claim to unique superiority is most deeply rooted in the belief-system, and where the pluralistic vision is therefore most challenging and most troublesome. And for this reason it is difficult, if not impossible, to avoid giving offence to conservative believers and to appear to be undermining faith and even, in the eyes of some ultra-conservatives, doing the work of the devil. I can only say that having once been within that thought-world, I can appreciate its fears. I have, however, discovered that there is nothing to fear in a greater openness to God's presence within the religious life of all humankind; on the contrary, there is a release from an artificially restricted vision into a greater intellectual honesty and realism and a more mature Christian faith.

As I have been suggesting, conservatives' claims regarding the unique superiority of Christianity are belied by the observable facts. But in what way does conservative theology entail the unique superiority of Christianity? Traditional orthodoxy says that Jesus of Nazareth was God incarnate – that is, God the Son, the Second Person of a divine Trinity, incarnate – who became man to die for the sins of the world and who founded the church to proclaim this to the ends of the earth, so that all who sincerely take Jesus as their Lord and Saviour are justified by his atoning death and will inherit eternal life. It follows from this that Christianity, alone among the world religions, was founded by God in person. God came down from heaven to earth and launched the salvific movement that came to be known as Christianity. From this premise it seems obvious that God must wish all human beings to enter this new stream of saved life, so that Christianity will supersede all the other world faiths. They may perhaps have some good in them and be able to function to some extent as a preparation for the gospel, but nevertheless Christianity alone is God's own religion, offering a fullness of life that no other tradition can provide; it is therefore divinely intended for all men and women without exception.

All this follows logically from the central dogma of the deity of Jesus. And the other traditionally central doctrines of Trinity and Atonement in turn follow logically from this. For when God was on earth as Jesus Christ, there was at the same time God in heaven; and when we add the Holy Spirit – which was not, however, distinguished in the earliest strata of the New Testament from the spirit of Jesus and was not originally hypostatized as a third entity – we have the Trinity. The traditional Atonement doctrines, whether the early ransom theory, the later Catholic satisfaction theory or the Reformed penal-substitutionary theory, presuppose the deity of Jesus. Thus the three pillars of traditional orthodoxy inevitably come under criticism in any attempt to develop our theology in the light of the realization that Christianity is not the one and only salvific path, but is one among others.

To revise the traditional doctrine of the Incarnation is thus, by implication, to revise also the traditional Trinity and Atonement doctrines. This has in fact already been effected in the minds of many Christians, quite independently of the pressures of religious pluralism. Many have found that they can love, revere, and seek to follow Jesus of Nazareth as he is known to us through the New Testament documents, without having to believe that he was literally God incarnate. For there are two main problems with the traditional dogma.[12]

The first problem is that the historical Jesus did not teach this doctrine. It is a creation of the church, one that Jesus himself would probably have regarded as blasphemous. Here we are on the edge of the 'bottomless pit' of biblical interpretation, for virtually nothing that any scholar has said in this field has remained uncontradicted by some other scholar. We must, however, distinguish between biblical fundamentalists, who hold to the verbal inerrancy of the Bible, and mainstream biblical scholars, such as those teaching in academically accredited universities and colleges. For fundamentalists, the Incarnation issue can be settled by such texts as 'I and the Father are one' (John 10: 30) and 'He who has seen me has seen the Father' (John 14: 9); and the pluralism issue by such texts as 'I am the way, and the truth, and the life; no one comes to the Father, but by me' (John 14: 6). But among mainline New Testament scholars, both conservative and liberal, Catholic and Protestant, there is today a general consensus that these are not pronouncements of the historical Jesus but words put into his mouth some 60 or 70 years later by a Christian writer expressing the theology that had developed in his part of the expanding church. To create speeches in this way for famous or revered figures of the past, embodying the writer's sense of the real significance of that past figure, was standard practice in the ancient world; and the discourses attributed to Jesus in the Fourth Gospel are seen today by most contemporary scholarship as examples of this.

However, not everyone within the evangelical wing of Christianity is aware of this. I shall, therefore, quote from one or two conservative New Testament scholars who wholeheartedly believe in the Incarnation doctrine but who acknowledge that it was not taught by Jesus himself. C.F.D. Moule, a pillar of orthodox Christology, wrote, 'Any case for a "high" Christology that depended on the authenticity of the alleged claims of Jesus about himself, especially in the Fourth Gospel, would indeed be precarious.'[13] The late Archbishop of Canterbury, Michael

Ramsay, another pillar of orthodoxy and, like Moule, a New Testament scholar, wrote, 'Jesus did not claim deity for himself', and, 'The title "Son of God" need not of itself be of high significance, for in Jewish circles it might mean no more than the Messiah or indeed the whole Israelite nation, and in popular Hellenism there were many sons of God, meaning inspired holy men.'[14] Professor James Dunn, a distinguished moderately conservative New Testament scholar and one who accepts an orthodox Christology, concludes in a widely used book on Christian origins that 'there was no real evidence in the earliest Jesus tradition of what could fairly be called a consciousness of divinity'.[15]

This judgment is today so generally accepted that conservative theologians defending the traditional incarnation doctrine now accept it among the basic data of which they must take account. Thus Canon Brian Hebblethwaite, in a major defence of the traditional incarnation doctrine, acknowledges that 'it is no longer possible to defend the divinity of Jesus by referring to the claims of Jesus'.[16] And Professor David Brown, another moderately conservative theologian, writes that 'there is good evidence to suggest that [Jesus] himself never saw himself as a suitable object of worship', and that it is 'impossible to base any claim for Christ's divinity on his consciousness once we abandon the traditional portrait as reflected in a literal understanding of St. John's Gospel'.[17]

That Jesus himself did not claim to be God cuts the ground from under the feet of the old apologetic – which I myself used effectively several times as an evangelical student at Edinburgh – that one who claims to be God must be either mad, or bad, or God, and that since Jesus was obviously neither mad nor bad he must have been God. For it now seems clear that Jesus did not claim to be God. Upholders of a literal incarnation doctrine have thus had to retreat from a dominical authority for their belief to the highly debatable argument that Jesus' words and actions *implicitly* claim deity. Certainly Jesus declared God's forgiveness to individuals, as indeed priests and ministers do. And according to Mark, he said that 'the Son of Man has authority on earth to forgive sins' (Mark 2: 10); but while there are various theories concerning the meaning of 'Son of Man', none of them suggests that he is more than either an intermediary being or simply a son of man, that is, a man.

The first problem about the traditional incarnation doctrine, then, is that Jesus did not teach it and that the suggestion that he implied it is highly debatable. It is precarious to base one's faith on a debatable interpretation of ancient texts. So the question has to be faced: On what ground can we properly claim to know who Jesus was, better than he knew himself?

The second problem is that it has not proved possible, after some 15 centuries of intermittent effort, to give any clear meaning to the idea that Jesus had two complete natures, one human and the other divine. The paradoxical character of the idea is evident. In order to be genuinely and fully human, Jesus must have had all the attributes that are definitive of humanity, and in order to be genuinely and fully God, he must also have had all the attributes that are definitive of deity. It is relatively easy to say what the essential divine attributes are, according to Christian theology. They include being the eternal, uncreated, self-existent creator of everything other than God; being omnipotent; being omniscient; being omnipresent; being a spirit, without a body; and being infinite in such moral qualities as goodness, love, justice, mercy and wisdom. A being who lacks any of these attributes is not fully God. The essential human attributes are less easy to list, since we have no orthodox anthropology corresponding to the orthodox theology. But these attributes presumably include being or having a human body with a specific location, and thus not omnipresent; being a creature, and thus not the creator of everything other than God; being limited in power and thus not omnipotent; being limited in knowledge and thus not omniscient; and having moral qualities in a finite, not an infinite, degree.

The question, then, that has so vexed theology and that has never been satisfactorily answered, is how a historical individual, Jesus of Nazareth, could have both sets of attributes at once, and indeed, whether we really want to claim that he did. Consider, for example, omniscience. Do we really want to say that the historical Jesus had the infinite knowledge that God has and only pretended ignorance, as in Matthew 24: 36? And even if we do want to say this, is it really possible for infinite knowledge to be housed in a finite human brain? The number of human brain cells, although truly vast, is nevertheless finite and therefore can only contain a finite amount of information. How then could the historical Jesus be omniscient?

Again, consider omnipotence. Do we really want to claim that Jesus was literally omnipotent but pretended not to be, as in Mark 6: 5? Furthermore, the historical Jesus would clearly seem from the Synoptic Gospels to have been a human creature, not the creator of the universe; to have come into existence at a certain time, rather than being eternally self-existent; and to have been limited to one place at a time, and thus not omnipresent. And while he was good, loving, wise, just and merciful, there is an obvious problem about how a finite human being could have these qualities in an *infinite* degree.

The Council of Chalcedon (A.D. 451), which first authoritatively defined the orthodox Christology, simply asserted that Jesus Christ was 'at once complete in Godhead and in humanity', and as such had two natures, divine and human, which exist 'without confusion, without change, without division, without separation; the distinction of natures being in no way annulled by the union, but rather the characteristics of each nature being preserved and coming together to form one person'. Thus Jesus had all the divine and all the human attributes, 'the characteristics of each nature being preserved'. But the Council did not say how this is possible. It insisted that Jesus was both fully human and fully divine and intended to exclude any doctrine that denied either of these, but it did not spell out what it is to be simultaneously fully human and fully divine.

The simplest possible model would be a divine mind in a human body. But this was not acceptable, because a being without a human mind would not count as a genuinely human being. More sophisticated models were attempted. For example, Apollinaris suggested that a human being consists of body, mind and spirit, and that in the case of Jesus the mind and body were human but the spirit was the eternal Logos. But this too was rejected, because if Jesus had no human spirit he was, once again, not fully human. Many other attempts, some very ingenious, were made during the Christological controversies from about the third to the ninth centuries; but all had to be declared heretical because they failed to do justice either to Jesus' deity or to his humanity. These attempts continue today, perhaps the most interesting contemporary one being the two-minds theory of Thomas Morris and others.[18] I have criticized this rather fully elsewhere.[19]

Cannot all these problems, however, be avoided by the idea of divine *kenosis*, self-emptying? Can we not say, with a whole school of Christological thinking, that in becoming man, God the Son emptied himself of his divine attributes in order to become genuinely and fully human? But this kenotic theory has also been strongly criticized. Is God without the attributes of God still God? In what sense was Jesus God incarnate if he lacked the characteristics in virtue of which God is God? But perhaps we can divide the divine nature – contrary, however, to the Chalcedonian 'without division' – and say that Jesus had some of the divine attributes but not others? Perhaps God the Son divested himself of such attributes as self-existence, omnipotence, omniscience and omnipresence, but retained such other attributes as goodness, love, wisdom, mercy and justice? It would, of course, need to be explained how a self-existent being can ever cease to be self-existent. But even if that could be made clear, the idea of half-divinity still has major problems. For the divine moral attributes are infinite, and how can infinite qualities be embodied in a finite human being? A finite being *cannot* have infinite attributes. We would have to say instead that Jesus embodied *as much* of the infinite divine moral qualities as could be expressed in a finite human life – rather than that 'in him the whole fullness of deity dwells bodily' (Col. 2: 9).

## A pluralist proposal regarding the incarnation

But this reduction of Jesus' deity is barely distinguishable from the understanding of him as a man who was so open to God's presence and so responsive to God's will that God was able to act on earth through him and could thus be said to have been 'incarnate' in his actions. Here incarnation is a metaphor, as in 'Abraham Lincoln incarnated the spirit of American independence' or 'Hitler was evil incarnate'. And in this metaphorical sense we can say that in so far as any human being does God's will, God is 'incarnated', embodied in a human action. Whenever anyone acts in love on behalf of the sick in body or mind, the weak and oppressed, refugees, vulnerable children, the exploited poor, or the bereaved and grieving, there God's love becomes incarnate on earth.

Thus, on the one hand, the idea of Jesus being God incarnate has no acceptable literal meaning, or at least none that has yet been discovered. On the other hand, it does have a powerful metaphorical meaning, in that Jesus was so open to divine inspiration, so responsive to the divine spirit, so obedient to God's will, that God was able to act on earth in and through him. This, I believe, is the true Christian doctrine of incarnation.

The kind of Trinitarian doctrine that is compatible with such a Christology is one in which the three 'Persons' are not persons in our modern sense of three centres of consciousness and will, but in the ancient sense in which a *persona* is a role that someone plays. (On the Roman stage, a *persona* was a mask that an actor used to indicate his role in the play.) Thus the three 'persons' are three ways in which the one God is experienced as acting in relation to humankind – as creator, as transformer or redeemer, and as inner spirit. And no Atonement doctrine, in the sense of a theory about how God has been enabled to forgive our sins by the death of Jesus, is required, because Jesus taught us in the Lord's Prayer to approach God directly as our heavenly Father, and to ask for and expect to receive divine forgiveness without any mediator or atoning sacrifice.

Again, in his parable of the prodigal son, Jesus taught us that God freely forgives and accepts those who truly repent. When the erring son returns in deep penitence, his father does not say, 'Because I am a just as well as a loving father, I cannot forgive you until your sin has been fully atoned for', but 'his father saw him and had compassion, and ran and embraced and kissed him ... [and said], "Let us eat and make merry; for this my son was dead, and is alive again; he was lost, and is found"' (Luke 15: 20, 23–24). In the story of the Pharisees and the tax collector, the latter 'standing far off, would not even lift up his eyes to heaven, but beat his breast, saying, "God, be merciful to me a sinner"'. Jesus then said, 'I tell you, this man went down to his house justified rather than the other' (Luke 18: 13–14). And yet again, there is Jesus' insistence that he came to bring sinners to a penitent acceptance of God's mercy: 'Go and learn what this means, "I desire mercy, and not sacrifice"' (Matt. 9: 13).

Unlike the traditional doctrines, all this is compatible with religious pluralism. We can see Jesus as the one who has made God real to us, who has shown us how to live as citizens of God's kingdom, who is our revered spiritual leader, inspiration and model. And we can do this without having to deny that other spiritual leaders and other revelatory histories function in the same way and to the same extent (so far as we can tell) for other people within other religious traditions.

## Notes

1. John Hick, *Faith and Knowledge*, 2nd edn. (Ithaca: Cornell University Press, 1966 / London: Macmillan, 1966; reprint, London: Macmillan, 1988; orig. edn. 1957).
2. For more about this, see my *Faith and Knowledge*, 2nd edn., or 'Religious Faith as Experiencing-as', in my *God and the Universe of Faiths* (1973; reprint, London: Macmillan, 1988 / Chatham, N.Y. and Oxford: One World Publications, 1993).
3. The Scripture quotations in this chapter are taken from the Revised Standard Version.
4. For details, see my *The Metaphor of God Incarnate* (Louisville: Westminster/John Knox, 1994 / London: SCM, 1994), ch. 11.
5. John Hick, *Death and Eternal Life* (1976; reprint, London: Macmillan, 1985; Louisville: Westminster/John Knox, 1994), ch. 13.
6. Thomas Aquinas, *Summa Theologica*, II/II, Q. 1, art. 2.
7. Gregory of Nyssa, *Against Eunomius*, 1.42.
8. St. Augustine, *De Vera Religione*, 36.67.
9. St. Anselm, *Proslogion*, 15.

10. Thomas Aquinas, *Summa contra Gentiles*, 1.5.3.; 1.14.3.
11. Nicholas of Cusa, *De Pace Fidei*, 7.21.
12. There is an extensive literature about this, some of which I have summarized in *The Metaphor of God Incarnate*.
13. C.F.D. Moule, *The Origins of Christology* (Cambridge: Cambridge University Press, 1977), p. 136.
14. Michael Ramsay, *Jesus and the Living Past* (Oxford: Oxford University Press, 1980), pp. 39, 43.
15. James Dunn, *Christology in the Making* (Louisville: Westminster / John Knox, 1980 / London: SCM, 1980), p. 60.
16. Brian Hebblethwaite, *The Incarnation* (Cambridge: Cambridge University Press, 1987), p. 74.
17. David Brown, *The Divine Trinity* (LaSalle, Ill.: Open Court, 1985 / London: Duckworth, 1985), p. 108.
18. Thomas V. Morris, *The Logic of God Incarnate* (Ithaca, N.Y.: Cornell University Press, 1986); Richard Swinburne, *The Christian God* (Oxford: Clarendon Press, 1984).
19. John Hick, *The Metaphor of God Incarnate*, ch. 5.

# A response by Clark Pinnock[1]

John Hick is the scholarly author of many excellent books on various aspects of the philosophy of religion and religious pluralism. All my life I have admired him as an effective communicator of profound theological ideas. This essay does not add anything new in his thinking about religious pluralism but rather reports those ideas in a chatty way to a conservative readership. In his choosing to tell the story of his own pilgrimage, we learn the truth he has discovered through narrative.

I would not be honest if I did not express a little annoyance that I felt by his testimonial about how he successfully escaped the evangelical faith. As an evangelical myself, I ordinarily like testimonies but do not like being talked down to. I received the distinct feeling that the reason he wants us to know he was once an evangelical is to make liberals of us all and that he is using his chapter to this end. I suppose it touched a nerve in me because I too, converted by evangelicals from bland liberalism and genuinely sympathetic with Hick's early concerns about getting serious about the universal salvific will of God, have not found his recent moves so helpful. On the contrary, I look upon his recent direction with sadness as I contemplate the loss to God's kingdom of a theologian who could be commending God's plan to save the world through Jesus effectively but who has decided not to.

The fateful turning point in Hick's life came in Birmingham, where he had positive experiences with people of other faiths that turned him towards an ideology of pluralism, which postulates an unknown God behind all the religions. He has seemingly changed his whole theology on the basis of meeting saintly members of other faiths. Ironically, Hick could just as easily have sustained a high doctrine of Christ by opting for inclusivism on the basis of this experience. An inclusivist can see God's grace at work in other people's religious lives – saintliness is not a sufficient argument for pluralism. The holy pagans of the Old Testament, like Job and Melchizedek, prove that the God of Israel operates in the lives of those outside the covenant with Abraham. I have no difficulty, for example, accepting the fact that there are holy people in other faiths – my inclusivism leads me to expect that. But it does not lead me to radical theological revision. His own telling of the story shows readers where he made his mistake. He had an experience of saintliness and misinterpreted the theological significance of it. He drew radical conclusions that the experience simply did not require.

## The moral parity of the religions?

From that point on, Hick tries to turn his discussion into a logical argument. The first argument is that religions seem equally good at producing morally and spiritually good people and must therefore be presumed to operate on the basis of the same sanctifying divine Power. Every religion produces saints, so it doesn't really matter what one believes about God. What about this argument?

First, as Hick says, some will disagree with this estimate. How do we know that other faiths transform sinners as effectively as Jesus Christ? What exactly is saintliness anyway? Is it a life of service to the poor or a life of other-worldly contemplation? Hick can be so vague. I look and see blessings such as universal human rights, the demythologizing of the state, the care of the sick and the poor, the importance of preserving the earth, and the ideal of self-giving service, and I notice that it is mostly the fruit of the Christian gospel and possibly proof of its superior sanctifying power. Eastern religions seem to produce stagnant societies, and Islam, intolerant ones.

Second, even if Hick is right about the equity of transformative power, it would not settle the truth question. Mormons are nice people as a whole, but that does not make Mormon theology and history true. There are other tests for truth we would want to apply. There is no need to rush to rash metaphysical conclusions on the basis of sanctity alone.

Third, Hick says that it doesn't matter what you think as long as you act morally, as if beliefs and behaviour were not more closely linked than that. It makes a big difference if one believes salvation is release from the karmic cycle, or if the poor are getting what they deserve for previous lives, or if evil is an illusion, or if the material world is of no importance. Ironically, what Hick as a western liberal probably wants is the kind of social activism agenda favoured by the politically correct. But most world theologies do not give the ground or support for that. Being a liberal Christian sustains Hick's ideal of saintliness best.

## The unknown Real

In a second argument, Hick leaps to the conclusion that all religions are human responses to the Ultimate. Since they all produce saints, he assumes that there is an unknowable ultimate Reality behind them. Why not consider God to be an undifferentiated unity beyond any specific designation? This is certainly possible, but questions arise.

First, while claiming to be a view of God that transcends all the culturally generated models of God in the world's religions, it is in fact a truth claim familiar to the Eastern monistic traditions. This means that it is a claim every bit as *particular* as the Christian one, which sounds covertly imperialistic. Second, how does Hick know that the Real exists and that it is unknowable? Has this been revealed to him? Third, even if there exists a Real, we have no idea what it might be like. Does it love us or hate us, or is it sleeping? It strikes me as a bad deal to trade in the God of Jesus for an unknown God. Such a trade would make it impossible to identify as evil religions that are really false and demonic.

A better solution would be to keep the truth question open rather than to fall into agnosticism. In science one does not give up trying to figure out what is out there just because people do not agree about it. Let's keep the truth question in play and share with each other what we have found to be true. This would also allow the Christian mission to go forward.

## Christology

Hick's third argument relates to Christology. He wants Christians to value the metaphor of God incarnate but not suppose there actually is a divine Logos that became flesh. Let them understand Jesus as embodying the ideal of a human life lived in faithful response to God and in which God was active. Let them value this faith as one of a number of human responses to God. He says that this would better serve the cause of world peace and inter-religious dialogue.

Hick wants to leave the impression that his Christology is based primarily upon historical (that is, Jesus did not teach this doctrine) and theological (that is, it never did make sense) considerations. It seems more likely that this analysis is a rationalization of the position his system requires. Readers have been told that Hick made his move to pluralism before the problem of Jesus was solved. He had already reached the conviction that there *cannot be* a definitive revelation of salvation if the equality of religions on the basis of an unknown Real is to be maintained. A belief in the Incarnation and Trinity would spoil everything. Therefore, the effort to get rid of the Incarnation has less to do with evidence than with the ideology. Be clear – for Hick, Jesus *cannot be* more than an inspiring example, whatever the evidence is! The bias against the Incarnation is invincible going in.

At the same time, Hick is a good scholar and launches a strong critique that cannot just be dismissed. *The Metaphor of God Incarnate* is a very challenging book. Let me make a few comments. First, did Jesus teach the doctrine of the Incarnation? The answer partly depends on which biblical critics you believe. Sceptics such as those in the 'Jesus Seminar' discard all evidence for Jesus' claim and for his bodily resurrection. N.T. Wright and Richard B. Hayes, on the other hand, do not. I would say that the claim of Jesus underlies and authenticates what later came to be known as the doctrine of Incarnation.

Second, does the doctrine possess clear meaning? The answer partly depends on how far one expects human reason to go in explaining the mystery of God incarnate. I would not expect it to be made rational without remainder. For me kenotic Christology comes the closest to explaining it, though it does not eliminate a dimension of mystery. After all, the Incarnation is a gift of the divine freedom.

Third, does the Anselmian soteriology, built around the Incarnation in western theology, add up? No, it does not, and Hick himself points to a better way when he refers to early Greek theologians who saw the work of Christ as recapitulation, not appeasement.

There is no question that Hick is an intelligent critic of historic Christology. His unitive pluralism is backed up by impressive attempts to demolish traditional beliefs. The impact on me is to hope for a new generation of evangelical scholars to arise who can defend the Incarnation as effectively as Hick is able to critique it.

In Hick's mind these revisions leave Christianity untouched – he has only winnowed away non-essential beliefs that have fostered superiority. Liberalism typically thinks that way. If we could just discard the element of the gospel that the current culture dislikes, we would ensure a future for it. What actually happens is that the salt loses its savour. There is no future for liberal Christianity because it just listens to culture and has nothing to contribute. It allows itself to be led around by the nose, while ruining the churches and robbing the world of the gospel. If we follow Hick, people will no longer be told about the light of the world. They will not know that, although no one has seen God, the only Son of the Father has made him known (John 1: 18). They will not learn of a new creation or of God reconciling the world to himself (2 Cor. 5: 17,19). The Christian faith should not make people feel superior – it should make them feel happiness for the nations because now there is hope and a knowledge of salvation.

## Note

1.  Clark Pinnock is Professor of Theology at McMaster Divinity College, Ontario.

# Part III
# In Dialogue with Catholics

# 7
# Cardinal Ratzinger on Religious Pluralism

In September 1996, Joseph Cardinal Ratzinger, Prefect of the Congregation for the Doctrine of the Faith (formerly known as the Holy Inquisition), addressed a group of 80 Catholic bishops about the central threat to the Christian faith today. He said that whereas ten years earlier this had been (in his view) Liberation Theology, it was now Relativism. The original text of the Cardinal's address is in German, and the English translation was published in the Catholic *Origins, CNS Documentary Service* (Vol. 26, no. 20, 31 October 1996). The following section deals with my own particular version of religious pluralism. (The footnotes do not all have the same numbers as in the original text because sections on other topics are omitted here.) After criticizing Liberation Theology again, Cardinal Ratzinger continued:

Relativism has thus become the central problem for the faith at the present time. No doubt it is not presented only with its aspects of resignation before the immensity of the truth. It is also presented as a position defined positively by the concepts of tolerance and knowledge through dialogue and freedom, concepts which would be limited if the existence of one valid truth for all were affirmed.

In the area of politics, this concept is considerably right. There is no one correct political opinion. What is relative – the building up of liberally ordained coexistence between people – cannot be something absolute. Thinking in this way was precisely the error of Marxism and the political theologies.

However, with total relativism, everything in the political area cannot be achieved either. There are injustices that will never turn into just things (such as, for example, killing an innocent person, denying an individual or groups the right to their dignity or to life corresponding to that dignity) while, on the other hand, there are just things that can never be unjust. Therefore, although a certain right to relativism in the social and political area should not be denied, the problem is raised at the moment of setting its limits. There has also been a desire to apply this method in a totally conscious way in the area of religion and ethics. I will now try to briefly outline the developments that define the theological dialogue today on this point.

The so-called pluralist theology of religion has been developing progressively since the 1950s. None the less, only now has it come to the centre of the Christian conscience.[1] In some ways this conquest occupies today – with regard to the force of its problematic aspect and its presence in the different areas of culture – the place occupied by the theology of liberation in the preceding decade. Moreover, it joins in many ways with it and tries to give it a new, updated form. Its means and methods are very varied; therefore, it is not possible to synthesize it into one short formula or present its essential characteristics briefly. On the one hand, relativism is a typical offshoot of the western world and its forms of philosophical thought; while, on the other hand, it is connected with the philosophical and religious intuitions of Asia, especially, and surprisingly, with those of the Indian subcontinent. Contact between these two worlds gives it a particular impulse at the present historical moment.

The situation can be clearly seen in one of its founders and eminent representatives, the American Presbyterian John Hick. His philosophical departure is found in the Kantian distinction between the phenomenon and noumenon: We can never grasp ultimate truth in itself, but only its appearance in our way of perceiving through different 'lenses'. What we grasp is not really and properly reality in itself, but a reflection on our scale.

At first Hick tried to formulate this concept in a Christ-centred perspective. After a year's stay in India, he transformed it – after what he himself calls a Copernican turn of thought – into a new form of theocentrism. The identification of only one historical person, Jesus of Nazareth, with what is 'real', the living God, is now relegated as a relapse into myth. Jesus is consciously relativized as one religious leader among others. The Absolute cannot come into history, but only models and ideal forms that remind us about what can never be grasped as such in history. Therefore, concepts such as the *church, dogma* and *sacraments* must lose their unconditional character. To make an absolute of such limited forms of mediation or, even more, to consider them real encounters with the universally valid truth of God who reveals himself would be the same as elevating oneself to the category of the Absolute, thereby losing the infiniteness of the totally other God.

From this point of view, which is not only present in the works of Hick but also in other authors, affirming that there is a binding and valid truth in history in the figure of Jesus Christ and in the faith of the church is described as fundamentalism. Such fundamentalism, which constitutes the real attack on the spirit of modernity, is presented in different ways as the fundamental threat emerging against the supreme good of modernity: that is, tolerance and freedom.

On the other hand, the notion of *dialogue* – which has maintained a position of significant importance in the Platonic and Christian tradition – changes meaning and becomes both the quintessence of the relativist creed and the antithesis of conversion and the mission. In the relativist meaning, *to dialogue* means to put one's own position, that is, one's faith, on the same level as the convictions of others without recognizing in principle more truth in it than that which is attributed to the opinion of others. Only if I suppose in principle that the other can be as right, or more right than I, can an authentic dialogue take place.

According to this concept, dialogue must be an exchange between positions which have fundamentally the same rank and therefore are mutually relative. Only in this way will the maximum cooperation and integration be achieved.[2] The relativist dissolution of Christology, and even more of ecclesiology, thus becomes a central commandment of religion. To return to Hick's thinking, faith in the divinity of one concrete person, as he tells us, leads to fanaticism and particularism, to the dissociation between faith and love, and it is precisely this which must be overcome.[3]

In Hick's thinking, whom we are considering here as an eminent representative of religious relativism, there is a strange closeness between Europe's post-metaphysical philosophy and Asia's negative theology. For the latter, the divine can never enter unveiled into the world of appearances in which we live; it always manifests itself in relative reflections and remains beyond all worlds [words?] and notions in an absolute transcendency.[4]

The two philosophies are fundamentally different both for their departure point and for the orientation they imprint on human existence. None the less, they seem mutually to confirm one another in their metaphysical and religious relativism. The areligious and pragmatic relativism of Europe and America can get a kind of religious consecration from India which seems to give its renunciation of dogma the dignity of a greater respect before the mystery of God and of man.

In turn, the support of European and American thought to the philosophical and theological vision of India reinforces the relativism of all the religious forms proper to the Indian heritage. In this way it also seems necessary to the Christian theology in India to set aside the image of Christ from its exclusive position – which is considered typically western – in order to place it on the same level as the Indian saving myths. The historical Jesus – it is now thought – is no more the absolute Logos than any other saving figure in history.[5]

Under the sign of the encounter of cultures, relativism appears to be the real philosophy of humanity. As we pointed out earlier, this fact, both in the East and in the West, visibly gives it a strength before which it seems that there is no room for any resistance.

Anyone who resists, not only opposes democracy and tolerance – that is, basic imperatives of the human community – but also persists obstinately in giving priority to one's western culture and thus rejects the encounter of cultures, which is well known to be the imperative of the present moment. Those who want to stay with the faith of the Bible and the church see themselves pushed from the start to a no-man's land on the cultural level and must as a first measure rediscover the 'madness of God' (1 Cor. 1: 18) in order to recognize the true wisdom in it.

In order to help us in this effort to penetrate the hidden wisdom contained in the madness of the faith, it will be good for us to try to know the relativist theory of Hick's religion better and discover where it leads man. In the end, for Hick, religion means that man goes from 'self-centredness', as the existence of the old Adam, to 'reality-centredness', as existence of the new man, thus extending from oneself to the otherness of one's neighbour.[6] It sounds beautiful, but when it is considered in depth it appears as empty and vacuous as the call to authenticity by Bultmann, who in turn had taken the concept from Heidegger. For this, religion is not necessary.

[*Cardinal Ratzinger then goes on to criticize the Catholic theologian, Paul Knitter, whose* No Other Name? A Critical Survey of Christian Attitudes Toward the World Religions *(Maryknoll, NY: Orbis, 1985) has, as Cardinal Ratzinger says, been translated into many languages. In more recent works (such as* One Earth Many Religions. Multifaith Dialogue and Global Responsibility, *New York: Orbis, 1995) Knitter emphasizes the common search for liberation in the form of political and economic justice on earth. The Cardinal then proceeds.*]

The relativism of Hick, Knitter and related theories are ultimately based on a rationalism which declares that reason – in the Kantian meaning – is incapable of metaphysical cognition.[7] The new foundation of religion comes about by following a pragmatic path with more ethical or political overtones. However, there is also a consciously anti-rationalist response to the experience of the slogan 'Everything is relative', which comes together under the pluriform denomination of *New Age*.[8]

For the supporters of the New Age, the solution to the problem of relativity must not be sought in a new encounter of the self with another or others, but by overcoming the subject in an ecstatic return to the cosmic dance. Like the old gnosis, this way pretends to be totally attuned to all the results of science and to be based on all kinds of scientific knowledge (biology, psychology, sociology, physics). But on the basis of this presupposition it offers at the same time a considerably anti-rationalist model of religion, a modern 'mystic': The Absolute is not to be believed, but to be experienced. God is not a person to be distinguished from the world, but a spiritual energy present in the universe. Religion means the harmony of myself with the cosmic whole, the overcoming of all separations.

[*The Cardinal proceeds to criticize the New Age movement. He then turns to the task of theology today, and continues.*]

I would like to mention two evident points in the writings of Hick and Knitter. Both authors, for their attenuated faith in Christ, refer to exegesis. They state that exegesis has proven that Jesus did not consider himself absolutely the Son of God, the incarnate God, but that he was made to be such afterward, in a gradual way, by his disciples.[9] Both Hick, in a clearer way, and Knitter also refer to philosophical evidence. Hick assures us that Kant proved beyond dispute that what is absolute or the Absolute can neither be recognized in history nor can it appear in history as such.[10] Because of the structure of our cognition, what the Christian faith maintains cannot be, according to Kant. Therefore, miracles, mysteries or sacraments are superstitions, as Kant clarifies for us in his work *Religion within the Limits of Reason Alone*.[11]

It seems to me that the questions from exegesis and the limits and possibilities of our reason, that is, the philosophical premises of the faith, indicate in fact the crucial point of the crisis of contemporary theology whereby the faith – and more and more the faith of simple persons as well – is heading towards crisis.

Now I would only like to outline the task before us. First, with regard to exegesis, let it be said from the outset that Hick and Knitter cannot be supported by exegesis in general, as if there were a clear result shared by all. This is impossible in historical research, which does not have this type of certainty, and it is even more impossible with regard to a question that is not purely historical or literary but includes value choices that go beyond a mere verification of the past and a mere interpretation of texts. However, it is certain that an overall glance at modern exegesis can leave an impression that is close to Hick's and Knitter's.

What type of certainty corresponds to this? Let us suppose – which can be doubted – that most exegetes think in this way. None the less, the question still remains, To what point is that majority opinion grounded?

My thesis is the following: The fact that many exegetes think like Hick and Knitter and reconstruct the history of Jesus as they do is because they share their same philosophy. It is not the exegesis that proves the philosophy, but the philosophy that generates the thesis.[12] If I know *a priori* (to speak like Kant) that Jesus cannot be God and that miracles, mysteries and sacraments are three forms of superstition, then I cannot discover what cannot be a fact in the sacred books. I can only describe why and how such affirmations were arrived at and how they were gradually formed. . . .

If we consider the present cultural situation, about which I have tried to give some indications, frankly it must seem a miracle that there is still Christian faith despite everything, and not only in the surrogate forms of Hick and Knitter and others, but the complete, serene faith of the New Testament and of the church in all times.

Why, in brief, does the faith still have a chance? I would say the following: because it is in harmony with what man is. Man is something more than what Kant and the various post-Kantian philosophers wanted to see and concede. Kant himself must have recognized this in some way in his postulates.

In man there is an inextinguishable yearning for the infinite. None of the answers attempted is sufficient. Only the God himself who became finite in order to open our finiteness and lead us to the breadth of his infiniteness responds to the question of our being. For this reason, Christian faith finds man today too. Our task is to serve the faith with a humble spirit and the whole strength of our heart and understanding.

# Notes

1. An overview of the most significant authors of the pluralist theology of religion is offered by P. Schmidt-Leukel, 'Das Pluralistische Modell in der Theologie der Religionen. Ein Literaturebericht', in *Theologische Revue* 89 (1993), 353–70. For the discussion, cf. M. von Bruck-J Werbick, *Der einzige Weg zum Heil? Die Herausforderung des christlichen Absolutheitsanpruchs durch pluralistische Religions theologien* (QD 143, Freiburg 1993); K.-H. Menke, *Die Einzigheit Jesu Christi im Horizont der Sinnfrage* (Freiburg 1995), especially pp. 75–176. Menke offers an excellent introduction into the thinking of the two significant representatives of this theology: John Hick and Paul F. Knitter. The following reflections are mainly based on this author. The discussion of the problem in the second part of Menke's book contains many important and relevant elements, but other questions remain open. An interesting systematic attempt to cope with the problem of religions from the Christo-logical point of view is given by B. Stubenrauch, *Dialogisches Dogma. Der christliche Auftrag zur interreligiosen Begegnung* (QD 158, Freiburg 1995). The question will also be treated by a document of the International Theological Commission, which is in preparation.

2. Cf. the very interesting editorial in *Civilta Cattolica* 1 (20 January 1996), 107–20: 'Il christianesimo e le altre religioni'. The editorial examines most of all the thinking of Hick, Knitter and Raimondo Panikkar.

3. Cf. for example John Hick, *An Interpretation of Religion. Human Responses to Transcendent* (London, 1989); Menke, p. 90.

4. Cf. E. Frauwallner, *Geschichte der indischen Philosophie*, two vols. (Salzburg 1953 and 1956); S.N. Dasgupta, *History of Indian Philosophy*, 5 vols. (Cambridge, 1922–55); K.B. Ramakrishna Rao, *Ontology of Advaita With Special Reference to Maya* (Mulki, 1964).

5. An author belonging clearly to this trend is F. Wilfred, *Beyond Settled Foundations. The Journey of Indian Theology* (Madras, 1993): 'Some Tentative Reflections on the Language of Christian Uniqueness: An Indian Perspec-tive', in the Pontifical Council for Interreligious Dialogue's *Pro Dialogo*, Bulletin 85–86 (1994/1), pp. 40–57.

6. John Hick, *Evil and the God of Love* (Norfolk, 1975), pp. 240f; *An Interpretation of Religion*, pp. 236–40; cf. Menke, p. 81f.

7. Both Knitter and Hick base their refusal of the Absolute in history on Kant; cf. Menke, pp. 78 and 108.

8. In the middle of this century the concept of *New Age* or of the *Time of the Waterman* has been introduced by Raul Le Cour (1937) and Alice Bailey, who in messages received in 1945, spoke about a new world order and a new religion of the world. Between 1960 and 1970 the Esalen Institute was established in California. Today Marilyn Ferguson is the best-known repre-sentative of New Age. Michael Fuss ('New Age: *Supermarkt alternativer Spiritualitat*', in *Communio* 20 [1991], 148–57) defines New Age as the result of a mixture of Jewish and Christian elements with the process of seculariza-tion, with Gnosticism and with elements of Oriental religions. The pastoral letter, translated in many languages, of Cardinal G. Danneels, *'Le Christ ou le Verseau'* (1990) offers useful orientations for this problem. Cf. also Menke, pp. 31–6; J. LeBar (ed.), *Cults, Sects and the New Age* (Huntington, Ind.).

9. See questions in Mencke, pp. 90 and 97.
10. Cf. note 7.
11. B 302.
12. This can be seen very clearly in the confrontation between A. Schlatter and A. von Harnack in the end of the last century, presented carefully by W. Neuer, Adolf Schlatter, *Ein Leben für Theologie und Kirche* (Stuttgart, 1996), pp. 301ff. I have tried to show my own view of the problem in the *questio disputata* edited by myself: *Schriftauslegung im Widerstreit* (Freiburg, 1989), pp. 15–44. Cf. also the collection of I. De la Poitiere, G. Guardini, J. Ratzinger, G. Colombo and E. Bianchi, *L'esegsei christiana oggi* (Piemme, 1991).

# 8
# A Response to Cardinal Ratzinger

Last year Cardinal Ratzinger, head of the Vatican's Congregation for the Doctrine of the Faith, addressed gatherings of 80 bishops and of the presidents of the doctrinal commissions of the bishops' conferences of Latin America, on the subject of Relativism as the central problem for the Faith today. In religion, what he calls relativism is what most writers in this area today call pluralism. He says of the 'so-called pluralist theology of religion' that 'only now has it come to the centre of the Christian conscience'. On studying the text I find that Cardinal Ratzinger, speaking of contemporary religious pluralism, identifies me as 'one of its founders and eminent representatives' (p. 150).

If I were a Catholic, owing allegiance to the Pope, I would probably not feel able to question Cardinal Ratzinger's pronouncements. But as what he calls an American Presbyterian (I am not in fact an American, although I taught for a number of years very happily in the United States), I feel entitled to respond to the Cardinal as a fellow theologian – a much more eminent one than myself, but nevertheless subject to the same canons of accuracy when expounding views which one intends to criticize. The tone of the Cardinal's address is courteous throughout and I can appreciate the concerns which he expresses from his own very conservative point of view. My regret, however, is that internal evidence reveals that he has relied on a secondary source which has provided him with a misleading version of what I have written. He refers (footnote 6) to two of my books, *Evil and the God of Love*, which is on a different subject altogether and makes no mention of religious pluralism, and *An Interpretation of Religion*,[1] which is indeed largely about religious pluralism. In the case of *Evil and the God of Love* (whose place and date of publication are wrongly listed) the pages cited have nothing whatever to do with the point which they are supposed to support. In the case of *An Interpretation of Religion* the pages cited are, again, on a different topic. The impression of reliance on a secondary source is confirmed when, in a footnote at the beginning of his address, Cardinal Ratzinger cites a book by the theologian K.-H. Menke and acknowledges that 'The following reflections are based mainly on this author'. It is surprising that neither Cardinal Ratzinger nor his assistants seem to have checked on the reliability of his informant.

Before coming to the misleading aspect of Cardinal Ratzinger's account of my own position, I want to make the wider point that his address mixes together several different issues under the elastic heading of Relativism. These are (1) the moral relativism which *denies* that 'There are injustices that will never turn into just things (such as, for example, killing an innocent person, denying an individual or groups the right to their dignity or to life corresponding to that dignity)' (pp. 149–50); (2) the religious pluralist denial that Christianity is the one and only true faith and that the sacramental life of the church is the one and only place of direct human contact with God; and (3) the contemporary New Age movements. As a result of presenting these as coming from the same source, the one that I espouse, namely no. 2, becomes tainted with 'guilt by association'. But I am not in fact a moral relativist, and I have no connection with the New Age movements. I shall therefore not discuss here the relativisms which I join with the Cardinal in rejecting, or the liberation theology, with its 'preferential option for the poor', which he also attacks extensively in the same address – although his use of Professor Paul Knitter's writings in this area is as flawed as his use of mine.

Turning, then, to religious pluralism, Cardinal Ratzinger is right in saying that my own version hinges upon the distinction between, on the one hand, God – or, as I prefer in a global context to say, ultimate Reality or the Real – as that reality is in its infinite mystery beyond the scope of the human intellect, and on the other hand as concretely known through the 'lenses' of the human mind. Our awareness of the Transcendent is, I believe, necessarily mediated to us through our own conceptual apparatus. As St Thomas said long ago, 'Things known are in the knower according to the mode of the knower'.[2] This is the great theologian's much earlier anticipation of the basic Kantian insight that the mind interprets the impacts of its environment in terms of the concepts and categories which structure our consciousness. In the case of religion, 'the mode of the knower' differs between the different ways of being human expressed in the varied cultures of the earth. Accordingly, I see the great religions as embodying different ways of conceiving, and therefore of experiencing, and therefore of responding in life, to the infinite reality that we call God. Cardinal Ratzinger correctly relays this suggestion in so far as this can be done in two sentences.

However, he then goes on to misrepresent it radically by missing out the vertical dimension of transcendence and reducing it to a purely horizontal horizon. 'In the end,' he says, 'for Hick, religion means that man goes from "self-centredness", as the existence of the old Adam, to "reality-centredness", as existence of the new man, thus extending from oneself to the otherness of one's neighbour', which is, however, he says, 'empty and vacuous' (p. 152). But any reader of *An Interpretation of Religion* knows that by 'the transformation of human existence from self-centredness to reality-centredness' I am referring to a radically new orientation centred in the transcendent divine reality as mediated to us in our religion.

Such a suggestion will, of course, be totally unacceptable from the standpoint of a Christian absolutism which insists upon the unique superiority of Christianity, or of the church as the sole channel of divine saving grace. But in my view that traditional absolutism has failed to take account of the apparently more or less equal presence of the salvific transformation within the other great traditions. For it does not seem to me that Jews, Muslims, Buddhists, Hindus are in general less good human beings, or less responsive to the Transcendent, than are Christians in general – as, however, surely they ought to be if we alone are able directly to encounter God and feed on the divine substance in our eucharistic worship. In humanity there is, as Cardinal Ratzinger says, an inextinguishable yearning for the infinite, and I believe that the infinite divine reality is present equally to us all throughout the world, when our hearts are open to that presence.

I have already said that there are points in Cardinal Ratzinger's address with which I am happy to agree. But, as I have also said, there is a very major point to which I have to take exception as misleading and as evidently not based on a proper study of the texts. There are also other matters in the Cardinal's remarks that I would dispute, but I prefer to keep this present response short. I now submit it to the judgement of the wider theological world.

## Notes

1. John Hick, *An Interpretation of Religion* (London: Macmillan and New Haven: Yale University Press, 1989. German translation: *Religion*, Munich: Diederichs, 1996).
2. *Summa Theologica*, II/II, Q. 1, art. 2.

*There are other aspects of the Cardinal's speech – his rejection of liberation theology, his rejection of the Enlightenment, his lack of serious response to the modern historical study of the New Testament and of Christian origins – that I would dispute in a full critique; but in this piece I was only concerned to point out the grave distortions in his account of my own work, due to his reliance on an unreliable secondary source.*

*I sent a copy of this Response to Cardinal Ratzinger and in due course received the following letter from his Personal Secretary, published here with the writer's permission:*

19 November 1997

Dear Reverend Professor,

His Eminence Joseph Cardinal Ratzinger has asked me to thank you for having provided him with some reflections on his presentation of the question of theological relativism, in which you question certain elements of his analysis that were based on the study by Professor Karl-Heinz Menke, *Die Einzigkeit Jesu Christi im Horizont der Sinnfrage.*

The Cardinal was very grateful to receive your opinion and wishes to assure you that it will be given attentive and careful consideration.

With kind regards and prayerful best wishes, I remain

Sincerely yours in Christ,

(Msgr) Josef Clemens, Personal Secretary

# 9
# The Latest Vatican Statement on Religious Pluralism

In 1997, the Vatican issued a document, *Christianity and the World Religions*, prepared by its International Theological Commission and approved by Cardinal Joseph Ratzinger as Prefect of the Congregation for the Doctrine of the Faith.[1] The document arises from a recognition that 'The question of the relations among religions is becoming daily more important', and that circumstances today 'make interreligious dialogue necessary'. Accordingly, the Commission sets out to 'clarify how religions are to be evaluated theologically' by offering 'some theological principles which may help in this evaluation'. And the Commission adds that 'In proposing these principles we are clearly aware that many questions are still open and require further investigation and discussion' (pp. 3–5).

Although the Report's title continues the traditional conceit that Christianity is not itself one of the world religions, these opening statements suggest a tentative and relatively undogmatic approach which contrasts with the 1996 address by Cardinal Ratzinger himself, in which in presenting the traditional absolutist position he attacked two theologians extensively by name, seriously misrepresenting their views as a result of not having read their writings for himself.[2] His Eminence's failure to check the accuracy of the tendentious secondary source on which he relied is all the more surprising in view of the accurate and up-to-date section on the state of the discussion, based on a wide knowledge of the existing literature, in this Report of his own Theological Commission. Here all the main competing schools of thought, both Catholic and Protestant, are included and discussed. The Report was first drafted in 1993 and its expertise must have been available to the Cardinal, had he wished to have more reliable information.

The central issue is defined by the Commission as 'Do religions mediate salvation to their members?' (p. 8). It recalls that prior to Vatican II two views were current within the Church. The older view was that the (other) world religions do not themselves have salvific efficacy. They have to be fulfilled in Christ and the Church. The newer view, advocated by Karl Rahner, was that the other world religions are responses to the universal divine grace, so that their adherents may, without knowing it, have an implicit faith in Christ which is sufficient for salvation. There is, then, salvation outside the Church, although not outside the atoning work of Christ.

In the burgeoning discussions since Vatican II a three-fold typology has developed and a form of it is adopted by the Commission: exclusivist ecclesiocentrism, inclusivist Christocentrism and pluralist theocentrism. They note that the first was implicitly rejected by Vatican II. But 'Christocentrism accepts that salvation may occur in religions, but it denies any autonomy in salvation on account of the uniqueness and universality of the salvation that comes from Jesus Christ. This position,' the authors add, 'is undoubtedly the one most commonly held by Catholic theologians' (p. 10) – and the same can be said today of Protestant theologians. But it is interesting that this is seen here as the current majority view but apparently not as the only one worthy to be considered.

The third option, pluralist theocentrism, 'claims to be a way of going beyond Christocentrism, a paradigm shift, a Copernican revolution' (p. 10) in which, instead of Christ being seen as the centre of the universe of faiths, all the religions, including Christianity, are seen as revolving around God, the ultimate transcendent divine reality. Here salvation is not seen as universally dependent on the work of Christ, but as consisting in a transformation, reached along different paths, from natural self-centredness to a new orientation centred in God, the Ultimate, the Real. Many today see this most prominently realized in the struggle for social justice and peace on earth.

The Report as a whole seems to include three different inputs, whose authors I shall dub the Accurate Reporter, the Interesting Theologian and the Absolute Dogmatist.

The Absolute Dogmatist ignores current debates and reiterates the traditional church teaching without taking any account of criticisms and alternatives. This is done by means of biblical quotations, and by citations from dogmatic pronouncements of the magisterium, treated as absolutely authoritative. The Dogmatist's use of the Bible is pre-critical with, for example, the Fourth Gospel sayings of Christ treated without question as historical (on pp. 21, 25, 34, 39, 40 and 41). Modern Catholic as well as Protestant New Testament scholarship is apparently regarded as irrelevant to the viability or otherwise of the traditional dogmas. There is no arguing with an absolute dogmatist – one has to submit or reject. Here we can only note that such anachronistic dogmatism is still at work in the Vatican.

We now turn to the work of the Interesting Theologian, based on the work of the Accurate Reporter. In contrast to the Absolute Dogmatist he is someone with whom those who differ from him could nevertheless hold a profitable dialogue. He rejects the pluralist's central focus on the salvific transformation of human life. 'One should take more account,' he says, 'of the Christian perspective of *salvation as truth* and of *being in the truth as salvation*' (p. 12) – the truth in question being, of course, that taught by the Catholic Church. He objects to the distinction between, on the one hand, God in Godself, the ineffable ultimate reality (the divine *noumenon*) beyond the scope of our human conceptual systems, and on the other hand that reality as humanly conceived, experienced and responded to through the different conceptual systems and spiritual practices of the different religious traditions. For on this view, what are literal or analogical truths about the known deities of the theistic traditions (Holy Trinity, Adonai, Allah, Vishnu, etc.) are mythological truths about the Godhead *a se* – true myths being stories or descriptions which are not literally true but that tend to evoke an appropriate response to the ultimate referent of the myth.

Concerning this pluralistic theocentrism, the Interesting Theologian says that 'such contrasting expressions of the *noumenon* (i.e. the ultimate reality) in fact end up by dissolving it, obliterating the meaning of the mythological truth. Underlying this whole problematic is also a conception which separates the Transcendent, the Mystery, the Absolute, radically from its representations; since the latter are all relative, because they are imperfect and inadequate, they cannot make any exclusive claims to the question of truth' (pp. 12–13). The pluralist position does indeed make this distinction between the ineffable Godhead and the humanly defined and experienced God-figures. But I would point out that virtually all the great theologians have affirmed the ultimate ineffability of God's eternal self-existent nature. For example, Gregory of Nyssa said that God is 'incapable of being grasped by any term, or any idea, or any other device of our apprehension ... unthinkable, unutterable, above all expression in words' (*Against Eunomius*, 1, 42), whilst St Augustine said that 'God transcends even the mind' (*De Vera Religione*, 36, 67), and St Thomas that 'by its immensity, the divine substance surpasses every form our intellect reaches' (S.c.G., I, 14, 3). Pseudo-Dionysius, the most influential of the Christian mystics, wrote concerning God, the 'transcendent One', 'It is not soul or mind, nor does it possess imagination, conviction, speech, or understanding. It cannot be spoken of and it cannot be grasped by understanding . . .' (*The Mystical Theology*, 105D). What we are aware of in religious worship is not, then, the ineffable divine reality as it is in itself, but that reality as impacting human life and as conceived in human terms. For as St Thomas said, 'Things known are in the knower according to the mode of the knower' (ST., II/II, Q.1, art. 2). And in relation to God the mode of the knower differs among the religious cultures of the earth. As a result, according to religious pluralism, different 'faces' of God, or different divine personae, have come about at the interface between the ineffable divine Reality and our human spiritual receptivity, a receptivity that has been variously formed within the different traditions.

The Interesting Theologian also criticizes the idea that our criterion of a religion's authenticity has to be its fruits in human life. He says, 'But one can see that such expressions [as from self-centredness to Reality-centredness] either manifest a dependence on a specific tradition (Christian) or they become so abstract that they cease to be useful' (p. 13). And yet to be centred in God, the ultimately Real, is to be released from self-centredness to love one's neighbour; and the Commission endorses this criterion when it says that 'The religions can be carriers of saving truth only insofar as they raise men to true love' (p. 56). This is also the criterion that operates within the other world traditions. The fruits of a life centred in the divine reality are most clearly seen in the truly holy individuals, the saints, of the different faiths, who show a spiritual similarity that transcends their historical and cultural differences.

But whilst this 'fruits' criterion seems intuitively right, and is in practice operated by us all, it opens up a major problem. It is often assumed – though not often stated – that because of the special divine grace flowing to us through the life of the church, and especially in the eucharist, Christians taken as a whole must be better human beings, morally and spiritually, than non-Christians taken as a whole. But as a factual claim this is extremely dubious. In fact, I would say that it is manifestly false. It would certainly be most unwise to let the church's claim to unique centrality stand or fall by it. But then we have to face the alternative – namely that Christians in general do not seem to be better human beings than Jews in general, or Muslims in general, or

Buddhists, etc., in general. We now have to ask, 'What then is the religious advantage, the spiritual plus, attached to being a Christian rather than a Jew, etc.?' Or putting it the other way round, 'What is the religious deprivation, the spiritual minus, attached to being a Jew, etc., rather than a Christian?' Any theologian and any Theological Commission dealing with 'Christianity and the World Religions' must face this question.

The Interesting Theologian addresses it by implication when he suggests that non-Christians are on a lower religious level because the saving grace that Christians presently enjoy is available to others only at the end of their lives. He says, 'According to the New Testament the necessity of the Church for salvation is based on the unique salvific mediation of Jesus' (p. 44), but 'those non-Christians who are not culpable of not belonging to the Church enter into the communion of those called to the kingdom of God; they do so by putting into practice love of God and neighbour; this communion will be revealed as the *Ecclesia universalis* at the consummation of the Kingdom of God and of Christ' (p. 48). At first sight, this makes Christian salvation available to the rest of humanity, if on less favourable terms because only at the end of their earthly life. But on closer examination this is not the case. For any Jew, Muslim, Hindu, Sikh, Buddhist, Taoist, etc. who deliberately adheres to his or her own faith, although well aware of the church's claims, is presumably culpable of not belonging to the church. What, then, is their fate? And again, how can Buddhists, however full of compassion (*karuna*) and loving-kindness (*metta*), be said to love God when they reject the idea that the ultimate reality is a personal God? Are Buddhists, therefore, excluded from the possibility of salvation?

At another point, however, the Interesting Theologian introduces the much broader and more permissive notion of people of good will. He says that 'What it [the *magisterium*] says about Christians is also valid for all men of good will, in whose hearts grace works in an invisible way. They also can be associated with the Paschal Mystery through the Holy Spirit, and they can consequently be conformed to the death of Christ and be on the road to the encounter of the resurrection' (pp. 46–7). Does this ambiguous formulation mean that Christians and non-Christians are to an equal extent recipients of divine grace, with the one knowing and the other not knowing its source? That is certainly a possible position. But later statements indicate that the writer's intention is rather that people of good will, even if culpable of not belonging to the church, can be saved in the end, in that they may already be 'on the road to the encounter of the resurrection' – 'on the road' meaning not yet. So, once again, a delayed salvation, but one that can eventually include Buddhists and all who now 'culpably' adhere to other faiths.

So the religious plus consists in being now within the saved community, and the religious minus in being, so to speak, 'on hold' until a fateful encounter with the risen Christ at or after death. Christianity thus retains its unique priority and normativeness, its higher status, although the difference is no longer the stark difference of salvation versus damnation.

The Interesting Theologian now goes further than this. For in answer to the question, 'whether the [other] religions as such can have salvific value' (p. 52) he answers that the Holy Spirit is at work 'not only in men of good will, taken individually, but also in society and history, in peoples, in cultures, *in religions*, always with reference to Christ' (pp. 52–3, my italics). He thus advocates an 'explicit recognition of the presence of the Spirit of Christ in the [other] religions' (p. 54). This does not, of course, entail that every aspect of every religion is good: it is accepted that there is both good and evil within each. But at this point it might seem that the other world religions are on the same level as Christianity, with the Holy Spirit present within them all.

However, what is apparently thus offered with one hand is taken back with the other. For 'the universal presence of the Spirit can not be compared to his special presence in the Church of Christ.... Only the Church is the body of Christ, and only in it is given in its full intensity the presence of the Spirit. The religions can exercise the functions of a *"preparatio evangelica"*; they can prepare different peoples and cultures for welcoming the saving event which has already taken place' (pp. 54–5). Thus the Spirit of Christ is present in the other religions, but not as fully or closely as in the Church. Jews, Muslims, Hindus, Buddhists still live under the shadow of a religious 'minus' in comparison with Christians.

Continuing his dialogue with religious pluralism, the Interesting Theologian points out that pluralism implies that the religions (including Christianity) are all imperfect because all formed within imperfect human cultures, and that no one of them can properly make an exclusive claim to absolute truth. What makes this unacceptable to him is the conviction that Jesus was God incarnate (that is, God the Son, Second Person of the Holy Trinity, incarnate). For if Jesus was God, and if he founded a new religion, then that religion is the only one to have been founded directly by God, and must therefore be uniquely superior to all others.

However, New Testament scholarship, since the modern rediscovery of the Jewishness of Jesus, strongly suggests that Jesus himself would have regarded as blasphemous the idea that he was God incarnate. Nevertheless the Church continues, on this extremely doubtful premise, to affirm its unique religious status and authority. It is therefore to the Interesting Theologian's credit that, confronted today with the spiritual reality of the other world religions, he asks the question, 'How can one enter into an interreligious dialogue, respecting all religions and not considering them in advance as imperfect and inferior, if we recognize in Jesus Christ and only in him the unique and universal Saviour of mankind?' (p. 15). He faces the dilemma: 'To break the [exclusive] link between Christ and God deprives Christianity of any universalist claim about salvation (and thus authentic dialogue with other religions would be made possible), but by implication one would then have to confront the Church's faith and, specifically, the dogma of Chalcedon' (p. 16). The Interesting Theologian notes the suggestion of some contemporary Christian thinkers that the idea of divine incarnation is not a literal but a metaphorical concept: 'The meaning of the incarnation, in this view, is not objective, but metaphorical, poetic and mythological. It aims only to express the love of God which is incarnate in men and women whose lives reflect the action of God. Assertions of the exclusive salvific meaning of Jesus Christ can be explained in terms of the historico-cultural context' (pp. 16–17). This is indeed the pluralist position, and the Commission's implicit recognition of it as an option to be considered is welcome.

The Interesting Theologian's conclusion, then, is firmly inclusivist. That is to say, salvation is through Christ alone, but is nevertheless not confined to Christians. 'There is not a *Logos* which is not Jesus Christ, nor is there a Spirit that is not the Spirit of Christ' (p. 51). But the possibility of salvation within other religions remains as a lesser blessing, incomplete until the eschaton.

But now the Interesting Theologian becomes enmeshed in what I shall call the Ecumenical Catholic's Dilemma – namely, that he wants both to engage in authentic dialogue with people of other faiths on an equal footing, and yet also to retain his belief in the unique superiority of his own religion. And so, 'Faced with this way of setting the stage, we must show that Catholic theology in no way undervalues or does not appreciate the other religions when it affirms that everything true and worthy of value in the other religions comes from Christ and the Holy Spirit' (pp. 59–60).

At this point the Interesting Theologian engages again in debate with the pluralist theology of religions which, he says, 'not only is not justified in consideration of the truth claim of one's own religion but also because it simultaneously destroys the truth claim of the other side' (p. 62). In other words, since each religion professes to have the final truth, the pluralist denies not only the Christian claim to be the one and only fully true religion, but also the similar claim of each of the other religions. And this is indeed the case. But does not the Christian inclusivist do exactly the same in relation to every religion other than his own? Does not the inclusivist believe that all claims to be the one and only true religion are false – except for his own Christian claim? In inter-religious dialogue, Catholic inclusivists believe – although they are too polite to say so face to face – that they alone have the final and absolute truth, whilst their dialogue partners have only lesser elements of truth. For 'the religions talk "of" the Holy, "of" God, "about" him, "in his place" or "in his name". Only in the Christian religion is God himself the one who speaks to man in his Word' (p. 66). Is this an acceptable answer to the initial question, 'How can one enter into an interreligious dialogue, respecting all religions and not considering them in advance as imperfect and inferior, if we recognise in Jesus Christ and only in him the unique and universal Saviour of mankind?' (p. 15). The answer is manifestly, No. One can be personally totally friendly and courteous to the dialogue partner, leaving one's true belief out of sight in the background; but nevertheless one cannot logically affirm the unique superiority of the Christian faith without 'considering [other religions] in advance as imperfect and inferior'. It is impossible to reconcile the traditional claim to the unique superiority of Christianity with the outlook required for genuine inter-religious dialogue. The Theological Commission has struggled with this dilemma but leaves it unresolved.

The conclusion that follows is that the 'further investigation and discussion' (p. 5) at which the Report hints, is indeed required.

## Notes

1. *Christianity and the World Religions* (Rome: Vatican Press, 1997).
2. Cardinal Ratzinger, 'Relativism: The Central Problem for Faith Today', *Origins: CNS Documentary Service* (31 October 1996).

# 10
# The Possibility of Religious Pluralism: A Reply to Gavin D'Costa

In 'The Impossibility of a Pluralist View of Religions' (*Religious Studies* **32**, June 1996) Gavin D'Costa[1] argues that 'pluralism must always logically be a form of exclusivism and that nothing called pluralism really exists' (p. 225). He sees himself as doing a 'conceptual spring cleaning exercise' (p. 225). However, the result is to obscure clear and useful distinctions by confused and confusing ones. Some further spring cleaning is therefore called for.

The religious pluralism that D'Costa is referring to is the view that the great world religions constitute conceptually and culturally different responses to an ultimate transcendent reality, these responses being, so far as we can tell, more or less on a par when judged by their fruits. And the religious exclusivism to which he refers holds that one particular religion, Christianity, is alone fully true and salvific, the others being either wholly misleading, or inferior imitations of or lesser approximations to the one 'true' religion.[2]

To say that the former of these two views, religious pluralism, is a version of the latter, religious exclusivism, would be so totally implausible that this cannot be what D'Costa means. Even if we banished the word 'pluralism', the two rival views would remain so manifestly different that we would still need different names for them.

D'Costa's real concern is, I think, that in distinguishing between, on the one hand, those religious phenomena (Christianity, Judaism, Islam, Hinduism, Sikhism, Buddhism, Taoism ...) that are held to be different culturally conditioned responses to the Transcendent, and on the other hand those religious, or quasi-religious, phenomena (he cites Nazism and the Jim Jones cult) which are held not to be responses to the

Transcendent but products of individual or collective egoism, the pluralist is obviously using a criterion: and D'Costa's thesis is that to use a criterion is to be an exclusivist. For in operating with a criterion one is accepting something and rejecting something else; and this is what D'Costa chooses to mean by exclusivism. 'I want to suggest,' he says, 'that there is no such thing as pluralism because all pluralists are committed to holding some form of truth criteria and by virtue of this, anything that falls foul of such criteria is excluded from counting as truth' (p. 226).

That religious pluralists do employ criteria is certainly true, even though D'Costa at one point slips into saying that 'Hick holds that *all* religions are paths to the "Real"' (p. 227; my italics). The main criterion is whether a movement is a context of human transformation from natural self-centredness to a new orientation centred in the Transcendent, this salvific transformation being expressed in an inner peace and joy and in compassionate love for others. (More about where this criterion comes from presently.) But to think that using criteria, as such, constitutes exclusivism, although intelligible in a purely notional and trivial sense, is much more misleading than helpful. In this trivial and misleading sense one is an exclusivist when one admires Mahatma Gandhi and the Dalai Lama but condemns Hitler and Stalin; or when an umpire declares a foul in football; or even when one distinguishes between left and right, or night and day, or makes such an innocent statement as that it is raining! For to make an assertion about anything is to deny its contrary, and to propose a theory or view about anything is to reject alternative views. But to label all judgements, all proposing of theories and hypotheses, all expressions of opinion, as exclusivist would be to empty the term of any useful meaning. For there could then be no non-exclusivist statements, so that the term would cease to mark any distinction. We can hardly suppose that D'Costa means to affirm the self-destructive principle that to use criteria is to be an exclusivist.

But in the special field of religion, when we hold that such religious and quasi-religious movements as Nazism, which set out to exterminate the Jewish race, or (on a much smaller scale) the People's Temple of the 1978 Jonestown mass suicide, or the Branch Davidians of the 1993 Waco massacre, or the Order of the Solar Temple of the 1994 Swiss mass suicide, or the Aum Shin Rikyo cult which put sarin nerve gas in the Tokyo underground system in 1995, are not authentic human responses to God/the Divine/the Dharma/the Real/the Transcendent, are we perhaps being exclusivist in a more substantial sense? It is, of course, possible to use the term in this very extended way; but it would in my view be confusing and unhelpful to do so. For it would obscure the important distinction between, on the one hand, claiming that one's own religion is the only 'true' religion, for which 'exclusivism' is surely the natural descriptive term[3] and, on the other hand, the idea that there is a plurality of 'true' religions, for which 'pluralism' is surely the natural descriptive term. Gavin D'Costa and others will still want to argue against this latter position, and rather than having to invent a new name for it, would it not be more sensible to continue to use the established name?

However, D'Costa believes that he is making a logical point: 'pluralism,' he says, 'operates within the same logical structure as exclusivism' (p. 226). But in fact religious exclusivism and religious pluralism are of different logical kinds, the one being a self-committing affirmation of faith and the other a philosophical hypothesis.[4] The hypothesis is offered as the best available explanation, from a religious as distinguished from a naturalistic point of view, of the data of the history of religions. Pluralism is thus not another historical religion making an exclusive religious claim, but a meta-theory about the relation between the historical religions. Its logical status as a second-order philosophical theory or hypothesis is different in kind from that of a first-order religious creed or gospel. And so the religious pluralist does not, like the traditional religious exclusivist, consign non-believers to perdition, but invites them to try to produce a better explanation of the data.

D'Costa has not taken note of this basic point. He asks, 'how does John Hick know that the Real is beyond all language, incapable of any description?' (p. 229). The answer, of course, is that he does not *know* this. He is offering a hypothesis to explain how it is that the great world religions, with their different concepts of the Ultimate, nevertheless seem to be equally effective (and of course also equally ineffective) contexts of the salvific human transformation.

With this clarification we can now take up the legitimate question that D'Costa raises. When we judge that Nazism, the People's Temple, the Branch Davidians, etc. are not authentic responses to the Divine/Ultimate/Real, where did we get the criterion which entitles us to say this?

The answer is very simple; but before coming to it I must point to a regrettable misrepresentation which has crept into D'Costa's article. D'Costa professes to see 'an ambiguity as to how Hick would answer this question' (p. 228), an ambiguity between thinking of the Ultimate as a personal deity and thinking of it as an ineffable transcendent reality ('the Real') to which, because it is ineffable, the personal/impersonal distinction does not apply.[5] The two different ideas of the Ultimate as a divine Person, and as an ineffable Reality that cannot be described as either personal or impersonal, both occur in my writings, the theistic view in writings in the 1970s and those embodying the concept of the Real in the 1980s and 1990s, the latter being presented as an explicit departure from the former position. However, D'Costa suggests that 'in parts of *An Interpretation of Religion* (1989)' (p. 228) 'Hick's incipient theism leaks out' (p. 229), so that the two incompatible positions are held simultaneously and there is thus ambiguity as to which is intended. He does not say which parts of *An Interpretation* he thinks embody a theistic view, and in fact there is none. There is no 'incipient theism' in the book; and to treat an earlier position, and a later one which replaces it, as jointly constituting an ambiguity is as inappropriate as it would be to say that D'Costa's position is ambiguous because in his present article he renounces an earlier view for which he had previously argued! For he says, 'This paper could be an act of public self-humiliation as in what follows I am going to suggest that a typology that I have promoted and defended against critics I now come to recognize as redundant' (p. 223). I would encourage him to think, however, that there is neither contradiction nor humiliation in sometimes changing one's mind.

Returning from this corrective we come to the question of the source of the criterion by which we judge Nazism, the Order of the Solar Temple, etc. not to be authentic responses to the Divine/Ultimate/Real. The answer is that this criterion is a basic moral insight which Christians have received from Christian teachings, Jews from Jewish teachings, Muslims from Islamic teachings, Hindus from Hindu teachings, Buddhists from Buddhist teachings, and so on. This criterion represents the basic moral consensus of all the great world faiths. The Golden Rule, in which this basic consensus is encapsulated, is common to (in historical order) Hinduism, Judaism, Buddhism, Confucianism, Taoism, Zoroastrianism, Christianity and Islam.[6]

But why select *these* particular traditions in the first place, rather than Satanism, Nazism, the Order of the Solar Temple, etc., as providing the right criterion? The answer arises out of the route by which the pluralistic hypothesis is arrived at. It starts from the basic faith that religious experience is not purely imaginative projection but is also (whilst including such projection) a cognitive response to a transcendent reality. The hypothesis is thus explicitly a *religious* interpretation of religion, and as such it originates within a particular religious tradition – in my own case Christianity. As a Christian, then, one accepts that the sense of the presence of God within the Christian community is indeed an awareness of a divine presence; and one sees as confirmation of this the self-evidently valuable and desirable 'fruit of the Spirit' which St Paul listed as 'love, joy, peace, patience, kindness, goodness, faithfulness, gentleness, self-control' (Galatians 5: 22). It is important to recognize that religious experience and its fruits in life cohere; for if the fruits in this case were hatred, misery, aggression, unkindness, impatience, violence and lack of self-control, this would lead us to deny the authenticity of the experience.

One then becomes aware that there are other great religious traditions within which people conceive and experience the Divine/ Ultimate/Real differently, but the moral and spiritual fruits of which nevertheless seem to be essentially similar to those of Christian faith and experience. And so one extends to them the basic faith that their religious experience also is a cognitive response to a transcendent reality.

At this point, it would be possible to see the theistic traditions as responses to different deities, Christians responding to the Holy Trinity, Jews to Adonai, Muslims to Allah, theistic Hindus to Vishnu or to Shiva, and so on. But on reflection such a polytheism, although theoretically possible, creates more problems than it solves. Does the Holy Trinity preside over Christian countries, Allah over Islamic countries, Vishnu and Shiva over different parts of India? And what about the increasing number of places in which more than one religion is practised? In the city of Birmingham (England) for example, where I now live, does the Holy Trinity answer prayers in Edgbaston, but Allah in Small Heath, the *war guru* of the Sikh faith in parts of Handsworth and Vishnu in other parts of Handsworth? And when we enlarge our vision to take account of the non-theistic faiths, particularly Buddhism, the problem escalates.

And so if we are looking for the most reasonable, the least problem-prone, explanation of the data, the pluralistic hypothesis offers itself as an obvious solution. The process of reasoning which I have described from a Christian point of view is also, of course, appropriate for adherents of any other of the world religions who are also philosophers seeking to understand our global human situation in relation to the Transcendent.

One further point. Possibly the real heart of D'Costa's concern is that according to the pluralist hypothesis the claim made in varying degrees by each of the great religions to embody the full and final truth, and to be in that respect uniquely superior to all other religions, has to be modified. Thus the pluralist theory denies an aspect of the self-understanding of each faith in so far as each sees itself as having the only fully authentic revelation or enlightenment. D'Costa is very critical of this. But people who live in glass houses should not throw stones! Has it escaped D'Costa's notice that he also contradicts the self-understanding of every religion except his own? If Muslims or Hindus or Buddhists, etc. think that their tradition has the final truth, D'Costa confidently holds that they are mistaken. His difference from a religious pluralist is that he regards his own tradition as the sole exception to the general principle that claims to be the one and only 'true' religion are mistaken! But whilst the difference between religious pluralism and religious exclusivism is, in their logical structure, as narrow as this, there is still an important difference in their religious outlooks and practical outworkings.

I have been replying here to D'Costa's attack upon what he calls 'philosophical pluralism'. But this is not really distinct from what he calls 'practical or pragmatic pluralism', as is clear from the discussion above about the moral criterion. Paul Knitter's distinctive contribution (with which I am fully in agreement) is to stress the liberative social and political aspects of this. There are good answers to the questions that D'Costa raises about this also, but the present response is already long enough.

## Notes

1. Gavin D'Costa is Senior Lecturer in Theology at the University of Bristol (England).
2. D'Costa presents himself in this article as an exclusivist when he says that inclusivism (which he has previously advocated) and pluralism are both 'sub-types of exclusivism' (p. 225).
3. There is, however, now a difference within the camp of those who hold that Christianity is the only true religion. Some (such as Alvin Plantinga, 'Pluralism: A Defense of Religious Exclusivism', in Thomas D. Senor (ed.), *The Rationality of Belief and the Plurality of Faith* [Ithaca and London: Cornell University Press, 1995]) continue to speak of themselves as Exclusivists, whilst others (such as Alister McGrath, in Dennis Ockholm and Timothy Phillips (eds), *More Than One Way? Four Views on Salvation in a Pluralistic World* [Grand Rapids, Michigan: Zondervan, 1995]), perhaps feeling that 'exclusivist' sounds unattractive to many people today, now call themselves Particularists.
4. The relevant chapter in my *An Interpretation of Religion* (London: Macmillan, and New Haven: Yale University Press, 1989) is called 'The Pluralistic Hypothesis'.
5. D'Costa describes my position as 'transcendental agnosticism' (p. 228). But it is a mistake to equate the concept of ineffability with agnosticism. Agnosticism

in this context is the view that the Ultimate is either personal or non-personal but we don't know which. That the Ultimate is ineffable means that it is beyond the scope of our human conceptual systems, including the personal/impersonal dichotomy.

6.  For supporting details, see *An Interpretation of Religion*, ch. 17, section 5.


*Since this was originally published Gavin D'Costa has replied to it in his book,* The Meeting of Religions and the Trinity *(2000), particularly pp. 45–7, and I have continued the dialogue in a review of this book in* Reviews in Religion and Theology *(Vol. 8, no. 3, June 2001).*

# Part IV
# In Dialogue with Theologians

# 11
# The Theological Challenge of Religious Pluralism

In our own time a new challenge to the structure of Christian belief has come from our awareness, not merely of the existence of the other great world faiths – there is nothing new in that – but of their spiritual and moral power. The challenge is to the traditional assumption of the unique superiority of the Christian gospel, or faith, or religion. If I am right, we are in the early stages of an adjustment that may take another 50 or more years. This is the transition from a view of Christianity as the one and only true religion to a new Christian self-understanding as one true religion among others. This will certainly mean a considerable restructuring of Christian theology.

I shall for the most part confine what I say here about other religions to the 'great world faiths', meaning those traditions that have existed for upward of a thousand years, which have profound scriptures and have produced great saints and thinkers, and which have provided the foundations of civilization for many millions of people. Oral primal traditions, and the many smaller and newer religions, and also the modern secular faiths, are not intrinsically less important, but in the case of the great world religions one can assume a certain common background of knowledge that facilitates discussion. If we can achieve a viable Christian view here, it will then be easier to cope with the further problems posed by the yet wider religious life of the world.

Christians have, of course, always been aware of other religions. However, during the second half of the twentieth century a new kind of awareness developed. The cause that I would single out here was the large-scale immigration from the East to the West, bringing millions of Muslims, Sikhs, Hindus, Taoists and Buddhists into a number of European and North American cities. The population of the Los Angeles area, for example, includes the third largest Jewish community in the world, the biggest Buddhist temple in North America, supported by a large Buddhist population, and quite large Muslim and Hindu, and smaller Sikh and Taoist, communities. And when one meets some of one's neighbours of these other faiths, and gets to know individuals and families, and is invited to their weddings and festivals and community events, one discovers that, while there are all manner of fascinating cultural differences, Muslims and Jews and Hindus and Sikhs and Buddhists in general do not seem to be less honest and truthful, or less loving and compassionate in family and community, or less good citizens, or less religiously committed, than are one's Christian neighbours in general. The ordinary people of these other faiths do not generally seem to be better human beings, morally and spiritually, than Christians, but neither do they seem to be worse human beings. Further, reading a fair amount of the literature of these other faiths, and encountering several outstanding individuals of the kind whom we call saints, confirms the impression that these other traditions are, to about the same extent as Christianity, contexts of a salvific human transformation from natural self-centredness to a new orientation centred in the divine or the transcendent. And, although this is another dimension of the subject which there is not time to go into here, I think we have to conclude that the civilizations in which these faiths have been expressed, although very different, have been more or less on a par with Christendom as regards their moral and spiritual fruits.[1]

I appreciate that these last statements can be contested. Indeed, probably most Christians assume as a matter of course that Christian religious life and Christian civilization exhibit a manifest superiority. Rather than debate this here, I would like to focus attention on the procedural issue. Just as it has been asked whether Christianity stands or falls by historical evidence concerning the truth of the Gospel accounts of Jesus, so also it can be asked whether it stands or falls by historical evidence concerning the moral quality of Christian civilization. And I imagine that just as there have been theologians (such as Kierkegaard, Barth, Tillich, Bultmann) for whom knowledge about the historical Jesus does not affect the core of their faith, so also there will be theologians for whom the superiority of Christianity is accepted *a priori*, without depending on historical evidence.

Indeed, such an *a priori* judgment comes very naturally to us all. It is where we most naturally start. But it evokes a 'hermeneutic of suspicion', arising from the fact that in perhaps 99 per cent of cases the religion to which one adheres (or which one specifically rejects) is selected by the accident of birth. When someone is born into a devout

Muslim family in Pakistan or Egypt or Indonesia, it will nearly always be a safe bet that he or she will become a Muslim, either observant or non-observant. When someone is born into a devout Christian family in Italy or Mexico, it will nearly always be a safe bet that he or she will become a Catholic Christian, again either observant or non-observant. And so on. And, of course, it normally seems obvious that the religion that has been part of one from infancy is normative and basically superior to all others.

This relativity of religious conviction to the circumstances of birth and upbringing is so obvious that we seldom stop to think about it. But it nevertheless has immense significance. If there is a religious 'plus', a spiritual gain, advantage, benefit, in being a Christian rather than a Jew, Muslim, Hindu or Buddhist, then there is a corresponding 'minus', a spiritual loss or disadvantage, in being a Buddhist, Hindu, Muslim or Jew. It then becomes a proper question why only a minority of the human race have been awarded this religious 'plus'. For if the 'plus' is a reality, divine providence has favoured those born into a Christian society over those born in non-Christian countries. And the greater the religious 'plus' for Christians, the greater the 'minus' for everyone else and the greater the discrimination that needs to be accounted for in our theology. Should we conclude that we who have been born within the reach of the gospel are God's chosen people, objects of a greater divine love than the rest of the human race? But then, on the other hand, do we not believe that God loves *all* God's creatures with an equal and unlimited love?

There is obviously a problem here, and yet it is very rare to find it discussed. I am aware of only two responses to it. One is to stress the imperative of evangelization, the duty to bring all humankind to enjoy the religious 'plus' of knowing Christ. But the general failure of the Christian mission to Jews, Muslims, Hindus and Buddhists leaves the original problem very largely intact. (The Christian population of the entire Indian subcontinent, for example, after 200 years of fairly intensive missionary activity, is about 2.5 per cent.) The other response is the horrific suggestion, based on the concept of middle knowledge – the idea of a divine knowledge of what everyone would freely do in all possible circumstances – that God knows concerning all those who lack any real access to the Christian gospel that they would reject it if they heard it. They thus deserve the religious 'minus' under which they suffer, which, according to the evangelical Christian philosophers who propound this theory, consists of eternal damnation.[2] This theory declares completely *a priori* that each one of the hundreds of millions of men and women in each generation who have lived without knowledge of the Christian gospel are depraved sinners who would have rejected it if they had heard it. This is *a priori* dogma carried to terrifying lengths.

Suppose, then, we accept (1) that most of us are not Christians as a result of a deliberate choice resulting from a comprehensive study and evaluation of the religions of the world, but because we were born into a Christian rather than some other society; and (2) that the moral and spiritual fruits of faith seem to be more or less on a par within the different world religions. The question that I am then raising is, 'How should this affect our inherited Christian belief-system?'

It might at this point be said that our belief-system has already been adjusted to take account of all this. The older exclusivist position was, in its Roman version, that outside the church there is no salvation or, in its Protestant version, that outside Christ (that is, outside a personal faith in Christ as our Lord and Saviour) there is no salvation. But through the discussions and debates of the last 30 or so years a new majority consensus has emerged, which is generally known as Christian inclusivism. This is both continuous and discontinuous with the previous exclusivism. The continuity is in the claim that salvation is, exclusively, Christian salvation, made possible solely by the atoning death of Jesus. The new element however, the discontinuity, is in the claim that this Christian salvation is not limited to Christians but is available to all human beings without restriction.

I should perhaps remind us at this point that the question of salvation for non-Christians as well as Christians is distinct from the question of universal or restricted salvation, which is not the issue here. The inclusivist position is that all who are saved, whether they constitute the whole human race or only part thereof, are saved by Christ, but that this is not dependent on their accepting Jesus as their Lord and Saviour, at least not in this life.

This inclusivist type of theology of religions takes three forms. The first (in the arbitrary order in which I shall discuss them) is based on the idea developed within Catholic thinking of implicit faith, or the baptism of desire, the idea that at least some individuals of other faiths, and indeed of no faith, may be so rightly disposed in their hearts that they *would* respond to the Christian gospel if it were properly presented to them. But they have in fact never encountered it, or only in inadequate ways, and have thus had no real opportunity to respond to it. Such people, who may be said to have an implicit faith in Christ, have been dubbed by Karl Rahner anonymous Christians. Only God knows who they are; but we can at least know that non-Christians who in their hearts sincerely desire to know the truth and to serve the good are not excluded from salvation by the fact that, through no fault of their own, they are not presently Christians. This was the view of some of the early church fathers concerning persons who lived before Christ. But Rahner and others have now gone further in applying this principle to people of the other world religions since the time of Christ. Not only those who lived B.C.E. (Before the Common Era), but also non-Christians today, may be anonymous Christians.

The second form of inclusivism holds that salvation does require a conscious personal faith in Christ but that although this is not possible for hundreds of millions in the present life, it will be possible in or beyond death. Thus the devout Muslim living, let us say, in Pakistan and insulated from the gospel by a powerful Islamic faith, will encounter Christ after or in the moment of death and will thus have an opportunity to receive salvation.

Among contemporary Catholic theologians perhaps the most explicit recent expression of this idea is Father J.A. Dinoia's 'Christian theology of religions in a prospective vein'.[3] Father Dinoia, who is the secretary for doctrine and pastoral practice of the National Conference of Catholic Bishops in the United States, rejects Rahner's suggestion that some non-Christians can now, in this present life, be accepted as having an implicit faith in virtue of which they are anonymous Christians. 'Rather,' he says, 'than attributing an implausible implicit faith in Christ to the members of other religious communities, theology of religions in a prospective vein contends that non-Christians will have the opportunity to acknowledge Christ in the future. This opportunity,' he says, 'may come to them in the course of their present lives here on earth or in the course of their entrance into the life to come.'[4] And he invokes the doctrine of purgatory, adding that the interval in which the necessary purification or transformation takes place 'may be thought of as instantaneous and coterminous with death'.[5] Thus, he says, 'The doctrine of purgatory permits Christians a wide measure of confidence about the salvation of non-Christians.'[6]

Among Protestant theologians George Lindbeck is probably the most influential proponent of what he calls 'an eschatologically futuristic perspective'.[7] Like Dinoia he is critical of the Rahnerian idea of implicit faith. He speaks of 'the temptation to religious pretentiousness or imperialism implicit in the notion that non-Christians are anonymously Christians',[8] and says that 'saving faith cannot be wholly anonymous, wholly implicit, but must be in the same measure explicit: it comes, as Paul puts it, *ex auditu*, from hearing'.[9] His alternative theory is eschatological. 'The proposal is,' he says, 'that dying itself be pictured as the point at which every human being is ultimately and expressly confronted by the gospel, by the crucified and risen Lord. It is only then that the final decision is made for or against Christ; and this is true not only of unbelievers but also of believers....Thus it is possible to be hopeful and trusting about the ultimate salvation of non-Christians no less than Christians.'[10]

The difference between the theories, on the one hand of the prospective or eschatological salvation of non-Christians, and on the other hand of their present anonymous salvation, is however not as great as it might seem. For Rahner also presumably holds that ultimately the implicit faith of the anonymous Christian will become explicit. I shall therefore not play these two kinds of inclusivism off against each other but shall bracket them together in the composite view that (1) salvation is in Christ alone, and (2) non-Christians may nevertheless receive this salvation by being related to Christ either implicitly in this life and explicitly beyond it or, as an alternative version, only explicitly and beyond this life.

It is to be noted that this kind of inclusivism, in either form, does not regard other religions as such as channels of salvation, but is a theory about individuals within them. A third form of inclusivism, however, validates those religions themselves as alternative mediators or contexts of salvation; and this is a large step closer to the position at which I think we must eventually arrive. But before coming to that, let me comment on the individualistic inclusivism of the 'anonymous Christians' and the eschatological salvation theories.

The appeal of inclusivism is, of course, that it retains the unique centrality of Christ as the sole source of salvation, and yet at the same time avoids the morally repugnant idea that God consigns to perdition the majority of the human race, who have not accepted Jesus as their Lord and Saviour. It is thus a comfortable and comforting package, enabling Christianity to go on regarding itself as superior while at the same time being charitable to the people of other religions.

But there are nevertheless two problems. One is its sheer arbitrariness. I referred earlier to the 'hermeneutic of suspicion' evoked by the presumed centrality and normativeness of the religion into which one was born. If I, who was born in England and who as a student experienced an evangelical Christian conversion, had instead been born in India or Egypt or Tibet, my religious awakening would almost certainly have taken a Hindu or a Muslim or a Buddhist form. Of course this is a misleading way to put it, because it would not then be the same I, since we are all so largely formed by our surrounding culture, including our religious culture. But when *someone*, anyone, is born as an Indian or an Egyptian or a Tibetan the belief-system that he or she internalizes will very likely not be Christian but Hindu, Muslim, or Buddhist, as the case may be. And just as it seems obvious to most devout Christians, without any argument being needed, that their familiar Christian set of beliefs is true and any incompatible beliefs therefore false, so likewise it seems obvious to devout people of the other world religions that *their* inherited beliefs are true and any incompatible beliefs false. They can also, if they wish, fit sincere and devout Christians into their own belief-system as anonymous Hindus, Muslims, or Buddhists, or as to be converted to one of those faiths beyond death, as indeed some of the thinkers of these traditions do. But is not the sheer arbitrariness of this procedure, whoever is using it, glaringly evident?

One can of course 'bite the bullet' and say, 'Yes, it is arbitrary; but why not? It so happens that the beliefs that were instilled into me by my Christian upbringing are true, while those instilled into Hindus, Muslims, Buddhists, and so on, in so far as they are incompatible with mine, are false.' As Karl Barth wrote, 'The Christian religion is true, because it has pleased God, who alone can be the judge in this matter, to affirm it to be the true religion.'[11] This is a theological cover for the fact that, having been brought up as a Christian, Barth assumed that Christian revelation is revelation and that other 'revelations' are not. And if this seems unilaterally dogmatic in a way that is difficult to defend rationally, one can add that happily the situation is not as harsh as it might seem, because we can believe that God is also able, in the end, to save by some indirect route those who presently lack the one true revelation.

This kind of armour-plated belief-system is logically invulnerable. What we normally do when faced with someone else's armour-plated conviction is to look at its practical fruits. In the case of the major world religions, we have to make discriminations, recognizing both good and evil elements. Some Christian beliefs, for example, have in the course of history proved extremely harmful to others. Thus the belief that the Jewish people are guilty of deicide authorized the medieval persecution of the Jews and created a prejudice that continued in the secular anti-Semitism of the nineteenth and twentieth centuries, culminating in the Nazi Holocaust of the 1940s. The belief, during the European wars of religion, that Protestants, or Catholics, are heretics who have forfeited divine grace, validated slaughter on a massive scale. The belief that white Christian colonists stood on superior religious ground to that of the pagan natives of what today we call the Third World, and were accordingly justified in conquering them, validated their enslavement and the exploitation of their human and natural resources. The belief that, because Jesus and his apostles were all men, women cannot serve the church as ordained priests, still continues to validate the ecclesiastical oppression of women. And similar discriminations have to be made within each of the other great world faiths. The belief that the caste system of India is divinely ordained; the belief that God has given the entire area of Israel and Palestine to the Jewish people; the belief that God demands the death of Salman Rushdie, are obvious examples of beliefs that validate evil. Thus while claims to be the sole possessors of the truth may start out as pure and innocent, they can all too easily become a cloak for human prejudice and self-interest, and their arbitrariness properly evokes, as I have suggested, a 'hermeneutic of suspicion'. In the case, to take recent examples, of such cults as the People's Temple of the 1978 Jonestown mass suicide, or the Branch Davidians of the 1993 Waco massacre, or the Order of the Solar Temple of the 1994 Swiss mass suicide, the fruits were manifestly evil, and we all condemn their arbitrary dogmatism.

The other main criticism of Christian inclusivism turns on what we mean by salvation. If this means being forgiven and accepted by God because of the atoning death of Jesus, then salvation is by definition Christian salvation and it is a tautology that Christianity alone knows and proclaims its possibility. Either an exclusivist or an inclusivist theology of religions then becomes virtually inevitable. But suppose we think of salvation in a much more concrete and empirically observable way as an actual change in men and women from natural self-centredness to, in theistic terms, God-centredness, or in more general terms, a new orientation centred in the Ultimate, the Real, as conceived and experienced within one's own tradition. Salvation in this sense is the central concern of each of the great world religions. Within Christianity it is conceptualized and experienced as the state in which Paul could say, 'It is no longer I who live, but Christ who lives in me' (Gal. 2: 20, RSV). Within Judaism it is conceived and experienced as the joy and responsibility of life lived in accordance with God's Torah. Within Islam it is conceived and experienced as a personal self-surrender to God in a life lived according to God's revealed commands. Within Advaitic Hinduism it is conceived and experienced as a transcending of the ego and discovery of unity with the eternal reality of Brahman. Within Buddhism it is conceived and experienced as a loss of the ego point of view in a discovery of the Buddha-nature of the universal interdependent process of which we are all part. And in each case this transformation of human existence from self-centredness to Reality-centredness is reached by a moral and spiritual path. The Golden Rule is taught by all the great traditions, as are love and compassion, justice and fair dealing, and a special concern for the vulnerable – in the societies within which the scriptures were produced, mainly the widows and orphans. Within Buddhism, for example, much of the Noble Eight-fold Path to enlightenment is ethical, including among its requirements kindness, truthfulness, abstaining from stealing, from dishonesty, from cheating, from illegitimate sexual intercourse, from intoxication, and from earning one's living by trading in arms or by killing animals. And each of the other world religions has its own overlapping though not identical moral requirements.

So, if we understand by salvation the transition to a life centred in the Divine, the Ultimate, the Real, we can properly look about us for the signs of it. To what extent is this transformation actually taking place among Christians, among Jews, among Muslims, among Hindus, among Buddhists? I suggest that, so far as we can tell, it is taking place to much the same extent within each of these traditions. It is true that we have no organized evidence or statistics to establish this. But we can properly put the issue the other way round. If anyone asserts that Christians in general are morally and spiritually better human beings than Jews, Muslims, Hindus or Buddhists in general, the onus is on them to produce the evidence for this. It cannot simply be affirmed *a priori*, without regard to the concrete realities of human life.

My conclusion, then, so far is that the salvific transformation seems to be taking place more or less equally within all the great world religions, including Christianity, and that for any one of them to assert that it alone is the source of this change within all the others is an arbitrary claim that cannot be refuted but on the other hand cannot be rationally justified.

But there is also a third kind of inclusivism. This goes farther than the other two in speaking, not only of non-Christian individuals, but of the other world faiths as such. It sees the divine Logos, or cosmic Christ, or Holy Spirit at work within these other religious histories. It holds that God, whether as second or third member of the Holy Trinity, has been and is savingly present within them. There are different ways of developing this thought. One is the Christocentric version, which gave rise to the idea of the unknown Christ of Hinduism, and likewise by implication the unknown Christ of Islam, and so on. Since Hinduism and Buddhism (and also Taoism, Confucianism, Zoroastrianism, and

Jainism) all long pre-date Christianity, the Christ who has been at work within them from the beginning cannot be the God-man Jesus, but must be the cosmic Christ or eternal Logos who later became incarnate as Jesus of Nazareth. And so we are in effect talking about a worldwide and history-long divine presence to and within the religious life of humanity, while insisting that this be named and thought of in exclusively Christian terms. The inevitable criticism of this insistence is, once again, its arbitrary and religiously imperialistic character. To claim that Christ is the real though hidden source of saving grace within other religions is a way of asserting the unique centrality of one's own tradition. The hermeneutic of suspicion that I referred to earlier is inevitably brought into play here.

The other version is the much more radical idea that the same God who saves Christians through their response to the incarnate Christ also saves Jews through their response to the Torah, and saves Muslims through their response to the Qur'an, and saves Hindus through their response to the Vedic revelation and the various streams of religious experience to which it has given rise, and saves Buddhists through their response to the dharma. This view validates the other world religions as alternative channels or contexts of divine salvation. One can then stress their complementarity, and the possibility that they may in the future converge as a result of friendly dialogue.

There are two comments to be made about this more promising theory. The first is a clarification. The test question for this position is whether it involves a renunciation of the missionary ideal of converting Jews, Muslims, Hindus, Buddhists to Christianity. Does it entail the conclusion that there is an equal possibility of salvation within whichever of the great world religions one has been born into, so that there is no salvific 'plus' in being a Christian rather than a Jew or a Muslim, for example? If it does not accept this implication, then it is only an elaborate manoeuvre for preserving belief in the unique superiority of Christianity. But if it does entail a renunciation of that supposed religious superiority, it then comes close to the kind of pluralism that I want to recommend.

There is, however, at this point a qualification to be made to the idea that no religious 'plus' is involved in being born into one rather than another of the great world faiths. Each tradition has its own distinctive religious 'pluses' and 'minuses', for each is a different and unique mixture of good and evil. But this fact does not amount to one of these complex mixtures' being superior as a totality to the others. If any of them claims this for itself, that claim must be established by objective evidence. Nevertheless, for the individual who has been spiritually formed by a particular tradition, that tradition does normally have an overall 'plus'. For our religion creates us in its own image, so that it fits us and we fit it as no other can. It is thus for us the best, truest, most naturally acceptable faith, within which we rightly remain. This is the point made by Ernst Troeltsch, at the beginning of the modern discussion of the problems of religious plurality, when he said, 'We cannot live without a religion, yet the only religion that we can endure is Christianity, for Christianity has grown up with us and has become a part of our very being.'[12] There are, of course, and will always be, individual conversions in all directions, for individual reasons. But broadly speaking we do best to live within the religion that has formed us, though with an awareness that the same holds for those who have been formed by a different tradition from our own.

My other comment on the idea that the Christian God is at work saving people through the medium of each of the world religions is that it does not take adequate account of the non-theistic traditions, most particularly Buddhism. If we are to proceed inductively from the actual religious experience of humanity, rather than deductively from an arbitrarily adopted premise, then we must see theism as a major form, but not the only form, of religious thought and experience. And if we accept that the fruits in human life of Buddhist faith are on a par with the fruits of the monotheistic faiths, we have to expand our theory to take account of this fact.

Such an expanded understanding of religion has been forming in many minds during the last 70 or so years and has come to be known as religious pluralism. This is the view that the great world faiths, both theistic and non-theistic, are different culturally formed responses to the Ultimate, and thus independently valid channels or contexts of the salvific human transformation. The general conception is ancient and widespread – from the basic Vedic declaration that 'the Real [*sat*] is one, but sages name it variously';[13] to the edicts of the Buddhist Emperor Ashoka affirming and supporting all the religions of his empire; to the Sufis of Islam, with Rumi, for example, saying of the religions of his time, 'The lamps are different, but the Light is the same';[14] to the Christian Nicholas of Cusa's statement that 'there is only one religion in the variety of rites'.[15] The problem comes when we try to spell out this basic insight in a philosophically coherent way. Some who take a broadly pluralist view think that it is not possible, or not necessary, or not desirable to spell it out. There are indeed many good Christians who in practice treat people of other religions on the implicit basis that it is perfectly acceptable in the sight of God for them to be, and to remain, Jews, Muslims, Hindus or Buddhists, but who shrink from making explicit the implications of this. If they are ecclesiastical officials, they probably do so to avoid controversy and division within the church. If they are lay people, they probably shrink from it because it would be unacceptable to their church leaders. All this is readily understandable. We are in an interim situation in which theological theory lags behind our practical religious insights. But it is the task of Christian theologians and philosophers to think through the implications of these insights. And so as a contribution to this I will now very briefly outline a positive suggestion.

## A positive suggestion

This rests on two basic principles. One is the view, widespread in philosophy since Kant, and confirmed by cognitive psychology and the sociology of knowledge, that consciousness is not a passive reception of the impacts of our environment but always an active process of selecting, ordering, integrating and endowing with meaning in accordance with our human systems of concepts. I suggest that this applies to awareness of our divine, or supranatural, environment as well as of our physical environment. The other basic principle is consequent on this: the distinction between something as it is in itself, independently of human observation, and as it appears to us, with our specifically human perceptual equipment and conceptual resources. This also, I suggest, applies to our awareness of the Ultimate.

To avoid using a string of alternative terms, such as the Divine, the Transcendent, the Ultimate, Ultimate Reality, the Real, I shall arbitrarily employ the last. The distinction then is between, on the one hand, the Real in itself and, on the other hand, the Real as variously conceived and experienced and responded to within the different world religions. These fall into two main groups. One group thinks of the Real in personal terms, as a great transcendent Thou, further specified as the Adonai of Judaism, or more complexly as the Holy Trinity of Christianity, or as the Allah of Islam, or as the Vishnu or Shiva of theistic Hinduism, and so on. The other thinks of the Real in non-personal terms, as Brahman, or the Tao, or the Dharmakaya and so on. According to this pluralistic hypothesis, the status of the various God-figures is as *personae* of the Real, that is, the Real as variously perceived by the personifying human mind, while the various non-personal absolutes are *impersonae* of the Real, that is, the Real as variously manifested in non-personal terms to a non-personifying religious mentality. Both are joint products of the universal presence of the Real above, below, around and within us, together with the distinctive set of concepts and accompanying spiritual practices of a particular religious tradition.

The Real in itself lies beyond the range of our entire network of concepts, other than purely formal ones. We therefore cannot experience it as it is in itself, but only as we conceptualize it in our human terms, organizing its impact on us in a particular form of religious experience. The religious traditions thus stand between us and the Real, constituting different 'lenses' through which we are aware of it. As Thomas Aquinas wrote, in a foreshadowing of the Kantian insight: 'Things known are in the knower according to the mode of the knower'.[16] And in relation to the Real or the Divine the mode of the knower is differently formed within the different religious traditions.

Here, then, are the bare bones of a pluralistic hypothesis. It is open, as probably all large-scale hypotheses are, to a variety of objections, and I will now in conclusion look briefly at a few of these.

First, is not the concept of the ineffable Real so featureless as to be redundant, incapable of doing any work? Reply: The concept of the Real does do vital work. For the Real is that which there must be if religious experience in its variety of forms is not purely imaginative projection but a response to a transcendent reality. The difference between affirming and not affirming the Real is the difference between a religious and a naturalistic interpretation of religion in this variety of forms.

But, second, how can we worship the noumenal Real? Surely an object of worship must have some definite characteristics, such as being good, loving, and so on. Reply: We do not worship the Real in its infinite transcendent nature, beyond the scope of our human categories, but the Real as humanly thought and experienced within our own tradition. In religious practice we relate ourselves to a particular 'face' or appearance or manifestation of the ultimate divine reality.

But, third, do not the different traditions make many mutually contradictory truth-claims – that the divine reality is personal, that it is non-personal; that it is unitary, that it is triune; and so on? Reply: These different and incompatible truth-claims are claims about *different* manifestations of the Real to humanity. As such, they do not contradict one another. That one group conceives and experiences the Real in one way is not incompatible with another group's conceiving and experiencing the Real in another way, each described in its own theology. There is contradiction only if we assume that there can be only one authentic manifestation of the Real to humanity.

Fourth, in seeing the various objects of worship and foci of religious contemplation as not being themselves ultimate, but appearances of the ultimate to human consciousness, does not this hypothesis contradict the self-understanding of each of the religions? And is this not gross presumption? The reply here is a counter-question: Does not the traditional Christian view contradict the self-understanding of every religion except itself? And is it not a lesser presumption to apply the same principle to one's own religion also?

Fifth, on what basis can we judge that the figure of the Heavenly Father, for example, is indeed an authentic manifestation of the Real? Answer: On the basis of its capacity to promote the salvific transformation of human life.

But then, sixth, if we say that the figure of the Heavenly Father is a manifestation of the Real because it is salvific, and that it is salvific because it is a manifestation of the Real, are we not moving in a circle? Reply: Yes, the hypothesis is ultimately circular, as indeed every comprehensive hypothesis must be. The circle is entered, in this case, by the faith that human religious experience is not purely imaginative projection but is also a response to a transcendent reality. The hypothesis should be judged by its comprehensiveness, its internal consistency, and its adequacy to the data – in this case, the data of the history of religions.

But, seventh, surely in denying that the Real in itself is personal, is one not asserting that it is non-personal, and thus arriving at a Hindu or Buddhist conclusion? Reply: The suggestion is more radical than that, namely, that these dualisms of human thought – personal/ impersonal, good/bad, substance/process, and so on – do not apply to the Real in itself. Its nature is beyond the scope of our human conceptual systems.

Eighth, so the Real is not properly thought of as being good or loving? Reply: No, these human concepts do not apply to the Real in itself. But we have found, within all the great world religions, that the Real is good, or benign, from our human point of view, as the ground of our highest good, which is the transformed state that we speak of as eternal life, or nirvana, or moksha, and so on.

Ninth, can we not, however, modify the ineffability of the Real in itself by saying that it has analogous attributes to those of its *personae* and *impersonae*? Thus, if the Heavenly Father of Christian belief is an authentic manifestation of the Real, must not the Real in itself be loving and fatherlike, at least in an analogous sense? The reply is again a counter-question: What could it mean for the Real to be both analogically personal and analogically nonpersonal, both analogically conscious and analogically not conscious, both analogically purposive and analogically not purposive, both analogically a substance and analogically a nonsubstantial process? Would this not be a mass of contradictions? If, however, these mutually incompatible attributes are attributes of different manifestations of the Real to human consciousness, the contradictions disappear.

Tenth, why postulate *one* Real? The different religions report different realities, so why not affirm all of them? Reply: For two reasons. One is the difficulty of making sense of the relationship between a plurality of ultimates. Does the Holy Trinity preside over Christian countries, Allah over Muslim countries, and so on? And what about those parts of the world where people of different religions live mixed together? And, more fundamentally, if there exists a God who is the creator *ex nihilo* of everything other than God, how can there also be the eternal uncreated process of *pratitya samutpada*?

The other reason is that the moral and spiritual fruits produced by response to the different experienced ultimates are so essentially similar, within the cultural differences of their different traditions, that it seems more reasonable to postulate a common source of this salvific transformation.

There are many other issues, and a growing literature about them.[17] But the task of this chapter has been the relatively modest one of introducing the newly perceived global context within which Christian theologians will increasingly feel obliged to think in the future.

## Notes

1. For more about this see, for example, John Hick, 'The Non-Absoluteness of Christianity', in *The Myth of Christian Uniqueness*, ed. John Hick and Paul Knitter (New York: Orbis Books; London: SCM Press, 1992).
2. For example, William Lane Craig, '"No Other Name": A Middle Knowledge Perspective on the Exclusivity of Salvation through Christ', *Faith and Philosophy* 6:2 (April 1989).
3. J.A. Dinoia, O.P., *The Diversity of Religions* (Washington, D.C.: Catholic University of America Press, 1992), p. 104.
4. *Ibid.*, p. 107.
5. *Ibid.*, p. 105.
6. *Ibid.*
7. George Lindbeck, *The Nature of Doctrine: Religion and Theology in a Postliberal Age* (Philadelphia: Westminster Press; London: SPCK, 1984), p. 63.
8. *Ibid.*, p. 61.
9. *Ibid.*, p. 57.

10.  *Ibid.*, p. 59.
11.  Karl Barth, *Church Dogmatics*, II/2 (English translation; Edinburgh: T. & T. Clark, 1956), p. 350.
12.  Ernst Troeltsch, 'The Place of Christianity among the World Religions' (1923), in *Christianity and Other Religions*, ed. John Hick and Brian Hebblethwaite (London: Collins; Philadelphia: Fortress Press, 1980), p. 25.
13.  *Rig-Veda*, I, 164. 46.
14.  *Rumi: Poet and Mystic*, trans. R. A. Nicholson (London and Boston: Unwin Mandala Books, 1978), p. 166.
15.  Nicholas of Cusa, *De Pace Fidei*, 6, trans. James Biechler and Lawrence Bond, in *Nicholas of Cusa on Interreligious Harmony* (Lewiston and Lampeter: Edwin Mellon Press, 1990), p. 7.
16.  Thomas Aquinas, *Summa Theologica*, II/II Q.1, art. 2.
17.  See, for example, John Cobb, *Beyond Dialogue* (Philadelphia: Fortress Press, 1982); Paul Knitter, *No Other Name? A Critical Survey of Christian Attitudes toward the World Religions* (New York: Orbis Books, 1985); Alan Race, *Christians and Religious Pluralism* (London: SCM Press; New York: Orbis Books, 2nd edn., 1993); Hans Küng et al., *Christianity and the World Religions: Paths of Dialogue with Islam, Hinduism, and Buddhism* (New York: Doubleday, 1986); John Hick and Paul Knitter, eds, *The Myth of Christian Uniqueness* (New York: Orbis Books; London: SCM Press, 1987); Gavin D'Costa (ed.), *Christian Uniqueness Reconsidered* (New York: Orbis Books, 1990); John Macquarrie, *The Mediators: From Moses to Muhammad* (New York: Continuum, 1996); John Hick, *An Interpretation of Religion* (New Haven, Conn.: Yale University Press; London: Macmillan, 1989), and *idem*, *A Christian Theology of Religions* (Louisville, Ky.: Westminster John Knox Press, 1995); S. Mark Heim, *Salvations: Truth and Difference in Religion* (New York: Orbis Books, 1995); Peter Byrne, *Prolegomena to Religious Pluralism* (London: Macmillan and New York: St. Martin's Press, 1995).

# 12
# Is Christianity the Only True Religion?

What do we mean by a true religion? To start with, one whose teachings are true. But there is more to it than that. For the central religious concern is undoubtedly salvation, which consists in a fundamental shift from a bad and humanly destructive situation of alienation from God to a new, healing and growing relationship of reconciliation and acceptance, increasingly expressed in a life lived in response to God. And so a true religion is an authentic channel or context of this salvific transformation. More about both of these elements presently.

Next a word about theology. In the medieval period Christendom constituted for its inhabitants the entirety of the civilized world, and Christian theology was a closed circle of belief, unaffected by anything outside. Indeed, down to our own day a great deal of theology has continued to be written as though Christianity were the only religion in the world, or at least the only one worth mentioning. However, beginning with the Age of Exploration and then the European Enlightenment, and culminating with the communicational unification of the world through ever easier travel and an ever expanding telephone and television network and now the global computer internet and e-mail, we find ourselves in a very different situation. We are all today aware of the reality of the other great world faiths; and indeed in Britain people of these other religions are visibly present in most of our cities, confidently practising their own faiths.

In response to this new situation it has become customary for theologians to add a chapter at the end of their books in order to take account of 'the non-Christian religions'. The most extravagant view, found among Protestant fundamentalists and extreme evangelicals (more in the United States than in Britain), and also among some pre-Vatican II Catholics, is that non-Christians who die without having accepted Jesus as their Lord and Saviour, or the church as the only ark of salvation, forfeit eternal life. But outside those extremes a new and more positive attitude to other religions has become widespread. The most common view today is that, whilst salvation is through Christ alone, made possible solely by his atoning sacrifice on the cross, this salvation is nevertheless available to all human beings without restriction. Non-Christians are thus *included within* the sphere of Christian salvation – hence the term 'inclusivism' to describe this position. From this standpoint, whilst Christianity is in the last analysis the only true, or only fully true, religion, this does not imply any lack of redeeming love on God's part for the remaining majority of the human race.

In an astronomical analogy, the medieval and contemporary funda-mentalist view corresponds to the old Ptolemaic picture, with our earth (our religion) at the centre of the universe of faiths. In contrast, the new inclusivist view sees the religions as all revolving around the sun (God), but with its life-giving light and warmth (the divine saving grace) falling directly only upon our earth (Christianity), but then being reflected off it, though with diminished intensity, to the other planets (other reli-gions). Christianity thus retains its unique, central, normative position within the divine dispensation, but without the harsh consequences of the old exclusivism. Salvation outside Christianity is a derivative effect, dependent upon the Christ-event, a kind of 'trickledown' from the spir-itually richer primary recipient; but on the other hand, non-Christians do have their place, even though a secondary one, within the economy of salvation. Yet a third picture, known as religious pluralism, which is growing today in its appeal, sees the light of the sun, the redeeming love of God, as falling directly and impartially on the entire human race throughout the world. On this view, all who are open to the divine influence, within whatever human tradition, have an equal opportunity of undergoing the salvific transformation.

I shall be saying more about this pluralist view presently, and also extending it to take account of the non-theistic religions, particularly Buddhism. But first, why should we not remain satisfied with the inclus-ivist option, which both preserves the uniqueness of Christianity, based on God's personal self-disclosure and direct presence in Christ, whilst avoiding the unacceptable idea that non-Christians are outside God's saving concern? For if God became incarnate in Jesus Christ, so that Christianity alone among the religions of the world was founded by God in person, it must in the nature of the case be religiously superior to all others. And yet at the same time the availability of Christian salvation to the whole world expresses love towards the non-Christian millions.

This is how it seems from a traditional Christian point of view. On the other hand, it must seem very different from a Jewish or a Muslim or a Hindu or a Sikh or a Buddhist, etc. point of view. Here this must appear as a way of asserting, though in as charitable a way as possible, the unique priority and normative character of the Christian gospel. For when the Jewish people believe that their redemption comes through the Covenant revealed in the Torah, and that Jesus was a prophet of God but not God himself in human form, Christian inclusivism entails that they are fundamentally mistaken and that their redemption comes from Christ alone. And when Muslims believe that their salvation depends entirely upon *Allah rahman rahim*, God gracious and merciful, self-revealed in the Qur'an, and that Jesus was one of the greatest of the prophets but emphatically not God incarnate, Christian inclusivism entails that they too are mistaken and that their salvation comes from Christ alone. And again, when Buddhists believe that attainment of the supreme good of *nirvana* comes through transcendence of the ego point of view in compassion for all life, Christian inclusivism once again entails that they are mistaken and that their salvation comes solely from Christ, who was God incarnate. And so on. It is important to be aware of this implication of inclusivism, because it is often made a point of criticism of the pluralist position that in taking a global perspective it presumes, imperialistically, to contradict some aspect of the self-understanding of each tradition. But the Christian inclusivist does precisely the same to every religion other than his or her own. Which is more imperialistic – to treat one's own religion as the sole exception to the general truth that structures of belief entailing an inherent superiority are in need of revision, or to acknowledge that this applies to one's own tradition also?

So the basic objection to Christian inclusivism is that, although it may seem to be purely an expression of love for Jews, Muslims, Buddhists, etc., it is also – however politely disguised – an expression of the traditional Christian claim to an unique priority.

Is this traditional claim justified? That depends upon how one conceives of salvation. If this means being forgiven and accepted by God because of the atoning death of Jesus, then by definition all salvation is Christian salvation, and Christianity alone knows and preaches its true source and nature. But suppose we think of salvation as an actual change in human beings from natural self-centredness, with all the wickedness and suffering that flow from this, to a radically new orientation centred in God and lived out in love of God and love of neighbour. The observable side of this will be what St Paul identified as the fruits of the spirit: love, joy, peace, patience, kindness, goodness, faithfulness, gentleness, self-control (Gal. 5. 22–23), and requiring social justice as distributive love. If salvation/redemption/becoming a servant or a child or a friend of God is thus in its varying degrees a concrete reality in human life (though not completed in this life), then we can look about us to see where it occurs and through what traditional structures it is mediated.

It used to be widely taken for granted within the church that Christian men and women, and Christian civilization, are morally and spiritually superior to all others. But in the light of contemporary experience of meeting people of other faiths, and in the light of modern readings of history, this no longer seems to be the case. Going no further than British cities, when one gets to know one's fellow citizens who are Muslim, Hindu, Sikh, Jewish, Buddhist, Taoist, Bah'ai, it is a common experience to find that they are not, in general, less loving in family and society, less caring for their neighbours, less honest and truthful, less good citizens, less devoted to their faith, than are our Christian fellow citizens in general. They do not seem to be *better* human beings, but neither do they seem to be *worse* human beings, than Christians. And when one goes abroad sufficiently to move beyond an often superficial tourist point of view, and particularly if one is fortunate enough to encounter a few of the remarkable individuals whom we call saints, it becomes increasingly clear that the salvific transformation is, so far as we can tell, taking place to more or less the same extent within each of the great world religions. It is admittedly impossible to establish such a conclusion by statistical evidence, and there will be some who deny the rough parity that I have affirmed. But today the onus of proof or of argument is upon any who claim that their own tradition produces morally and spiritually better human beings than all the others.

And when we turn to the large-scale events of history we find a similar situation. Each of the great religions has been responsible both for immense good and also for immense evil. In trying to assess these, it is not permissible to compare the best within our own history with the worst within another. But when we compare good with good and evil with evil, how do we weigh, for example, Buddhist compassion against Christian love, or on the negative side, the caste system of India against the class system of Europe, or the treatment of women in traditional eastern societies against the treatment of the Jews in Christian Europe? It does not seem possible to assign numerical values to such vast phenomena and then add them up to establish an objective conclusion.

So whilst this is all open to debate, the onus is squarely upon any who wants to assert the overall superiority of their own tradition.

It is also to be noted that the religion to which one belongs (or against which one rebels) depends, in the vast majority of cases, on the accident of birth. So if it is the case, both that religious allegiance usually depends on where one is born, and also that the great world faiths seem to be more or less equally effective contexts of the salvific transformation, why should we not develop our theology to take account of these facts? Surely it is the function of theology to make sense of facts, not to try to evade their implications?

How, then, can we make sense of these facts? If we are not simply to reiterate the long-established sense of the unique superiority of our own faith – a sense that attaches itself to whichever tradition we happen to have been born into – we must expand our horizon to do theology in a global context. Instead of fitting the religious life of humanity into our inherited set of categories, we must see Christianity as part of the world-wide and history-long religious life of the human race. This includes the non-theistic faiths of Buddhism, advaitic Hinduism, Taoism, Confucianism, as well as the more familiar monotheistic faiths. We have to take account both of the immense differences – conceptual, experiential, institutional, cultural – between the different great religions, and also of the fact that they all teach that the Ultimate, the Real, the Divine is benign in relation to humanity, and requires of us that we value others as we value ourselves.

In an attempt to do justice to this complex situation, I offer the constructive suggestion that we should distinguish between, on the one hand, the infinite divine reality in itself, transcending the scope of our human minds, and on the other hand, the ways in which that universal presence has taken concrete forms within human experience through the mediation of our different sets of religious concepts and their associated spiritual practices. This distinction can render intelligible the fact of the different God-figures and the different non-personal absolutes. For they have been jointly formed by the impact upon us of the ultimate, ineffable divine reality and the different culturally conditioned forms of human religious thought. In the words of St Thomas Aquinas, 'Things known are in the knower according to the mode of the knower' (*Summa Theologica*, II/II, Q. 1, art. 2). And the mode of the knower has been differently formed within the different religious traditions, so that the noumenal divine reality is humanly thought and experienced within different faith communities as a plurality of divine phenomena. Thus we do not all worship the same experienced God, but the different experienced Gods whom we worship are manifestations of the one ultimate ineffable reality.

This sets the problem of the 'conflicting truth-claims' of the different religions in a new light. For whilst their theologies are indeed often mutually incompatible, these theologies describe *different* manifestations to humanity of the ultimate divine reality, and so do not conflict with one another. For the fact that the divine reality is known to Christians as the holy Trinity, with Jesus as our window onto the divine life and with this life flowing through the church, does not conflict with the fact that the divine reality is known, for example, to Muslims in the holy Qur'an as a strictly unitary Being, and is responded to in the pattern of prayer, fasting, alms-giving and pilgrimage enjoined in the Qur'an. We have here something analogous to different maps of the world. For any two-dimensional representation of the three-dimensional globe has to distort it, and the various projections used by different cartographers are different ways of doing this systematically. But that one map is correct does not mean that another, drawn in a different projection, is incorrect. If they are made properly they are both correct – and yet at the same time they both inevitably distort. However, if both enable us to progress successfully from A to B, there is no need for a quarrel between them. For when we try to map the infinite divine reality in our finite earthly human terms we inevitably distort it, some of us within one theological projection and some in another.

Although the idea of the religions as involving different human perceptions of the one ultimate divine reality is not a component of any of the traditional religious belief systems – because it is a meta-theory about the relationship between them – it does nevertheless have a point of resonance within each. A distinction between the directly worshipped God, with a range of describable attributes, and the ultimate ineffable (or transcategorial) Godhead runs through much of the Christian mystical tradition, with Pseudo-Dionysius and Meister Eckhart as its earlier and later high points. The Jewish and Muslim mystical traditions likewise distinguish between the ineffable ultimate reality, referred to as *Ein Sof* (the Infinite) or *al-Haqq* (the Real), and the worshipped God of the scriptures. Hindu thought offers the distinction between *nirguna* Brahman (Brahman without attributes), and the human awareness of this as *saguna* Brahman (Brahman with attributes, that is, Ishwara, personal deity in many forms). Mahayana Buddhism has its parallel distinction between, on the one hand, the ultimate *Dharmakaya*, utterly beyond the scope of our human conceptual systems, and on the other hand the *Sambhogakaya* in which this is manifested as the heavenly Buddha figures, and the *Nirmanakaya* consisting of the succession of incarnate Buddhas. The Kantian distinction between the unexperienceable *noumenon* and its phenomenal appearances enables us to generalize these distinctions embedded within the great traditions of religious thought.

The great world religions then, I suggest, constitute different ways of conceiving, and therefore different ways of experiencing, and therefore different ways of responding in life to the ultimate eternal and ineffable reality; and so far as we can tell from their fruits in human life, they are more or less equally authentic. But there nevertheless remains an important sense in which Christianity *is*, for Christians, the only true religion. For we have been formed by it. It has, so to speak, created us in its own image, so that it fits us and we fit it as no other religion can. We should therefore adhere to it and live it out to the full. But we should also remember, whenever this is relevant, that precisely the same is true of the adherents of each of the other world faiths.

# 13
## Paul Knitter on the Person of Christ

In 1997 Orbis published *The Uniqueness of Jesus: A Dialogue with Paul F. Knitter*, edited by Leonard Swidler and Paul Mojzes, in which an article by Knitter, Professor of Theology at Xavier University, Cincinnati, was followed by a number of Responses by others, and then a reply by Knitter. What follows is my own Response and part of Knitter's reply to the Responses. Paul Knitter is a long-standing personal as well as theological friend and ally. We both advocate religious pluralism, but whereas my own mission aims beyond as well as within the churches, his has been primarily within the Catholic Church; and I have long been aware that it is very much harder, and also more dangerous, for a Catholic to take up this work than for a Protestant such as myself.

Paul Knitter's purpose in presenting his Five Theses on the uniqueness of Jesus[1] is clearly to commend the Christian pluralist point of view within the church by stressing its elements of continuity with the past tradition. This is a valuable service, and if his theses succeed in gaining a greater Christian acceptance for religious pluralism, the project will have been fully vindicated.

The misgivings that I shall register do not concern the Five Theses themselves. The five propositions seem to me, with the caveat that I shall enter below about thesis 4, to be excellent, but I shall take issue with Knitter's more detailed explanation of them. These seem to me at certain crucial points to be ambiguous, capable of being understood in both pluralist and inclusivist ways. He seems, in his desire to make the pluralist position as widely acceptable as possible, to be offering the illusory possibility of having it both ways.

My first misgiving concerns Knitter's account of pluralism. He defines it as announcing 'at least the possibility (some would hold the probability, if not the actuality) of many true religions, each carrying on a different though valid role in the divine plan of salvation' (note 2). But both exclusivists and inclusivists could hold that it is possibly but not actually the case that there are other true religions as well as Christianity. St. Thomas Aquinas argued with great cogency that there could in principle have been other divine incarnations. There could have been incarnations of the other Persons of the Trinity, for 'what the Son can do, the Father can do, for otherwise the three persons would not be equal in power. The Son had the power to become incarnate. So then did the Father and the Holy Spirit' (*Summa Theologica*, IIIa, Q. 3, art. 5); and there could have been other incarnations of the Son: 'It seems that after the Incarnation the Son has the power to take up another human nature distinct from the one he actually did' (IIIa, Q. 3, art. 7). Aquinas held, of course, that there has been only one incarnation, in Jesus Christ. However, if there had been other divine incarnations, they might well have founded other religions which would have been as true and salvific as Christianity. It is therefore perfectly orthodox to affirm the *possibility*, but not the actuality, of other true-and-salvific religions. And so the traditional exclusivist and inclusivist positions do not preclude what Knitter defines as majority pluralism, that is, apart from the 'some' who go beyond possibility to probability or actuality. Pluralism now ceases to be another option in addition to exclusivism and inclusivism. I conclude that Knitter's definition is too permissive to be useful.

In a later note Knitter argues that 'it is *probable* that God's love will be found in and through other religions, thus rendering them, at least to some extent, true' (note 15). This is an accurate delineation of Christian inclusivism. Some other religions are, or probably are, to some extent true. But pluralism ought not to be watered down into inclusivism. A pluralism that is worth agreeing or disagreeing with in its own right will hold that we have as much reason to think that the other great world religions are true and salvific as to think this of Christianity. The ground for this lies in their fruits in human life. If it seems to us that Judaism, Islam, Hinduism, Buddhism, Sikhism and Taoism have shown themselves to be contexts as effective as Christianity for human transformation from self-centredness to a new centring in the Ultimate Reality that we call God, then we must affirm not merely the possibility or probability but the actuality of their being true and salvific. This is not something to be determined by *a priori* dogma but by the observation of actual human behaviour. Judgments concerning human behaviour as reflecting our relationship to the Ultimate are of course difficult, to say the least. I would only claim that we have *as much* reason, on the basis of their fruits, to believe that Buddhism, for example, is true and salvific as we have to believe that Christianity is. This is what I, for one, understand by religious pluralism, that is, the affirmation not merely of a possible or probable but of an actual plurality of authentically true-and-salvific religious traditions.[2]

My second misgiving follows from this and concerns something on which Knitter rightly insists, namely that in inter-faith dialogue 'if Christians think that they are in possession of the "fullness" of revelation and the final norm for all truth, then no matter how much they might call for a dialogue "among equals", they retain the position of advantage'; or as he also puts it, there must in genuine dialogue be 'a level playing-field' (thesis 2). But is this position of advantage really renounced in dialogue, producing a genuinely level playing-field, when Christians affirm that Christianity is true and salvific but that the religion of their dialogue partner is only *possibly*, or at most *probably*, also true and salvific? I cannot help thinking that any impartial observer would judge that Christians here are setting themselves up in a 'position of advantage' rather than coming onto a 'level playing-field'. Does Knitter really recommend that we engage in dialogue on this basis?

I applaud Knitter's thesis that God was *truly* at work in Jesus, but not *only* in Jesus. This is, I think, an excellent formulation. But my third misgiving concerns his expounding the key word *truly* as meaning that 'Christians must announce Jesus to all peoples as God's *universal*, *decisive*, and *indispensable* manifestation of saving truth and grace' (thesis 3). 'Universal', yes, in the sense that God's work in the life of Jesus is relevant to everyone without restriction. Knitter adds that this is *probably* also true of other revelations of the divine. This is a halfhearted or less than halfhearted pluralism. I want to say that we have as much reason to believe that the Buddhist, Muslim and other messages are universally relevant as we have to believe that our own Christian message is. 'Decisive', yes, in the sense that, as Knitter says, the Christian gospel 'shakes and challenges and calls one to change one's perspective and conduct' (thesis 3). Again, he adds that this is *probably* also true of other gospels; and again I want to say that we have as much reason, from actual observation, to think that the Muslim and Buddhist messages, for example, are decisive in this sense as that the Christian message is. And 'normative', yes, in the sense that the Christian revelation is normative for Christians but is, as Knitter says, not 'the absolute, final, full, unsurpassable norm for all times and all religions' (note 13). But 'indispensable'? Indispensable for what? What is it that cannot occur without this indispensable message having been heard and accepted? Is it indispensable for salvation? This would be the old exclusivism that Knitter has rejected. Indispensable, then, for what? Knitter's answer is that 'those who have not known and in some way accepted the message and power of the gospel are missing something in their knowledge and living of truth' (thesis 3). That is to say, non-Christians will be spiritually enriched by hearing and appreciating the Christian message. Knitter adds, again, that it is *probable* that this is also true of the other great religious messages. But if several different messages are all indispensable in the sense that anyone is enriched by hearing and appreciating them, is *indispensable* really the right word? I appreciate that it will play well with the traditionally orthodox. But consider an analogy. If your life can be saved only by taking penicillin, then penicillin is indispensable to you in a very clear sense. But if your health will be enhanced by your taking multivitamin tablets, they cannot be said to be indispensable. And if several different brands of multivitamin tablets are more or less equally effective, a particular brand certainly cannot responsibly be advertised as indispensable. In my view, *indispensable* is not the right word, nor is it selected for the right reason.

My fourth misgiving concerns Knitter's comparative identification of each of the world religions in terms of a single unique feature, with Christianity's unique feature being a concern for social justice, for 'the betterment of human beings in this world', the transformation of this world 'from one of division and injustice into one of love and mutuality' (thesis 4). Historians of religion are today generally too conscious of the immense internal variety of each tradition to indulge in such one-dimensional stereotyping. But leaving that aside, is the stereotyping being done here in a fair and just way? Surely no impartial observer would pick out as the central and most obvious characteristic of Christianity a loving concern for social justice. Historically, Christianity has validated wars, slavery, patriarchy, immense hierarchical inequalities, colonial exploitation and anti-Semitism – the opposite of what Knitter identifies as the central thrust of the Christian message. And, as he is obviously well aware, elements of Christianity today are still involved in some of these same evils. To define Christianity in contrast to the other world religions as having social and political liberation at its heart is to make a recommendation concerning what it *ought* to be – not an objectively accurate statement of what it actually is. I fully agree with Knitter's recommendation. But to equate the very recent (dating from the 1960s), small, much-contested and officially condemned movement of liberation theology with the actuality of Christianity in the world today – while ignoring parallel minority movements for social justice within other traditions – seems to me another abandonment of the 'level playing-field'. I think it is clear that Knitter is in fact aware that he is making a recommendation. But must we claim it as an exclusively or uniquely Christian recommendation? Indeed, would not an impartial observer, looking for the most outstanding religious leaders in the service of peace and justice on earth in the twentieth century, be likely to see above all Mahatma Gandhi[3] and the Dalai Lama?

The creation of peace and a rational conservation of the earth's limited natural resources in a just and sustainable world economy ought to be the aim of people of all religions. It has, in fact, in recent years been increasingly on the agenda of inter-faith dialogue. Recall, for example, the National Inter-Religious Conference on Peace at Washington in 1966, the New Delhi Symposium sponsored by the U.S. Inter-Religious Committee on Peace and the Gandhi Peace Foundation in 1968, the Assembly of the World Conference on Religion and Peace at Kyoto in 1970, and continuing gatherings at Louvain in 1974, Princeton in 1979, Nairobi in 1984 and Melbourne in 1989, as well as very numerous other smaller dialogue occasions centred on the same concerns. This is indeed proving to be the most fruitful area of inter-religious cooperation. From a Third World Christian point of view, Aloysius Pieris has said,

> The irruption of the Third World [with its demand for liberation] is also the irruption of the non-Christian world. The vast majority of God's poor perceive their ultimate concern and symbolize their struggle for liberation in the idiom of non-Christian religions and cultures. Therefore, a theology that does not speak to or speak through this non-Christian peoplehood [and its religions] is a luxury of a Christian minority.[4]

Knitter himself has in another paper endorsed this and spoken of the liberating potential of Buddhism and Hinduism.[5] And he could well have added each of the other major world faiths. But the growing inter-faith dialogue on peace and justice will not be helped by a Christian claim to a uniquely authentic concern for justice and love. Does Knitter really want us to engage in dialogue on this basis?

A fifth misgiving is triggered by Knitter's statement that 'as a pluralist Christian, I can with no difficulty whatsoever announce – indeed, I feel impelled to proclaim – that Jesus is truly the Son of God and universal Saviour. The recognition and announcement of Jesus' divinity remains integral and essential to a pluralist christology' (note 20). The point of this language is, of course, that it sounds traditionally orthodox. But if it is meant in a traditionally orthodox sense, it is, in my view, incompatible with genuine religious pluralism. For if Jesus was God the Son, Second Person of a divine Trinity, incarnate, then Christianity is the only religion to have been founded by God in person and must be uniquely superior to all others. And so, presumably, when Knitter speaks of Jesus as the Son of God he does not mean this in the traditional sense that Jesus is the only source of salvation for all human beings. What he does mean is hinted at when he goes on to speak of Jesus' 'divinity' as meaning that he is 'the symbol, the story that makes God real and effective for me' – as to all of us who are Christians. But has not Knitter's desire to minimize the difference between Christian pluralism on the one hand and traditional orthodoxy on the other led to an ambiguous use of language?

My sixth misgiving is whether Christian pluralism, as Knitter is here presenting it, is able adequately to take account of the great nontheistic religions – Buddhism, Taoism and Advaitic Hinduism. It is natural and proper for a Christian normally to use our Christian term God for the ultimately Real. And Knitter does not forget that 'God is an unsurpassable Mystery, one which can never totally be comprehended or contained in human thought or construct' (thesis 3). But nevertheless he sometimes writes, like so many theologians, as though he had forgotten this! Perhaps this is allowable in a document that is intended for internal Christian consumption. But in dialogue with, for example, Buddhists, we cannot take it for granted that that which is ultimately real is a personal God, still less a Trinity of Three Persons. We cannot require that the dialogue be conducted in Christian terms. Knitter is, of course, well aware of this, having engaged extensively in the contemporary Buddhist–Christian dialogue.

But there is so much in Knitter's pages that I heartily applaud that I cannot end on a negative note. A short response has only space to pick out the most debatable points. Knitter has contributed as much as anyone to the development of contemporary Christian pluralism. His chosen mission is within and to the church. This is an entirely legitimate and important – and indeed indispensable – mission. But it carries with it the temptation to resort to easing ambiguities, and I have suggested that Knitter has not entirely avoided this. I nevertheless hope very much for the success of his mission.

## Notes

1. Strictly speaking, *uniqueness* is not the right word. Jesus, and of course everyone else, is unique; that is to say, there was only one of him. But the word is commonly used in the present context to signal the claim that Jesus uniquely was God (that is, God the Son, Second Person of the Holy Trinity) incarnate, the only saviour of the world from sin and perdition. The question is whether this claim is appropriate. So Knitter says correctly that he is 'not questioning *whether* Jesus is unique but only *how*' (*The Uniqueness of Jesus*, ed. Leonard Swidler & Paul Mojzes, New York: Orbis, 1997, p. 5).

2. I have no space here to take up the further questions of smaller, extinct or new religious movements, or of the criteria by which we judge a movement to be an authentic response to the Ultimate. I have done so, however, in Part V of *An Interpretation of Religion* (New Haven: Yale University Press; London: Macmillan, 1989).

3. The idea, cherished by some, that Gandhi received his most important ideas from Christianity cannot be sustained in the light of his own speeches and writings. See Robert Ellsberg (ed.), *Gandhi on Christianity* (Maryknoll, N.Y.: Orbis Books, 1991), and the discussion by Margaret Chatterjee in *Gandhi's Religious Thought* (London: Macmillan; Notre Dame, Ind.: University of Notre Dame Press, 1983).

4. Aloysius Pieris, S.J., 'The Place of Non-Christian Religions and Cultures in the Evolution of Third World Theology', in Virginia Fabella and Sergio Torres, (eds.), *Irruption of the Third World: Challenge to Theology* (Maryknoll, N.Y.: Orbis Books, 1983), pp. 113–14.

5. Paul Knitter, 'Towards a Liberation Theology of Religions', in John Hick and Paul Knitter (eds.), *The Myth of Christian Uniqueness: Towards a Pluralistic Theology of Religions* (Maryknoll, N.Y.: Orbis Books, 1987), p. 180.

## A response by Knitter

Granting that an active commitment to this-worldly well-being is something without which one wouldn't have authentic Christian faith, one must recognize that other religions are also so committed. Christians can't claim any uniqueness in this area. Raimon Panikkar attests that in his scholarly and personal pilgrimages throughout most of the religious landscapes of the world, he has found a broad display of 'inner-worldly actions of love and justice'. Michael von Brück, on the basis of similar experience, agrees: a 'genuine life of unbounded love and justice is happening also outside the Christian tradition'. Such a life, as Hick points out, has been embodied for all the world to see in Gandhi and the Dalai Lama, whose active historical work for peace and harmony is thoroughly Hindu and Buddhist. Finally, ... where did Jesus learn that to know God is to do justice? In announcing a God of history who calls us to historical engagement, Jesus was preserving a unique ingredient in Judaism. Islam, too, carries on this same unique concern for well-being in this world.

All of these reminders presume that if what characterizes me also characterizes others, it can't be unique to me. That is, indeed, the first definition Webster's dictionary gives for *unique*: 'being the only one'. But Webster tells us that *unique* can also signify 'distinctively characteristic'. And that's the meaning all of us, myself included, should feel and intend when speaking about the uniqueness of Jesus or Christianity – that which distinctively characterizes, or identifies, or constitutes identity. What makes one unique, in other words, is not what makes one different but what makes one oneself – that without which one would not be who one actually is. Uniqueness therefore need not depend on differences from others but on identity, or integrity, with oneself. . . .

Therefore, the fact that other religions or spiritual leaders affirm the value of this world and the need to act for its betterment does not weaken the claim that the same quality is unique to, or distinctive of, Jesus. In *One Earth Many Religions*[1] I spent a whole chapter trying to show that all (or at least most) religions that have survived the centuries have traditions within them that call their followers to respond to the terrestrial needs of others. In some way, I would venture to say, all religions are actually or potentially 'this-worldly'. *But* when we look at the distinctive characteristics of each religion, when we study their identities, we find, I believe, that each of them is 'this-worldly' in *different* ways. . . .

So even in attesting to the way all religions do or can promote this-worldly well-being, we have to be open to the differences in how they do it. Doing this, I think we will discover, first of all, that in the identities of many other religious communities the call to transform the world through concrete acts of love and justice does not occupy the same self-defining role that it does for the identity of Jesus. Historical involvement does not enter into the core of who they are as it does (or is supposed to) for disciples of Jesus. I think that this will be the case for many of the Asian or Indic religious traditions. For example, as Aloysius Pieris has pointed out, although *agape*, or active love of neighbour, is certainly alive in Buddhist spirituality, it does not occupy the focal place that *prajna* or contemplative wisdom does. . . .

At this point my understanding of Christian participation in the inter-faith dialogue exposes either its solid basis or its Achilles' heel. On what grounds am I raising such criticisms in the dialogue? Just why am I claiming so adamantly that encounter with the Mystical must include a concern for worldly well-being? John Hick speaks for the many Christians who would argue that to place liberation and world transformation at the heart of the gospel is more politically than biblically correct. Hick pointedly but gently tells me that what I am holding up as part of the unique core of Christianity is 'the very recent (dating from the 1960s), small, much contested, and officially condemned movement of liberation theology'. Hick would align himself with E.P. Sanders and those New Testament scholars who hold that Jesus' eschatological orientation – his conviction that the end was near – precluded any real commitment to changing things in this world. Jesus announced God's reign, but its coming was to take place soon, after the passing away of this world.[2]

Hick's words touch and weaken the bedrock of my suggestions for re-visioning Jesus' uniqueness. In differing ways and degrees, many other participants in this conversation share his concerns about placing a this-worldly liberation at the heart of Christian life and belief. I hope I can move the conversation forward by reflecting on these concerns and clarifying the reasons for designating love-with-justice as a unique and distinctive mark of Christian identity.

A subtitle for this part of these reflections might read: 'Jesus' notion of the Reign of God does make Christianity unique, but relationally so'.

Let me begin with the stickiest part of this conversation: what we can and cannot know about the historical Jesus. This is like stepping into a minefield where, with every assertion about what Jesus really said or did, one fears that the ground will blow up beneath one's feet. Still, I think it is relatively safe to claim that whatever else Jesus may have intended with his vision of the Reign of God, one of the essential pieces in his vision was the greater well-being of humans *right now*. This is so even though Jesus thought the 'right now' was going to be very abbreviated. What Jesus was after with his efforts as a healer (historically reliable, according to most scholars) the Christian communities have reaffirmed through the centuries: 'Thy Kingdom come, thy will be done *on earth* as it is in heaven.' To use an eschatological scalpel to remove this central concern of Jesus for the suffering and need of persons in this world is, I fear, to deform what Jesus, especially as a Jewish prophet, was all about. And if we survey the shifting terrain of New Testament scholarship, it seems that the once unanimous picture of Jesus as a thoroughly eschatological prophet has blurred. Already in 1987 Marcus Borg ventured an assessment that has gained firmer foundations over recent years: 'The consensus regarding Jesus' expectation of the end of the world has disappeared. The majority of scholars no longer thinks that Jesus expected the end of the world in his generation.'[3] . . .

I would like to go a step further in trying to articulate the distinctiveness of Jesus' vision. This step is prompted by the reminder . . . that many, if not all, religions are in some way concerned about the well-being of this world. I think more can be said about what distinguishes the way Jesus calls us to historical engagement; it is something that I have frequently noticed in the inter-religious conversations in which I have taken part. It can be summarized in the language of liberation theologians as the *preferential option for victims*. Affirming and embellishing a central note in the message of the Jewish prophets who preceded him, Jesus, as presented by the gospel writers (especially Luke), shows a special (not exclusive) concern for the little ones, those who are suffering most because, usually, they have been victimized most. Perhaps the clearest indication that the invitation to the table of the Kingdom was given especially to those who were excluded from the well-laden tables of the establishment was Jesus' scandalous 'table fellowship' or 'open commensality' with the riff-raff of Jewish society – beggars, prostitutes, tax-collectors.[4]

Aloysius Pieris confesses that it was in the course of an inter-religious exchange that a Buddhist reminded him that Jesus stands out from other religious messengers in revealing 'God's defence pact between God and slaves'.[5] Pieris's own experience confirms that such a claim is not made of any other founder of a religion, but also that such a claim has never been experienced by other religions as a threat to their integrity or value. So I would want to add to my thesis 4: Today, the uniqueness of Jesus can be found in his insistence that salvation, or the Reign of God, must be realized in this world through human actions of love and justice, *with a special concern for the victims of oppression or exploitation*. . . .

At this point, John Hick will patiently press his question: In this view of mission as dialogue, am I still saying that the truth revealed in Jesus is indispensable for others? Yes, I am. But what does that mean? For the most part, I would not understand this indispensability to be like that of penicillin for the dying patient. But neither is it like vitamins available under different brand names but fulfilling the same function. Rather, what I intend by indispensability (and remember, Buddha may be as indispensable as Jesus) is better compared to a skill or insight that enriches our life profoundly and becomes integral to who we are, but which, we know, is not necessary to lead an adequate, contented human existence. I'm thinking of something like learning how to read and write; we know that we could live happily without these skills (and sometimes we envy the depth and vitality of oral cultures), but still we recognize that to read and to write are indispensable parts of who we now are and want to be.

Perhaps a better image of what I mean by indispensability can be found in friendship. After we have made a good friend and experienced how much that friend has changed and expanded our life, we can say that this friend is an indispensable part of our identity; yet we know that our lives would have been quite liveable without that friend. Such a friendship can be indispensable and essential to one's life, and yet not make up one's primary relationship. This comparison touches my own experience, for, as a Christian, my primary relationship is with Jesus, and yet Buddha has become indispensable for who I now am and how I want to live – as a human being and as a Christian.

## Notes

1. Paul F. Knitter, *One Earth Many Religions* (Maryknoll, N.Y.: Orbis Books, 1995).
2. E.P. Sanders, *Jesus and Judaism* (Philadelphia: Fortress Press, 1985); John Hick, *The Metaphor of God Incarnate* (London: SCM Press, 1993), pp. 19–22.
3. Marcus Borg, *Jesus: A New Vision: Spirit, Culture, and the Life of Discipleship* (San Francisco: Harper, 1987), p. 14. In 1994 Borg reaffirmed: 'Over the last ten years, the image of Jesus as an eschatological prophet, which dominated scholarship through the middle of this century, has become very much a minority position' (*Meeting Jesus Again for the First Time: The Historical Jesus and the Heart of Contemporary Faith* [San Francisco: Harper, 1994], p. 29).
4. Albert Nolan, *Jesus before Christianity* (Maryknoll, N.Y.: Orbis Books, 1978), pp. 39–40; John Dominick Crossan, *The Historical Jesus* (San Francisco: Harper, 1991), pp. 261–4; Richard A. Horsley (with John S. Hanson), *Bandits, Prophets and Messiahs: Popular Movements at the Time of Jesus* (San Francisco: Harper, 1985), pp. 29–87.
5. Aloysius Pieris, 'Interreligious Dialogue and Theology of Religions', *Horizons* 20 (1993), pp. 111–12; *idem*, 'Whither New Evangelism?', *Pacifica* 6 (1993), p. 329. Both articles also published in Aloysius Pieris, *Fire and Water: Basic Issues in Asian Buddhism and Christianity* (Maryknoll, N.Y.: Orbis Books, 1996).

# Postscript

Looking back at this book as a whole two things now strike me as inviting a brief final comment.

The first is the repetitions in the presentation in different contexts of my own version of religious pluralism. But these are inseparable from the responses to them by critics, who reply to the particular way in which my position was formulated on that occasion. I can only ask the reader to accept the joint result as a whole.

The more significant point concerns the difficulty of even the most honest debates in these areas. When they are focused on specific and well-defined issues they are generally profitable. This is true in particular of the exchanges with William Alston, George Mavrodes and William Rowe, where we deal directly with one another's arguments. But on the other hand, when we are presenting the global differences between, on the one hand, a religious pluralism and, on the other, either evangelical Protestant or Catholic traditional Christian absolutism, or again between religious realism and non-realism, the arguments seem to go past each other instead of meeting head on. There are always some points of contact, and some points scored on both sides, but nevertheless the discussion seems to be based on two different agendas.

In the case of the realist/non-realist debate, respectively affirming and denying a transcendent reality as the object of ultimate religious concern, the division seems to run today within most of the churches, and indeed within the minds of many Christians. As the alternatives come to be seen more clearly they may well resolve themselves into two consciously different forms of religion, with and without the Transcendent. Here I myself remain on the realist side of the divide.

In the case of the Christian understanding of the other world religions, we may, within a generation or two, find that two Christianities are apparent – a traditional Christianity, which regards itself as the one true faith in a world of religious errors, and a second Christianity, which sees itself as one valid context of salvific transformation and liberation among others. Here I am on the pluralist side.

Can these divisions be avoided? The only possibility lies in further and more fruitful dialogue between those who see the issues clearly and are deeply concerned about them. But there can be no guarantee that the differences can be overcome. On the one hand, we must continue to try; on the other hand, pessimism as to the outcome may well be realistic!

# Index